SEARCH FOR THE MAYA

SEARCH FOR THE

MAYA

The Story of Stephens and Catherwood

VICTOR W. VON HAGEN

Saxon House

Saxon House
D. C. Heath Ltd
Westmead, Farnborough, Hants, England

ISBN 0 347 00007 X

Manufactured by Halliday Lithograph Corporation,
West Hanover and Plympton, Massachusetts
First American Edition

The author wishes to thank his
publishers, Barre of Barre, Massachusetts,
and the University of Oklahoma Press, who
allowed certain portions of the material
in this book to be used and recast.

Dedication

PARA ALBERTO BELTRAN, 'MI CATHERWOOD,'
QUIEN VIAJÓ CONMIGO POR MÉXICO,
YUCATÁN Y PERÚ, Y QUIEN
DIBUJÓ DIEZ DE MIS LIBROS TAN
MARAVILLOSAMENTE.
CON AFECTO Y
AGRADECIMIENTO.

CONTENTS

FOREWORD
WHICH INTRODUCES MR STEPHENS AND MR CATHERWOOD

Part 1
THE MEETING

CHAPTER I
WHO WAS CATHERWOOD? 3
His birth at Hoxton. Studies under Sir John Soane. To Rome with
Joseph Severn. Society of Englishmen. Sicily and Greece. To Egypt
and up the Nile. Employed by Robert Hay of Linplum. Arabia
Deserta. Jerusalem and the Dome of the Rock. London. The Panoramas
at Leicester Square.

CHAPTER II
WHICH INTRODUCES MR STEPHENS 35
The New York City of John Lloyd Stephens. Columbia College.
With Blackstone at Litchfield, Connecticut. The law suspended.
The Far West of Illinois.

CHAPTER III
MR STEPHENS' TOUR 43
Stephens: Attorney at Law. Fervor for politics. A 'mild trip' to
Europe proposed. Smyrna and the Levant. Mother Russia (and
Poland). Paris and the touch of the antique. The pleasure of ruins.

CHAPTER IV
THE GREY NILE 54
Alexandria: past and present. The firman of Mehemet Ali. Up and
around the Nile. The Temple of Dendera. The Luxor complex.
The graffiti on the Colossi of Memnon. Elephantine and the Temple
of Philae.

CHAPTER V
ARABIA PETRAEA 71
Stephens becomes Abdel Hassis. The way through Arabia Deserta.
Mt. Sinai and the Convent. Aqaba. Over the Roman Way to Petra.
Rose-Red City. A journey through Idumea to Palestine. The Jerusalem
map of F.C. The round-about way to London.

CHAPTER VI

THE MEETING   92

London and the new literary lion. The ruins of Jerusalem in
Leicester Square. The meeting of Stephens and Catherwood. New York
City in 1836. Politics and financial disaster. How Stephens became
an author. *Incidents of Travel in Arabia Petraea*. Catherwood follows
Stephens to New York. Catherwood & Diaper, Architects.
The Panoramas. Were there ancient ruins in Central America?

Part 2
THE FIRST JOURNEY

CHAPTER VII

THE MYSTERIOUS MAYA   103

The subject researched. Who were these mysterious people?
Humboldt's views. William Robertson denigrates the idea of American
ruins. Ancient Jews in America. Lord Kingsborough's obsession.
The contract: Stephens and Catherwood. Death makes Stephens a
diplomat. The sailing of the *Mary Ann* for Belize.

CHAPTER VIII

COPÁN AND THE WAY THITHER   114

Belize: the entrepôt. People, black and white. British Honduras in
History. The Copán conspiracy. Patrick Walker and Caddy. The way
thither. Problems and solutions. Arrival at Copán.

CHAPTER IX

THE RISE OF THE MAYA   133

The first glimpse of Copán: a description. Who had built these stone
buildings? Origins and dispersals. The peopling of the Americas.
American tribal societies. The Mayas: a city culture. Copán emerges.
Its literary and archaeological discoverers.

CHAPTER X

COPÁN: THE NEW GROUND   147

Threshold of a new cultural world. Who owned Copán? The purchase
of a ruined city. Catherwood maps Copán. Limns the first monuments.
The Hieroglyphic Stairway. The Maya conference altar. Departure.

CHAPTER XI

DIPLOMACY: ENDS AND MEANS 163

Guatemala and the chaos of liberty. The serarch for a government.
The bare bones of Central American history. Reform and chaos.
Rafael Carrera: dictator. Catherwod discovers the ruins of Quiriguá.
The plans for the Palenque expedition. Mr Chatfield's scepticism.
The padre's story. The way through jungle and barrancas.
Palenquian arrival.

CHAPTER XII

PALENQUE: THE SECOND CITY 181

The village of Palisade-Palenque. The city of Palenque in history.
Incredible Count Waldeck. Prescott's suspicions of Waldeck's
drawings. They assault the ruins. The 'Palace' discovered. Insects and
other problems. The importance of being a padre. The Temple of the
Inscriptions. The tomb beneath. A galaxy of ruins. Stephens bids
$1,500 for Palenque. Down the Usumacinta River to the Lagoon.
A glimpse of Uxmal. To Cuba and home.

CHAPTER XIII

INCIDENTS OF TRAVEL IN
CENTRAL AMERICA 216

The fascination of ruins. The Conquests of William Prescott.
The Stephens-Prescott letters. The advent of Baron Friedrichsthal.
Chaterwood's drawings challenged. *Central America* published.
Its impact on American archaeology.

Part 3
YUCATÁN REVISITED

CHAPTER XIV

YUCATÁN REVISITED 233

The conquest of the Maya. The three Montejos. Diego de Landa:
destroyer and preserver. Life and Leisure in Mérida. Daguerrotypes,
strabismus and Dr Cabot. A view of Uxmal. 'Savages could not have
carved these stones!' The coming of Chaipa Chi. Malaria.
Kabah comes into history. The 'Stephens' stones'. Labná in the Puuc.
The watery well of Bolonchen. The ancient chronicle of Yucatán.
White roads of the Maya. Farewell to the Puuc.

CHAPTER XV
THE WELLS OF ITZA   289
The island of Women. Cozumel. Tulum: walled and sea-girthed.
Aké, Silán and the colossal head of Izamal. The Temple of the
Warriors. Itzas. The pyramided Kulkulkan. Ball-courts with temples.
Challenge and change in Yucatán lands. Toltecs. The New Maya. Ave.

CHAPTER XVI
INCIDENTS OF TRAVEL IN YUCATÁN   310
New York City in 1843. America's literary world. Fire consumes
Catherwood's Panorama. *Yucatán* begins its publishing history.
Catherwood's scheme of publishing. The Mayan project.
Exhibitions and promise. Catherwood turns to London.
Sponsorship and *loco foco* motions. Frederick Catherwood, publisher.
The *Views of Ancient Monuments* issued (1844).

Part 4
YOU CAN'T GO BACK
CHAPTER XVII
MANIFEST DESTINY   329
Ocean to Ocean suzerainty. Railroads and telegraph. The call of the
wheels. The Demerara Railway of British Guiana. Catherwood assumes
the character of railway engineer. The colony of British Guiana.
Flies, floods and floosies. The first railroad in South America.
Rewards and disagreements.

CHAPTER XVIII
TROUBLES WITH THE RAILWAYS   337
Stephens turns toward Big Business. Navigation. A visit to Humboldt.
The Panama Rail scheme. Stephens' Congressional presentation.
The History of the Panama Isthmus. Stephens departs, Catherwood
arrives. The iron-road begins. Gold discovered in California.
Gold-pokes save the railway. Catherwood moves on to San Francisco.
The last correspondence. Stephens returns to Panama. Catherwood sails
to London.

CHAPTER XIX
DEATH MEETS MR STEPHENS   355
The insidiousness of malaria. Panama: entomological elysium.
A house on the Chagres. The Stephens' Tree. The final attack.
Stephens' last days in New York City. Death and Transfiguration.

CHAPTER XX

MR CATHERWOOD SINKS IN THE
STREAM OF TIME   358

Central America: Catherwood's last audible word. The Departure for
California's gold fields. The S.S. *Arctic* leaves Liverpool, arrives at
Newfoundland. The fatal collision. The last gun. The loss of the *Arctic*.
The obscurity of the artist of the Mayas. 'Mr Catherwood also
is missing.'

INDEX   362

List of Illustrations

Colour plates   *facing page*

I.   Catherwood's copies of details of Egyptian painting   140

II. Catherwood's reconstruction of the interior of an Egyptian Temple   140

III. Catherwood's drawing of the archway of the House of the Governor at Uxmal   141

IV. Catherwood's view of the Temple of the Plumed Serpent, Kulkulkan, at Chichén Itzá with one of the gigantic openmouthed serpents found on the north side   172

V. Catherwood's only self-portrait (the figure in the doorway). A sketch of the great doorway of the Temple of the Dwarf overlooking the Nunnery Quadrangle at Uxmal   172

VI. Catherwood's drawing of one of the Idols in the Great Plaza at Copán. Eleven feet high, it was erected at the end of a five year period and inscribed with the major events of that period   173

Half-tones   *page*

1. Catherwood's Plan of Jerusalem, published in 1835, which Stephens purchased and used. It brought them together (Courtesy of the British Museum)   2

2. A view of Cairo in the Nile Valley probably taken from one of Catherwood's many drawings which he sold or leased to other engravers   10

3. Catherwood's camera lucida sketch of an early excavation of the Temple of the Nobles on the west bank at Thebes (British Museum, Hays Collection, add. ms. 29832)   12

4. Catherwood's view of the riverbank at Luxor looking up to the site (British Museum, Hays Collection, add. ms. 29824)   12

5. The port of call of Luxor from the east bank looking across the Nile to the Necropolis at Luxor drawn by Catherwood in 1831 (British Museum, Hays Collection, add. ms. 29827)   13

List of Illustrations

6. Giza. Catherwood's water colour of the Pyramids in the Nile Valley. A letter from Catherwood to Robert Hay mentions the completion of his detailed drawings at Giza   13

7. Catherwood's sketch of his view of Thebes. It was given to viewers of his painted Panorama so that the monuments could be identified. It was destroyed by fire in New York in 1843 (Courtesy of the New York Historical Society)   12–13

8. Catherwood's view of the ruins at Philae sketched in 1833. 'A magnificent ruin' was Stephens' comment. Then buried in sand, now long buried under the waters of the Nile (British Museum, Hays Collection, add. ms. 29832)   16

9. The Colossi of Memnon. Catherwood's first *camera lucida* drawing of the two statues of Amen-hotep III (British Museum, Hays Collection, add. ms. 29829)   16

10. Another of Catherwood's drawings of the Colossi   16

11. Detail of Philae. A temple dedicated to Hathor, the goddess of distant places. 'It is a grand colonnade', Stephens wrote. 'It extends two hundred and forty feet'. On it he wrote his name under that of his friend Cornelius Bradford (British Museum, Collection add. ms. 29835)   18

12. Near Elephantine just below Aswan. Catherwood made this sketch in 1833. Stephens followed a few years later (British Museum, Hays Collection, add. ms. 29836)   18

13. Guide to Catherwood's panorama of Jerusalem. Figure 45 reads 'Messrs Catherwood and Bonomi', a rare autobiographical gesture from Catherwood (Courtesy of the New York Historical Society)   20–21

14. An etching by Finden from one of Catherwood's sketches of the Mosque of Omar El Aqsa at Jerusalem   23

15. An interior of the Golden Gate, Jerusalem. An etching from a drawing by Catherwood   23

16. Catherwood's plan of the ruins of Geraza (Jarash, Jordon) the first known plan of the Greco-Roman city (Courtesy British Museum)   27

17. A contemporary view of the ruins of the Temple of Zeus, Jarash, drawn by S. D. Harding from a sketch by Las Casas and published by John Murray in 1836   27

18. Woodcut illustration on the broadside for Catherwood's Panorama of Jerusalem in New York City   31

19. Stephens' map of his journey up the Nile   59

20. Watercolour by Catherwood about 1831 of the Temple of Dendera. 'One of the finest specimens of architectural art in Egypt', wrote Stephens. 'It was the first temple I had seen in Egypt' (British Museum, Hays Collection, add. ms. 29814)   59

21. Thebes. The hypostyle hall of the great Temple of Amun at Karnak. It was here that Stephens felt a surging interest in lost civilisations (British Museum, Hays Collection, add. ms. 29826)   61

22. The giant obelisk at Luxor, one of the few that remain in Egypt. Catherwood drew it after 1831 and in 1836 Stephens walked among the colossal figures and obelisks (British Museum, Hays Collection, add. ms. 29814)   64

23. A photograph of the same obelisk taken 150 years later by George Holton   64

24. The Gateway at Karnak believed to have been built by Evergestes I. Catherwood spent much time in and about Karnak (British Museum, Hays Collection, add. ms. 29826)   65

25. The Sik Gorge at Petra and the Temple of El Khaznah. Of it Stephens wrote, 'The first view of that superb façade must produce an effect which never would pass away' (George Holton photograph)   70

26. A sketch plan of Petra (Courtesy G. Lancaster Harding *The Antiquities of Jordan*)   81

27. Map of Petra sketched by Leon de Laborde in 1829   82

28. The travels of John Lloyd Stephens to Arabia Petraea in 1836 (From *Maya Explorer*, University of Oklahoma Press)   86

29. A view of New York from Governor's Island, 1844, from a lithograph by Catherwood (Courtesy New York Historical Society)   93

30. The back of an idol at Copán, from a Catherwood lithograph. The glyphic inscriptions of Stele F   102

31. The Huasteca ruins of Tajin-Chico in the state of Vera Cruz from *Antiquités Méxicaines*, Paris 1834   104

32. One of the first views of Palenque from *Antiquités Méxicaines*, Paris 1834   104

33. Catherwood's drawing of the Maya Lord of the Harvest, Yum Kax, discovered by the Author (Yale University Collections)   134

34. Catherwood's impression of the fallen 'idol', Stele D at Copán, since restored to an upright position. The drawing was discovered by the Author (Yale University Collections)   134

35. A Maya sculpture of a bat, one of the demon gods. Its Glyph is carved on its chest. Found at Copán   140

36. A naturalistic bull frog carved from a basaltic outcrop near Copán   140

37. A plan of Copán drawn by Catherwood. It is the first map ever attempted. Taken from *Incidents of Travel in Central America*   148

38. A modern ground plan of Copán, by Dr. S. Morley, a century later   148

39. The Serpent God at the base of the Hieroglyphic Stairway at Copán (Photographed by the Author)   154

40. The Maya system of numerical notation   157

41. Catherwood's exact copy from an altar at Copán. Its hieroglyphics are compared with those of the Dresden Codex underneath to show the similarity. Stephens' deduction was very apt   157

42. Stela and altar in Copán, from a lithograph by Catherwood. Zoomorphic altar in front of Stele D   160

43. Panorama of Palenque drawn by W. H. Holmes in 1895. Holmes was one of the surveyors of the American West. Later he turned to archaeology (W. H. Holmes, *Archaeological Studies Among the Ancient Cities of Mexico*, 1895)   192

44. Palenque. Catherwood's survey and the first correct ground plan of the Temple called the Palacio which is in the foreground of Holmes' drawings   192

45. Interior of Palenque. Cross section of the Temple of the Inscriptions   201

46. William Prescott as he appeared in 1856 when writing his *Conquest of Mexico*. Engraved by Holl after a photograph   219

List of Illustrations

47. Façade of stonework from Kabah (photographed by V. W. von Hagen)   232

48. Map of the exploration of the lost Maya cities by John Lloyd Stephens and Frederick Catherwood (From *Maya Explorer*, University of Oklahoma Press)   246

49. Panorama of Uxmal by W. H. Holmes, showing the House of Nuns in the foreground and the Temple of the Dwarf on the left (*Archaeological Studies Among the Ancient Cities of Mexico*, 1895)   248

50. Modern map of the Central section of Uxmal   248

51. Doorway of the Temple of the Dwarf, Uxmal   251

52. Catherwood's general view of the House of Nuns and the Temple of the Dwarf, Uxmal   253

53. Catherwood's drawing of the archway of Governor's Palace, Uxmal. The motif is the elongated snout of the Rain God   258

54. Modern view of the Governor's Palace, Uxmal   260

55. The masked façade from Kabah. Photographed by the Author   265

56. Stephens in a blue cutaway at the ruins of Kabah directing the removal of a carved stone door-jamb   265

57. Yucatán. Inset shows Stephens' travels from Sisal to Kabah (from the Author's edition of Stephens' *Yucatán*, University of Oklahoma Press)   269

58. An oval modern Maya house made of fascines plastered with mud. The thatch is of maize-stalks   272

59. A Maya house sculpted in the frieze of the Nunnery Quadrangle at Uxmal   272

60. The Temple at Zabacché in the Puuc area of Yucatán from an engraving by Catherwood   274

61. The ruins of Xlah-pak on the Maya road between Sayil and Labná   275

62. The façade of the principal temple at Sayil with Chac, the long-nosed God (the nose has broken off)   275

63. Catherwood's drawing of the Gateway at Lanbá. Its functions are unknown   277

List of Illustrations

64. Catherwood's sepia drawing of the Well at Bolonchen, discovered by the Author (Yale University Collections)   288

65. Catherwood's drawing of the Castle at Tulum, in Quintana Roo, Mexico, built about A.D. 560 and reoccupied in the 14th century   290

66. The gigantic head once on the side of the Pyramid at Izamal, now destroyed, from an engraving by Catherwood, also used by him in a lithograph   292

67. Modern drawing of central area of Chichén Itzá   294

68. The Nunnery of Chichén Itzá   296

69. The columns of the Temple of the Warriors at Chichén Itzá   297

70. A doorway in the Temple of the Warriors at Chichén Itzá   297

71. Panorama of Chichén Itzá drawn by W. H. Holmes in 1890 (*Archaeological Studies Among the Ancient Cities of Mexico*, 1895)   299

72. Catherwood engraving of the Ball Court, called 'the Gymnasium' at Chichén Itzá   300

73. The stone-carved ring in the Ball Court at Chichén Itzá   300

74. The Temple of Kulkulkan, the plumed serpent God, at Chichén Itzá   305

75. A modern view of the temple of Kulkulkan at Chichén Itzá   305

76. An engraving of Stephens (from Harper's *Monthly Magazine*, January 1859)   328

77. Stephens' cottage on the Rio Chagres (Harper's *Monthly Magazine*, January 1859)   349

78. Stephens' Tree in Panama. Stephens so admired this jungle monarch that he had the railway line diverted to preserve it (from Harper's *Monthly Magazine*, January 1859)   354

Which Introduces
Mr Stephens & Mr Catherwood

American archaeology had its effective birth with the explorations of John Lloyd Stephens and Frederick Catherwood. It was not merely forty-four archaeological sites that they found in Central America and Mexico between the years 1839–1843 but an entire civilization – one that had been irrevocably lost for four hundred years.

Heinrich Schliemann, who excavated the plains of Argos to find Troy and the topless towers of Ilium, did no more; nor did Paul Émile Botta, who dug out the remains of the Assyrians replete with their huge and terrible sculptures of winged bulls. The remains of ancient Greece, Egypt, and Mesopotamia were, in many instances, above ground and still within world memory. Even the Minoans had at least a known name and a timeless tradition. Thus when Sir Arthur Evans uncovered the Palace of Minos in Crete, archaeology was in effect illustrating the pages of Homer.

But Frederick Catherwood, British artist and architect, and John Lloyd Stephens, American lawyer by profession, traveler through inclination and archaeologist by choice, discovered a whole civilization so obscure that it had then neither name nor literature.

These two would have been famed alone for their discoveries and prescience but in addition they wrote three well-written and illustrated books which have aroused five generations of incipient archaeologists.

This then is their personal history.

V.W.vH.
First begun Copán 1937
Finished Rome 1973

PART I

THE MEETING

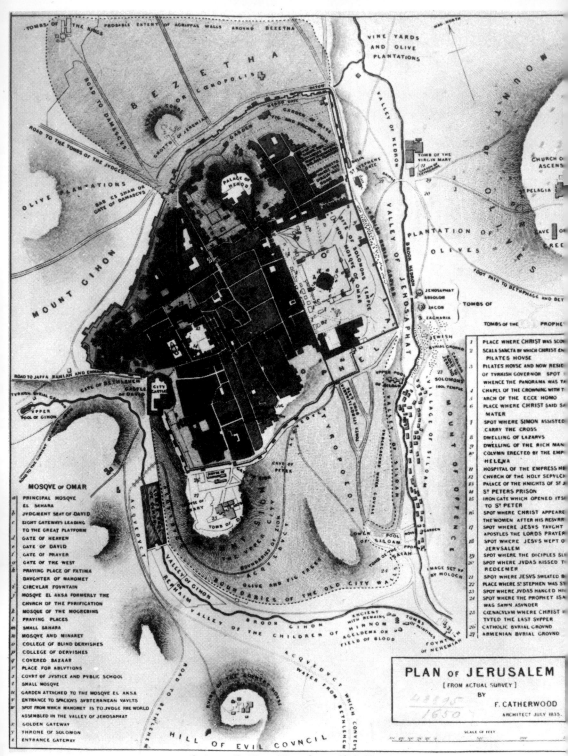

Catherwood's Plan of Jerusalem, published in 1835.

CHAPTER I

Who was Catherwood?

Frederick Catherwood began well enough. His eyes opened, in 1799, in London's Hoxton Parish during the late Georgian times, that period of candlelight and rhymed couplets.

The Catherwoods were neither well-placed nor mis-placed; they were gentry certainly of some financial competence since the house where Frederick Catherwood was born, and that still stands in Charles Square, is a graceful eighteenth-century building with architectural echoes of affluence and good taste.

Hoxton, in London's suburbs, was not then, as it was later to become, the 'Queen of Unloveliness.' It still carried an air about it. Shakespeare had acted in Hoxton at the theatre called The Curtain; Ben Jonson fought his duel there with Gabrial Spender; Keats lived close by; Mary Wollstonecraft Godwin, who wrote *Frankenstein* and lived with Shelley, was a Hoxtonian; and as a boy Catherwood walked past the local insane asylum, Balmes House (hence 'balmy'), where Mary Lamb had been confined after she had killed her mother with a carving knife.

There is not too much known about the other Catherwoods. The name appears occasionally in the public registers; in the middle of the 18th century a John James Catherwood enters the lists. This was Frederick's uncle, who resided at 21, Charles Square a small, charming square whose houses were 'occupied by a highly respectable class of persons'. Immediately next door at Number 20 was the residence of the other Catherwoods, Nathaniel and Elizabeth, the parents of our Mr Catherwood. He was born in that house on 27 February 1799.

While the Napoleonic wars raged in Europe, Frederick

Catherwood sought an education. For young people then without family position, an education or a place in the world was not easily acquired; education for those of meager circumstances was difficult. Catherwood doubtless attended one of those homespun day schools near to Charles Square which opened facilities to the children of Hoxton. There, presumably, Catherwood remained to the eighth form studying Accidence and Grammar, and becoming, at least to the satisfaction of the awarded certificates, 'a perfect grammarian, a good Orator and Poet, well instructed in Latin, Greek and Hebrew.' Short as it was, his education must have been basically good, for Catherwood became later an excellent linguist, able to speak Arabic, Greek and Italian, and to read, if not write, Hebrew. He also had enough 'Mathematicks' to prepare him for his profession.

Curiously enough, no one has ever described Catherwood so that his own self-portrait remains a luminous blur. Although he was known personally to almost every important artist or architect of his time and to many of the artists studying in Rome and to the regiment of artist-explorers (his colleagues) who toured Egypt (and although later he was a personal friend of most of the National Academicians in New York City), no one, for unfathomable reasons, ever drew or painted the reticent 'Mr Catherwood' – at least there is no known record of any portrait of him. Even among the hundred drawings of William Brockedon – now in the British Museum – containing pencilings of almost every one of Catherwood's contemporaries, there is none of him. In a rare autobiographical gesture Catherwood made a portrait of himself and his friend Joseph Bonomi for a 'Panorama of Jerusalem,' but this has been destroyed. There remains only his other self-portrait, in miniature and unclear, standing before one of the ruins of the Mayan site of Tulum. He is here pictured as a mature man of forty-two, and he drew himself as he undoubtedly was – light-haired and blue-eyed and as ruggedly constructed as a Dorchester fishing-boat. One can make out no more. Nor is there a word-picture of Catherwood; he is only referred to, even by his most intimate friends, as 'Mr Catherwood,' or very rarely as 'Cath'. John Lloyd Stephens, who knew him intimately for fifteen years, and traveled with him through strife-torn Central America, enduring with him imprisonment, disease, and incredible hardships, speaks of him only as 'Mr Catherwood.'

In 1820, under Joseph Severn's guidance, Catherwood began to attend the free art classes of the Royal Academy in London. Held at Somerset House, the school was open to qualified pupils.

It was in Soane's classes that Catherwood was introduced to Piranesi. It was a feverish moment when Soane exhibited the huge volume of Piranesi's *Della magnificenza ed architettura de' Romani* to his students. Catherwood, for one, was deeply moved by the manner in which Piranesi rendered the Roman ruins. It was Piranesi's treatment, his manner of conveying the impression of the great scale and magnificence of the buildings of ancient Rome that was astounding. For archaeology had early enmeshed him. After visiting Naples and the Paesteum he returned to Rome in 1740, where he spent the remainder of his life, 'quarreling with antiquarians and noble lords', but incessantly working and building for himself, by his skill as a draftsman and engraver, that monumental 'Acre perennius', which had been the admitted ambition of his life. Catherwood was influenced by Piranesi as by no other, and although he knew that the 'art of Piranesi is not a manner to be learnt,' he tried to capture in his own archaeological drawings the intense emotion of that master.

It was directly after Catherwood had exhibited his first drawing at the Royal Academy that his future itinerary developed, one that would determine his whole career; strangely enough, it came out of the circumstance of the illness of John Keats.

Keats was a friend of Joseph Severn, and being Hoxton-born, an intimate also of Catherwood. Severn had already begun to paint landscapes and portraits when he agreed to accompany Keats, who was then fatally ill with tuberculosis, to Italy where he expected to recover his health. After Keats's demise, Severn, who attended him up to his death, became famous for his death portrait of the young poet.

A painter of some renown, he later became British Consul in Rome. He now lies buried beside Keats in the renowned Protestant cemetery within the walls of Rome.

Joseph Severn's funds in 1821 consisted only of a pittance allowed him by the Royal Academy for a year's study in Rome, and Keats's of a small advance paid by John Taylor, his publisher, against his future poems.

Later, in response to the fervent entreaties of Severn, morose and melancholy after Keats's death, Frederick Catherwood joined him in Rome. This curiously enough is recorded; Joseph Severn, writing to his sister Maria on 15 September 1821, told of Catherwood's arrival at Severn's rooms at Via di San Isidoro 43 . . .

'. . . Mr Catherwood arrived here last night in perfect health and safety after a most favourable journey. I found him sitting in my Study with the same look and manner that I recollect in London – for he is the first Friend I have met here whom I knew there – his voice and face carried me to my dear home – it is a great pleasure and will be also a mutual improvement. We have this Morg. seen St. Peters – and the Vatican – with which he is quite delighted or I should say astonished – I have introduced him to many brother Artists here – Englishmen – there are three architects among them (T. J. Donaldson, Joseph Bonomi and J. J. Scoles) – whom he will begin to study with – and in the midst of many delightful Studies and speculations &c with many friends – The air in Rome is not unhealthy this season – so that I have remained here at the present time the weather and air is most delicious. Mr. C(atherwood) found this in the Morg. walk – he seems most gratified with what we tell of Rome and living in it. I think he has done wisely in coming whilst he is young – he will lay a foundation here that may direct nobly all through Life . . . Mr. Catherwood begs you to show my letter at Charles Square and prays them to excuse him writing this Post – his head is so full of Rome and Sleep and he is so tired . . .'

Catherwood was welcomed into the Society of Englishmen, 'all good fellows – twenty in number – Painters, Sculptors & Architects', wrote Severn. And it was in that exceedingly lively and enthusiastic group that he began his study of classical architecture. One of the four architects, Thomas Leverton Donaldson, the founder-to-be of the Royal Institute of British Architects and a life-long friend of Catherwood, was born in Bloomsbury Square in 1795, studied at the Royal Academy, and was awarded its Silver Medal. Thereafter, in pursuit of the antique, he left for Rome.

Two other architects of the 'Society of Englishmen', Scoles and Bonomi, arrived in Rome a few months after Catherwood. Scoles, the least remembered of them, had also studied the antique at the Royal Academy.

Born in 1798, Scoles is remembered now, if he is at all, as one of those present at Shelley's funeral; also for the great fiasco, the collapse of the suspension bridge, which he built in 1845 over the river Bure at Great Yarmouth.

Scoles was a constant companion of Catherwood in the Mediterranean, and long after he married and fathered four sons and eight daughters, he remained in touch with him. It is to Joseph John Scoles that we owe the only published biographical material of Catherwood – tantalizingly short though it is.

Joseph Bonomi, the famous curator of Sir John Soane's Museum at Lincoln's Inn Fields, is by far the best remembered of all these members of the Society of Englishmen. As the illustrator of Sir John Gardner Wilkinson's works on Egyptian archaeology, Bonomi's name is most enduringly linked to Egypt. He was a gay, small man, remembered in that circle of temperamental artists for his easy good nature. The son

7

of the Italian architect who had been brought from Rome on the invitation of the Brothers Adam, Joseph Bonomi was born in 1796 and inherited his father's talents. He went to Rome in company with Scoles and later, he and Bonomi and Catherwood were included as architectural artists on the famous Egyptian expeditions of Robert Hay.

Rome, in 1822, was filled with English aristocracy living elegantly in the villas of impecunious Roman nobles. At that time, everyone of consequence, it seemed, was in Rome; an endless succession of artists, sculptors, architects, and writers were working there under the munificence of the aristocracy, a society 'which was literary, athletic, dissipated and political.'

Catherwood soon found himself part of this dazzling group to which Joseph Severn had provided the key; he was admitted to the *conversazioni* of Roman society, a 'company numerous but very ill-sorted'. As Henry Fox complains, 'People of all descriptions without any connection or acquaintance with each other . . . gathered together and huddled up at the dinner table. . . .'

Catherwood also worked for a while with Elizabeth, Duchess of Devonshire, who was directing her own private excavations in the Forum. Then it was a pasture and an artist had to first scare off the cows before getting on with the serious work of limning the remains of Roman ruins. Although the 'antique' was in the air ever since the excavations had been begun in 18th century in Pompeii, archaeology had yet to leave the domain of the antiquarian, but with Henry Parke, one of the Society of Englishmen, Catherwood in turn excavated and made his first archaeological drawings, depicting the catacombs, which were published in the *Dictionary of Architecture*. Then, moving southward with drafting board and easel, he went to Sicily.

In the land of Demeter, Catherwood had his first glimpse of the remains of the Greeks. He followed the eastern shore, all along the way making sketches of the ruins in the effusive style of the Romantics. Of Taormina, lying midway between

Syracuse and Messina, all that visibly remained were the ruins of a Greek theater excavated twenty-three centuries ago out of the living rock of the northern face of Mount Taor, and a section of ancient walls with ruined columns facing Homer's 'purple sea.' The scene was stirringly picturesque. In the distance, snow-crowned Mount Etna acted as a superb backdrop, rising 10,800 feet into the blue Sicilian sky; the fabled Etna, where the Cumean Sybil abandoned Aeneas. It was this that Catherwood painted in tempera. It is a *pièce du milieu;* yet a superb one.*

After Rome, Greece was the architectural Mecca for young students; for Italy, the first to feel the pulse of archaeology, had given birth in 1733 to the Society of Dilettanti, composed of learned men – mostly Englishmen – who sponsored those superbly illustrated folios on classical architecture. Accompanied by Donaldson and Scoles, Frederick Catherwood went to Athens, arriving just about the moment that Lord Byron, volunteering for service with the Greeks, landed at Missolonghi with his retinue of twelve people, five horses, two cannons, and 50,000 Spanish pesos.

It had only been a few years before, in 1806, that Thomas Bruce, the 7th Earl of Elgin, had removed to the British Museum the Parthenon frieze by Phidias, so that Catherwood can well be counted among the early pioneer-artist-archaeologists in Greece. We do not know what Catherwood's itinerary was, nor precisely what ruins he drew, since none of his Grecian drawings are known. All we do know with certainty is what was succinctly revealed by his friend Stephens: 'Mr. Catherwood . . . shut up in Athens during the Greek revolution when it was besieged by the Turks, pursued his artistical studies and perforce made castings with his own hands.'

In the same year that Jean-François Champollion

*This picture was exhibited in 1839 at the National Academy of Design in New York and appears as Number 10 'Mount Etna from the Ruins of Tauramina.' It was purchased by Frederic Hoppin and has remained in the family in New York City for five generations; it is known only as 'the Catherwood'.

9

published in Paris (1824) his *Précis du Système Hieroglyphique des Anciens Egyptiens*, Catherwood (along with Henry Parks and Joseph Scoles) pooled their thin resources, hired a vessel with full crew and slowly went up the Nile. Drawing, sketching and making plans of ruins along the entire length of the navigable Nile up into the Nubian country, these young Englishmen were among the first to accurately record the ruins of Egypt. It had only been two decades since Napoleon, in 1798, had transported, in addition to his army, a whole corps of artists and antiquarians whose mission, among other things, was to compile a record of the ruins found in the valley of the Nile.

So, for more than one year, and at considerable risk of life, these young architects-artists systematically mapped and drew the clusters of ruins they found near to the Nile.

In more than one sense Catherwood's future was cast in the alembic of Egypt. For later in the October of 1824 he met Robert Hay, a young Englishman, rich and titled, who was then considering a large expedition up the Nile. It was Catherwood's drawings that delighted him and raised his enthusiasm, 'if such was possible,' he said. Later he dined with Catherwood who gave him, as he wrote in his still

2. *A view of Cairo in the Nile Valley.*

unpublished autobiography, 'much good and useful information of Egypt'.

Robert Hay of Linplum, heir to the marquisate of Tweedsdale, had thought out a most ambitious archaeological programme. With a retinue of experienced artists, architects, topographical draftsmen, and antiquarians (they were not yet called archaeologists), he planned to go up the Nile and investigate every ruined site, known and unknown. At each stop he planned to have his artists draw the murals with their inscriptions, and the architects make ground plans of the ruins; it was to be the greatest scientific expedition since Napoleon's. Composed mainly of Englishmen, many of whom in later years became famous for one reason or another, the group included Joseph Bonomi, Francis Arundale, James Haliburton (called Burton), Charles Laver, Edward W. Lane and Wilkinson (two incipient Egyptologists), G. B. Greenough, George A. Hoskins, and, to end the impressive list, Frederick Catherwood. These young men, during the years 1824–1833, were to lay down the basis of Egyptian archaeology.

Hay used his inheritance to good purpose; at his own expense he maintained this large expedition, which remained in the field for more than ten years. He bequeathed to the British Museum, in 1879, forty-nine folio volumes of paintings, drawings, plans and panoramas of Egyptian antiquities, a monument of archaeological research.

Hay himself published one book.

The expedition began its work at Memphis where Hay's artists drew to scale the great pyramids of Giza-Khufu, Khafre, and Menkawre, a work in which Catherwood's sketch of the pyramids of Gizeh was published. After Memphis, Saqqara and Abydos; by 1832, the expedition had set up its camp in the ruins of Thebes.

It was here, to the remains of the greatest cities of the ancient world – Thebes, Karnak, Luxor, and Deir el Bahri – that Robert Hay's company devoted their greatest attention. The magnificent temples built in the times of Queen

3. *Catherwood's sketch of the Temple of the Nobles at Thebes.*

4. *A sketch by Catherwood of the riverbank at Luxor looking up to the site.*

A Description of a View of THEBES, now exhibiting at the Panorama, Broadway, corner of Prince and Mercer Streets, New-Yo

1. ARAB VILLAGE.	6. GOURNOU.
2. THE NILE.	7. BEBAN EL MALOOR.
3. MEDEENET ABOU.	8. LIBYAN MOUNTAINS.
4. STATUES OF MEMNON, &c.	9. GRAND PROPYLON.
5. MEMNONIUM.	10. GREAT COURT.

11. SIDE TEMPLE.	16. FIRST COURT OF THE ANCIEN
12. LATERAL ENTRANCE.	17. SECOND COURT.
13. SECOND PROPYLON	18. THIRD COURT.
14. HALL OF COLUMNS	19. GRANITE SANCTUARY.
15. PROPYLON.	

5. *Catherwood's drawing of the port of call of Luxor.*

6. *Giza. Catherwood's view of the Pyramids in the Nile Valley.*

FINAL COURT.	23. WALLS OF UNBURNT BRICKS.	26. RESERVOIR.	29. LUXOR.
REMAINS OF A LARGE TEMPLE	24. CULTIVATED PLAIN AND DESERT.	27. RUINED PROPYLON.	30. GATEWAY OF PTOLEMY.
FINAL GATEWAY.	25. MOUNTAINS OF ARABIA.	28. PROPYLÆ.	31. TEMPLE AND PROPYLON.

Catherwood's sketch of his view of Thebes.

Hatshepsut in 1500 B.C. crowded the banks of the Nile. The Temple of Karnak, composed of red granite cut at quarries at Aswan, was so beautiful when completed that it brought insomnia to Hatshepsut, who said that 'she could not sleep because of this temple.' It had virtually the same effect upon the young English architects who pitched their tents among these superbly beautiful monuments of violently polychromed limestone.

Catherwood began work in September 1832 and, after careful measurements drew first a coloured plan of Thebes and then a detailed plan of the whole ruins. He then worked on a panorama of the valley showing Thebes* – a sketch that would one day be enlarged into a huge scenic panorama and displayed in London and New York. Later he drew to scale the obelisks that protruded above the ruins.

Toward the end of 1832 Catherwood, in company with James Haliburton, began work on the 'Colossi of Memnon.' Haliburton – of the Haliburtons of Roxburghshire – had come to Egypt in 1821 with Wilkinson, at the invitation of Mehemet Ali, to make a geological survey of the Nile. There, falling under the spell of the *antique*, he soon left the employ of the Pasha and went up the Nile. He had published in Cairo several bulky folios entitled *Excerpta Hieroglyphica*.

On the west bank of the Nile, between the ruined structure of Medinet Habu and the Ramesseum, stood the seventy-foot-high statue of Amen-Hotep III. An architectural sculpture three thousand years old, it had been fashioned out of a reddish conglomerate from the sandhills of Edfu, and floated down the Nile in eight especially constructed ships. Overawed by the size and grandeur of his work, the architect-sculptor of the 'Colossi' glowed with enthusiasm: 'They are wonderful' he said in hieroglyphics, 'for size and height, and they will last as long as heaven.'

*The huge circular canvass was destroyed in a fire that consumed Catherwood's rotunda in New York. The only representation of it is a wood engraving, printed in a pamphlet which guided the viewers as they moved around the circular mural. *A Description of a View of Thebes*, New York, 1836.

Catherwood raised a scaffold on the battered faceless sides of the statues, measured in detail these wonderful monuments of the 'vocal Memnon,' and drew them to scale, and then he excavated about their base and discovered that they reposed only on a stratum of sand. Catherwood's drawings, the first accurate ones ever made, were first published only recently; and still lie in the anonymity of the Hay collections in the British Museum. But his drawings of the Rameseum Court, the raised terrace and the Osiris pillars of Rameses II, had a history of publication, appearing in William Finden's *Landscape Illustrations of the Bible.*

Catherwood also etched his name among the hundreds of others, which included that of the Emperor Hadrian. Of all these graffiti his was most appropriate for he was the only one who drew them since the original Egyptian architect erected them.

The expedition continued up the Nile, working at Hierakonpolis, Edfu, and finally Elephantine and the Isle of Philae. There Catherwood copied the inscriptions on the intaglio walls relating to Ptolemy and Cleopatra. At the end of some weeks in the temples of Philae, he had a large portfolio of drawings, among others a watercolor that he thought was good enough to retain.*

The expedition ended, Catherwood was assigned to temporary oblivion. Of the hundreds of drawings and plans that form the huge Robert Hay collections, none of his work was published until the present author found and identified his drawings in the collections in the British Museum. The material contained in the 49 huge folios, is so vast that it would take a lifetime to interpret it. Doubtless much that Catherwood recorded in Egypt is now destroyed. Many of his drawings are signed merely 'F.C.' Many others are unsigned, so that only the experience gained from long contact with his style makes identification possible.

*297 Island of Philae, First cataract of the Nile – *Moonlight*; exhibited in 1845 at the National Academy of Design, New York.

8. *Catherwood's sketch of the ruins at Philae, 1833.*

9, 10. *The Colossi of Memnon. Catherwood's drawings of the statues of Amen-hotep III.*

Everyone, on that expedition, except Catherwood, it seemed, published a book illustrated with his own drawings. Henry Westcar, wrote *A Journal of a Tour made through Egypt, Upper & Lower Nubia* in 1823–1824. George Hoskins, another member of the expedition, who accompanied him to the Oasis of Khargam east of Thebes, wrote *A Visit to the Great Oasis of the Libyan Desert* (London 1837). Catherwood is often mentioned: 'A pistol with seven barrels belonging to Mr. C. was considered by all the Arabs who saw it a most formidable weapon and the fame of it was widely spread through the valley of the Nile. . . .' Robert Hay himself published a sumptuous *Illustrations of Cairo*. And finally there was Arundale. An architect who had aided the famed Augustus Pugin in collecting material for his *Architectural Antiquities of Normandy*, Arundale was one of the original members of the Robert Hay expedition. Francis Vyvyan Jago Arundale was an accomplished architectural draftsman, but suffered from epilepsy, and his seizures, which would come on without notice, were one of the trials of Catherwood.

Arundale published a book, *Illustrations of Jerusalem and Mt. Sinai* (London 1837), in which Catherwood figures. He himself seemed to be the mechanist of his own oblivion; he wrote nothing. Joseph Bonomi kept a diary.

Their project was an archaeological survey of the deserts east of Cairo, Sinai, and then north down the great rift through Jordan, Jerusalem, and into Lebanon.*

Catherwood, himself, must have been responsible for the meagerness of his personal history; there was some fundamental disequilibrium in his pysche. He was modest to a fault; he pushed the classic English virtues – dignity, serenity, reticence – to such a point that he diminished his own

---

*The present author is planning a retrospective work on Catherwood's work in Egypt, 'The Lost Egyptian Journals of Frederick Catherwood,' which will be based on personal exploration of all Egyptian sites and the Hay collections, British Museum Add Mss 29812–29860, and the Haliburton collections, British Museum Add Mss 25613–25675.

11. *Detail of the ruins at Philae. A temple dedicated to Hathor.*

12. *Catherwood's sketch of the view near Elephantine just below Aswan in 1833.*

personality. Formal and restrained, he exhibited early symptoms of melancholia. Yet he had enthusiasm, despite his reserved and retiring manner, and this was to sustain him while, in the narrow corners of some lost world, he delineated the remains of forgotten civilizations.

The long years in the Near East, under the benign action of the Mediterranean sun, had brought about an outward change in the appearance of Frederick Catherwood. He dressed as an Arab with robe and turban and, so says his friend Arundale, 'was well versed in Oriental manners.' He could speak fluent Arabic, Italian, and Hebrew; he seems also to have lost something of the reticence that early characterized him. By 1833 he had accumulated a great mass of material and observations such as no architect-archaeologist had up until then – or perhaps since. He had traveled the classical lands, Italy, Greece, and Sicily, delineating all with considerable skill, and after his journeys on the Nile he had been employed for a while as an engineer by Mehemet Ali to repair the mosques at Cairo. This permitted him to make the first architectural analysis of Saracenic structures (although these drawings, unhappily, are lost). In favour with Mehemet Ali, he carried the Pasha's personal firman, and traveled through Libya into West Africa, and in 1832 he was at the Regency of Tunis at Dugga, where he drew a twenty-foot plinth, a beautiful four-columned prostyle, built with an inscription on its façade stating that it had been erected by two brothers.*

In 1833 Catherwood, Arundale, and Bonomi, dressed as Turkish merchants, completed their preparations for an expedition into Sinai and Arabia Petra. They purchased, wrote Arundale, 'necessaries from the bazaar at Cairo,' and left for Mt. Sinai on 29 August, 1833. With the published

---

*'Frederick Catherwood: *Account of the Punico-Libyan Monument at Dugga and the Remains of an Ancient Structure at Bless near the site of Ancient Carthage,*' Trans. of the American Ethnological Society (vol. I), *New York, 1845.*

narrative of Arundale and the unpublished diary of Bonomi one can trace Catherwood's participation on this desert journey; they followed the camel-caravan route around the shore of the Red Sea. After leaving Suez, they passed hundreds of camels watering at Girgade, the nearest potable water to Suez. On the seventh day of travel they came to Wadi Mokateb – the Rock of Inscriptions. These inscriptions – in many languages, Greek, Arabic, and Latin – were 'copied by Cath and Arundale.' The Sinai peninsula is filled with ruins and in the Gebel el Igma, they came to the ruins of Sabit el Khadin. Later, when the road reached 5,000 feet altitude, they came upon the ancient Ummlugma mines, where they found the furnaces which melted gold and copper for the predynastic Egyptian cultures.

Many aspects of the sites which lie midway between two cultures, Egyptian and Nabatean, were copied by Catherwood.

On 16 September they arrived at the Convent of St Catherine. This Greek convent, famed for its hospitality, was the guardian of Mt. Sinai; Bonomi's diary records: 'Begun to ascend the mountain [we] made sketches of all the remarkable spots'.

During the last days of September and into October 1833, Catherwood, Arundale, and Bonomi travelled through the

13. Catherwood's panorama of Jerusalem.

A Description of A VIEW of JERUSALEM, now exhibiting at the PANORAMA, Broadway, corner of Prince and Mercer Streets.

onvent of St. Pelagia.
narch of Ascension.
here the Prayer was taught.
rotto of the Creed.
here Christ wept over Jerusalem.
arden of Gethsemane.
urial Place of the Virgin.
hrone of Solomon.

9. Graves of the Prophets.
10. Golden Gate.
11. Road to Jericho.
12. City Walls.
13. Praying Place.
14. Little Sahhara.
15. The Harem Scheriff.
16. Mountains of Arabia.

17. Dead Sea.
18. Judgment Seat of David.
19. Stoa Sahhara.
20. Invisible Bridge.
21. Mosque of Omar.
22. Gate of Heaven.
23. Praying Place of Fatima, Daughter of Mahomet.

24. El Mirage, Place of Ascension of the Prophet.
25. Mosque El Aksa.
26. Mount of Offence.
27. Mosque of the Mogrebins.
28. Fountain.
29. Minaret of the Seraglio.
30. Potters' Field.

31. Hill of Evil Council.
32. Habitations of Dervishes.
33. Mount Zion, with David's Tomb.
34. Armenian Church, and Convent.
35. Ruins of the Church and Convent of the Knights of St. John.
36. Castle of David.

20

Lands of Udemco where, through bouts of ague and illness ('Catherwood unwell so we tarried;' 'Arundale had three attacks of his old complaint'), they continued to draw the remains of whatever came within sight. By 6 October they arrived in Jerusalem.

It was Jerusalem and its environs that inspired Catherwood to undertake the most important of his architectural-archaeological researches in the Middle East; he was to complete the entire plan and details of El-Aqsa and the Dome of the Rock or the Mosque of Omar.

Throughout October 1833 he was essaying the first approaches to the Jerusalem 'problem'; 'Catherwood and I walked all this afternoon round the walls and returning by the pilgrims' gate . . . Monday 14th . . . put into effect two views of the house of Lazarus and the via Dolorosa . . . Monday 21st . . . sketching the Dome [of the Rock] and an outline of those strangely twisted columns. . . .'

Within days they were being troubled by Arabs who told them that they were not allowed 'to draw within the sacred enclosure for Cath went yesterday and the Governor saw him . . .' Later 'Cath was within the wall . . . he is now so bold that I think I must make my escape. . . .'

NEW-YORK HISTORICAL SOCIETY

of Unah.	43. Gate of Damascus.	51. Sheiks, Judges.	58. Turkish Soldier.	65. Church of St. Anna.
part of the Temple of the Holy	44. Arch of Ecce Homo, in the Via Dolorosa.	52. Pipe Bearer.	59. Arabs from the Borders of the Dead Sea.	66. Gate of St. Stephen.
ulchre.	45. Messrs. Catherwood and Bonomi.	53. Mufti.	60. Women of the same Tribe.	67. Pool of Bethesda.
of the Temple of the Holy	46. Servants Making Coffee.	54. Aga, or Governor.	61. Dervish.	68. Minaret, Ben Israel.
ulchre.	47. A Sheik and his Son.	55. Interpreter.	62. Merchant of Damascus.	69. Where the Angels appeared.
ouvent.	48. A Sheriff, or Descendant of Mahomet.	56. Greek and Latin Friars.	63. Site of Herod's Palace.	70. Chapel of the Crown of Thorns.
in the Via Dolorosa.	49. Scribes.	57. The Bastinado about to be administered.	64. Scopus.	71. Palace of Pontius Pilate, or Aga's Ho
on the Site of Pilate's House.	50. Albanian Servant, with Coffee.			

By 24 October Catherwood had set up his materials and 'apparati' on the roof of the House of Pontius Pilate: 'Cath is making his Panorama of Jerusalem'. Working with his camera lucida* he was able, by this simple yet effective instrument, to put down relatively quickly the entire outline of Jerusalem, as if he was using a panoramic lens in a modern camera.

When the Arabs swept into the Jordan Valley, over-whelming the armies of Heraclitus, all Palestine fell. The Arabs entered Jerusalem in A.D. 640. Behind the ancient city wall – the lower courses of which belonged to the period of Herod the Great – the Arabs, with the aid of Greek Christian architects and workmen, erected the magnificent Dome of the Rock. It and the adjoining Mosque of El-Aqsa were built in A.D. 691 by the Umayyad prince Abd el-Malik.

The Dome of the Rock had long been a subject of heated dispute between contending antiquarians, architects, and religious historians. A mosaic-walled mosque in a corner of ancient Jerusalem, it has long held a place in the Islamic diadem, for here Mohammed ascended on his eagle-winged horse to visit the seven heavens of Islam.

Mohammed's footprint is supposed to be impressed in that sacred black rock, a fact on which Mark Twain cast much impish doubt when he measured it and judged that Mohammed would have taken a size 18 shoe. In Catherwood's time, unbelievers took their lives in their hands when they entered. No architect up to that time had ever limned it nor its interior design.

By 7 November he is again at the Dome of the Rock despite the threat against him should he continue his drawing. 7 November '. . . Cath said he would go in even if it were necessary to say he was a Mussulman.' Then, on 13 November,

---

*The camera lucida was an instrument much used in the nineteenth century for copying the outlines of buildings. By means of a prism, formed by a certain arrangement of lenses, it causes an external image to be projected on a sheet of paper where outlines can be faithfully traced.

14.   *Etching by Finden from a drawing by Catherwood of the Mosque of Omar and El Aqsa at Jerusalem.*

15.   *Etching made from a drawing by Catherwood of the interior of the Golden Gate in Jerusalem.*

1833 Catherwood, dressed as an Egyptian officer and carrying, as he wrote, 'a strong firman expressly naming me as an engineer in the service of Mehemet Ali,' he returned to the mosque.

Mehemet Ali, born in 1769 in Albania, had his schooling in a Turkish regiment, where, between massacres, he learned the rudiments of speech and good custom. After trying his hand in the Latakia tobacco trade, he was sent as a lieutenant by the Turkish Sultan to command three hundred Albanian soldiers, to aid General Bonaparte's invasion of Egypt. Mehemet Ali played a superb game of trickery; he helped Napoleon against the British; then the British against Napoleon; then when Lord Nelson annihilated the French fleet, he remained in Egypt and consolidated his position.

In the chaos that resulted from the Napoleonic wars he aided the Mamelukes against the Turks; then he played off one faction against the other, finally inviting the heads of the factions to his palace in Cairo, where he slaughtered them all. Thus Mehemet Ali, 'whose every act,' wrote the French Consul to his government, 'reveals a Machiavellian mind'. To prove his theory he gave a copy of *Il Principe* to Mehemet Ali, which was translated to him ten pages a day. On the fourth day of reading Machiavelli Mehemet Ali spoke: '. . . in the first ten pages I discovered nothing great or new . . . I waited. But the next ten pages were no better. The last ten were merely commonplace. I can learn nothing from Machiavelli. And as regards cunning, I know far more than he did about it. Now stop and translate no more.'

It was with the firman of this formidable Mehemet Ali that Catherwood was able to enter the Dome and draw with impunity.

In this instance Catherwood has left a personal account. After making a survey of Jerusalem and a general plan of Harm es Shereef, and drawings of the exteriors of El-Aqsa and the Dome of the Rock, he entered the interior of the mosque 'feeling irresistibly urged to make an attempt.'

He wrote to the well-known travel-writer W. H. Bartlett: '. . . It was a proceeding certain to attract attention and expose me to dangerous consequences. The cool assurance of my servant, at once befriended and led me on. We entered, and arranging the camera [lucida] I quickly sat down to my work, not without some nervousness . . . I was completely surrounded by a mob of two hundred people who seemed screwing up their courage for a sudden rush upon me and, I believe, few moments would have passed ere we had been torn to pieces, when an incident occurred that converted our danger and discomfiture into positive triumph. This was the sudden appearance of the Governor on the steps of the platform. Catching sight of him, the foremost – rushed tumultuously up to him, demanding the punishment of the infidel, who was profaning the holy precincts. At this the Governor drew near, and as we had often smoked together, and were well acquainted, he saluted me politely, and supposing it to be beyond the reach of possibility that I could venture to do what I was about without a warrant from the pasha, he at once applied himself to cool the rage of the mob. "You see, my friends," he said, "that our holy mosque is in a dilapidated state, and no doubt our lord and master Mehemet Ali has sent this Effendi to survey it, in order to complete its repair. If we are unable to do these things for ourselves, it is right to employ those who can; and such being the will of our lord, the pasha, I require you to disperse and not incur my displeasure by any further interruption." And turning to me, he said, in hearing of them all, that if anyone had the hardihood to disturb me in the future, he would deal in a summary way with him. I did not, of course, think it necessary to undeceive the worthy Governor; and gravely thanking him, proceeded with my drawing. All went on quietly after this.

During six weeks, I continued to investigate every part of the mosque and its precincts, introducing my astonished companions as necessary assistants in the work of the survey.

But when I heard of the near approach of *Ibrahim Pasha,*
I thought it was time to take leave of Jerusalem . . .'

So Catherwood finished the drawings of the mosque,
made sections of the Dome, measuring the exterior wall, and
within six weeks had enough details of the most famous
mosque in the whole Mohammedan world to erect another
like it. It was up to that time his greatest single effort.

He had intended on his return to London to publish his
work in book form, utilizing all the superb drawings that he
had made. He found the London publishers indifferent; in
disgust he put his drawings away.

Not many years after Catherwood had worked there, a
violent controversy developed between various schools of
architecture over the origin of the Dome of the Rock.
Mr James Fergusson, the eminent historian of architecture,
conjectured that this mosque had been built by Constantine,
over the tomb of Christ. Challenged by antiquarians, he
sought out Catherwood, in order to see the drawings and
prove his archaeological theory. In 1846 he made contact
with him.

'The only means,' Fergusson wrote, 'that occurred to me
of getting out of this dilemma was trying if possible to gain
access to Mr. Catherwood's drawings which I knew did exist
somewhere. Mr. Catherwood in answer to a letter I wrote
him . . .' in January 1847 turned over his collections to
Fergusson. Thus disappeared another phase of Catherwood's
own archaeological monument. He lost his identity. Now all
his drawings of the Mosque of Omar have disappeared.

After the harrowing weeks in the interior of the Mosque of
Omar, Catherwood was anxious to see those ruins – not
less than fifty miles from Jerusalem – that had been discovered
by the German traveller Ulrich Seetzen in 1806.

Under its Roman name, Gerasa, it was one of the members
of the Greek commercial league known as the Decapolis.
The Romans, when they rebuilt the city and incorporated it

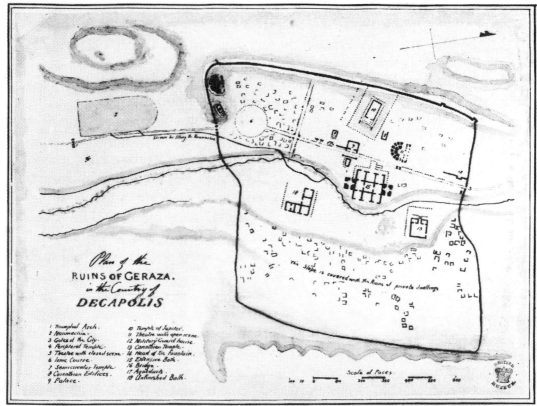

Plan of the
RUINS OF GERAZA.
in the Country of
DECAPOLIS

1 Triumphal Arch.
2 Naumachia.
3 Gates of the City.
4 Peripteral Temple.
5 Theatre with closed scene.
6 Ionic Course.
7 Semicircular Temple.
8 Corinthian Edifices.
9 Palace.
10 Temple of Jupiter.
11 Theatre with open scene.
12 Military Guard house.
13 Corinthian Temple.
14 Head of the Fountain.
15 Extensive Bath.
16 Bridge.
17 Aqueduct.
18 Unfinished Bath.

16. *Catherwood's plan of the ruins of Geraza (Jarash, Jordan).*

17. *A contemporary view of the Temple of Zeus, Jarash, by S. D. Harding.*

into Provincia Arabia, wisely allowed the Greek culture and language to remain.

The Emperor Vespasian had erected a wall around it in A.D. 75, and through it flowed a perennial stream, making the land about it vividly green and giving Gerasa an Arcadian setting. It is the finest and most completely preserved Roman provincial city in the Middle East. The Roman road passes through a triumphal arch, runs beside the amorphous remains of a Hippodrome, and leads into an immense stone-laid Forum, irregularly elliptical, and unique. The road, which becomes the principal street of Gerasa, is colonnaded from one end to the other. The paving stones – the polished white limestone slabs – still lie in their original form, wonderfully engineered with a drainage system underneath.

Shops once lined the streets; a nymphaeum, lovingly created to receive and then dispense the water of a brook which flowed into it, still stands mid-distance in the street. There are two theaters with Greek inscriptions, one at each end of the city; temples, baths, a vast scattering of house sites. At the north gate the road moves under an inscription. 'Built in A.D. 115 by Claudius Severus, legate of Trajan.' It seems incredible that this city should have slipped from memory until Seetzen came across it in 1806.

Catherwood tried to work rapidly within the time at their disposal, but there were problems: 'I made a sketch or two, found the people extremely troublesome . . .' In order to dominate the situation, he displayed his famous gun (the one with the seven barrels). The Arabs, wanting to know how it could be fired without a flint, fell prostrate when it went off. Bonomi's mule bolted 'so that I was obliged to offer ten piasters to some Arabs to catch him'.

Then there was Arundale; epileptic fits came on now with greater frequency and most of Catherwood's time was spent attending him. Under these circumstances there was not too much archaeological rendering and yet . . .

And yet Catherwood completed the first ground plan ever

to be made. He also did a drawing of the Temple of Artemis – perhaps the first ever made by a capable artist. This had reasonable recognition, it was engraved by Finden for his *Landscape Illustrations of the Bible* (London 1836).

It was inevitable that Catherwood should be drawn to the ruins of Baalbek. A pass through the mountains inland from Beirut led to the verdant valley that lay between Lebanon and Anti-Lebanon, fertile and well watered from the snow-covered peaks that surrounded it. The Orontes River had its origin there. It was famed for its cult of the god Baal; it had been Phoenician, then Greek, and finally Roman. They retained its Greek name, Heliopolis, the Sun City, and under the Antonines the Romans lavished much attention upon it; the huge complex of the temples of Baalbek rose from the ruins of early Phoenician structures. The Temple of Bacchus rested upon monolithic cut limestone; the largest single piece of stone ever cut, transported and fitted into place, was sixty feet long, seventeen feet across, the weight of each stone was 1,500 tons. On this base the Temple of Bacchus rose; the roof had been made from tiles.

Pitching his tent among the fallen columns, Catherwood, with Arundale in attendance, began the survey of the Temple of Jupiter. With careful attention to detail Catherwood drew the architectural lyrics of Baalbek, the Propylaea, the forecourt, the Great Forecourt with its altar pure and pristinely classical, the Heliopolis-Temple of Jupiter-Baal, and the sections of the Temple of Bacchus with its exquisite stone doorway and motif of fig leaves that time and man had spared. It had been erected in the era of Antoninus Pius (86–161), pilleged in 748 by the Seljuka, fell in 1134 into the bloodstained hands of Genghis Khan, and was taken by the Turks in 1517, in whose territory it remained until 1918.

The six remaining columns of the Temple of Jupiter, sixty-two feet in height, commanded a panorama of the watered greensward. The beautiful Roman temple, which had been turned into a basilica by the Byzantines, transformed by the Moslems into a mosque, and destroyed by the Mongols, was now only winter stalls for nomadic shepherds. Now there remained only six pillars, still retaining architrave, frieze, and cornice. Composed of three immense marble drums, the columns had been cemented by molten lead. This led to their destruction, for Arabs tumbled the columns to obtain the lead. The stupendous ruins have been figured and described over and over again. They had been known to the British ever since Robert Wood published, *The Ruins of Baalbek* in 1753.

There is no other record of Catherwood's visit to Baalbek than passing reference by Arundale who accompanied him. All else we know about his work in Baalbek is bibliographical.*

On 16 March, 1834, as we know from a letter dated from Damascus, Catherwood was preparing to go to Palmyra. This fabled desert city, first seen by Englishmen in the eighteenth century, lay 125 miles south-east from Damascus directly in the desert. Since Palmyra was an oasis and offered a perennial water supply it was an important station on the caravan traffic route. The Roman road enters Palmyra through the gateway of the great wall of Justinian, built in the sixth century A.D.

At once one enters the long colonnaded street of which 150 columns remain standing. As at Gerasa, the street of white limestone proceeds between the columns. A water conduit ran beside the road and it still can be seen ramifying into buildings which were the residential centre.

A well-preserved theatre, only the seats being weathered by wind and sun, is directly beside the road, and around it a whole city of shops, residences, fountains, temples and caravanserais. These give an impression of the wealth of the city that governed the vast caravan trade with the East.

Palmyra acquired its pre-eminence in trade and power in Trajan's time. It became a desert emporium. Cotton was

*Robert Burford: Description of a View of the Ruins of The Temple at Baalbek . . . Painted from drawings by F. Catherwood. London 1844.

brought in by bales, golden trinkets from Parthia, jewels from Babylon and, silk dyed with Tyrian purple. There was myrrh from Ethiopia, rare woods and spices from Persia, richly woven textiles, and live birds.

In an animated letter to Joseph Bonomi, dated 16 March, 1834, Catherwood asks him to 'join us in an excursion to Palmyra. We hear from Sheriff Bey that the road is safe and intend to leave as soon as possible after the return of the messenger . . .'

The Panorama of Damascus he must have done within the same period because he writes: 'At present [the month

18. Catherwood's Panorama in New York City.

of March] the trees are not out and consequently I cannot begin my Panorama.' That it was completed we know from the 'puff' that John L. Stephens gave his Rotunda in New York.

'Catherwood . . . has under his control large panoramas of Jerusalem,* Thebes, Damascus, Baalbek, Algiers, Carthage, and Athens.' Since Catherwood had lived in all these cities it is apparent that he did make panoramas of them all. And all are lost.

In the last days of the reign of King William IV, Great Britain was poised to enter an unprecedented era of material prosperity. In 1835 after nine years of unprofitable research amid the ruins of ancient empires, Frederick Catherwood returned to London. Spurred by the need of money he entered business as a panoramist, mortgaging his art services for Robert Burford.

Leicester Square had long been the centre of panoramic attractions. Its outsized rotundas housing colossal circular murals, paintings of battles, coronations, cities remote and romantic, drew, as does the cinema today, immense numbers of curious people. This cloud of panoramas, dioramas, poluphusikons, and eidophusikons, 'where the eye was pleased without the brain being duly exerted,' had a great hold over the public. Although many of art's immortals painted panoramas at one time or other in their careers, little is known about the medium. The panorama has had a neglected history.

A certain Herr Breisig, a German architectural painter of Danzig, is credited with the idea of the panorama in the late eighteenth century. It was soon taken up with much profit by Robert Barker of Edinburgh, who went to London in 1793 with his sketch of a panorama of Edinburgh.

Leicester Square had been well chosen as a site for the panoramas; it had a long art tradition. Sir Joshua Reynolds

*F. Catherwood: Plan of Jerusalem, published 1 August, 1835; F. Catherwood, 21 Charles Sq., Hoxton, London.

had lived there since 1760, painting in his studio the portraits that had made him famous. Hogarth, his contemporary, had lived near by at the Sign of the Golden Head until his death, so that a certain exotic air continued to bring artists to the Square. Long a favourite resort for dualists it became also a home for French Huguenots. Peter the Great had been entertained there when he came to England, in 1698, to learn shipbuilding, and this atmosphere of the foreigner continued to the end of the century when aristocratic émigrés, fleeing the revolution, took refuge in the *pensions* facing the Square that had been called after Robert Sindet, the Second Earl of Leicester.

So apparent was this 'foreign air' that Charles Dickens in *Bleak House* complained of it as 'a centre of attraction to indifferent foreign hotels and indifferent foreigners. Old China, gaming houses, exhibitions and a large medley of shabbiness and drinking out of sight.'

And 'Sex shops too,' writes the author of the *Encyclopaedia of London*, 'sex shops, birth control devices by Mrs Philips', announced at 5 Orange Street near Leicester Fields at the Sign of the Golden Fan and Rising Sun, where she 'sells implements of safety having thirty-five years' experience in making them and selling them.'

Decidedly, Leicester Square was well chosen for Robert Barker's panoramas!

In the rotunda, the people of London saw a muralistic history of their times. Whenever some noteworthy event occurred, Barker sent his own son or other artists attached to the panorama to make sketches, and within the time of memory a large, dramatically lighted panorama was set up in the rotunda.

The medium became so popular that many famed British artists, at one time or other in their apprenticeship, contributed to the panoramas: Thomas Girtin, the famous English water colourist was one of these.

In 1826 Barker turned over his interests to the Burfords,

father and son, and thereafter the rotunda in Leicester Square was known as 'Robert Burford's Panorama.'

Robert Burford, who trained Catherwood as a panoramist, had actively engaged in the enterprise ever since he had left the Royal Academy. An excellent artist and much traveled he made the original sketches for the panoramic murals of Waterloo, Athens, the Niagara Falls, Constantinople, the Ruins of Pompeii and in 1830, the View of New York City. In constant search for new material, Burford sought out British artists as they returned from their tours. So in 1835 he got in touch with Catherwood, newly arrived from the Holy Land. If this did not enhance his reputation as an architect it at least provided him with money.

It also gave his career a new direction, and was to bring him in contact with John Lloyd Stephens.

CHAPTER II

Which Introduces Mr Stephens

The New York City of John Lloyd Stephens* was then in 1805, only fourteen miles round. It was a little overgrown village of crooked and winding streets, with houses, mostly built in the Dutch style: high-roofed, gables on which weathercocks perched.

But this little old New York was cosmopolitan enough; beyond the Dutch and Americans its 60,000 population included a generous sprinkling of French, mostly émigrés from the French revolution (one of whom was Anthelme Brillat-Savarin, the author of *Physiologie du goût*) and sizeable groups of Germans, Swedes, and Irish. The Battery then at the tip of Manhattan was the place of promenade and elegance while Bowling Green was the centre of popular riots and popular sports, a spot which Stephens associated with his earliest recollections:

'It had been my playground as a boy: hundreds of times I had climbed over the fence to get my ball. I was one of those who held it long after the city of New York invaded our rights . . .'

At that time Brooklyn was a small village, reached only by ferry boat; Greenwich Village was a Potters' Field.

This America still looked to Europe for its standards in manners and taste. Its society was, quite naturally, a microcosm of England, and New York prided itself as being a 'little London'. Men dressed as they did in London town, albeit two seasons behind, in powdered queue, white-topped boots, silk stockings, breeches and cocked hats. The dress of women was 'Empire,' high waisted with the long sweep skirt hiding all but the points of prunella slippers.

*He was born in Shrewsbury, New Jersey, on 25 November, 1805 and moved to New York at the age of thirteen months.

With all its promise America was still no Arcadia. Despite its hustle and bustle there were ominous political rumblings over the land. New Yorkers were still nerve-strained by the aftermath of the presidential campaign of 1804, that batrachomyomia that had sent Thomas Jefferson to the White House and Alexander Hamilton to his grave. It had been one of unbridled bitterness, reaching its climax on the heights of Weehawken; for not only had Alexander Hamilton been killed in honourable combat with Aaron Burr, but with him had died Federalism, and as a corollary in its demise the dream of Jefferson that America would continue to be a land of husbandmen 'free from the corruptions of industrialism'.

Pressure from abroad, the centuries-old struggle between Great Britain and France for continental dominance, had lapped up to America's shores. There were impressments of sailors at sea and seizures of American vessels, giving rise to hostilities that produced the Embargo Act of 1807. This act began the era of American industrialization; manufacturing began to spring up almost everywhere so as to fill the void of the continental blockade. The 'corruption by industrialism' had begun.

Young John Lloyd Stephens grew as America grew. He was taking his first faltering steps while the Expedition of Lewis and Clark was examining the vast real estate that America had acquired with the Louisiana Purchase.

He had been learning to babble his first sentences when Robert Fulton's steam-boat *Clermont* anchored directly in front of his Greenwich Street home. He was a bright-eyed, mischievous boy when Zebulon Pike placed his standard on a peak in the Rocky Mountains: as John Stephens matured, so did his country, and this left a deep impression on him.

The evolving of John Lloyd Stephens in this young America gave him an enthusiasm and interest, with a boundless curiosity in people and places. This was discernible at an early age.

Learning then, in 1812 was 'driven in'; young Stephens was incessantly birched, beaten on that part which was then considered, as he remembered, 'the channel of knowledge into a boy's brain.' In 1815, at the age of ten, he entered the preparatory Classical School which was the gateway to Columbia College.

At the age of thirteen – there was then no intermediate school – John Stephens moved on to Columbia College. Its five faculty members arranged the admission into college by examination: 'No student shall be admitted into the lowest class of Columbia College unless he be accurately acquainted with the grammar of both the Greek and Latin tongues . . . He shall be versed in the four rules of arithmetic, the rule of three direct and inverse, decimal and vulgar fractions, with Algebra as far as the end of simple equations. And with modern geography.'

The classical examination was to be *ad aperturam libri*. On these terms Stephens was admitted in March 1818 to Columbia College, from which he was graduated in 1822.

At 17 years of age, Stephens looked now towards a profession. He elected law, and being articled out as a law clerk in the office of Mr Daniel Lord he began to read Blackstone.

An able lawyer, Daniel Lord was 'strictly professional, no politics.' He attended Yale University and had then read law at Tapping Reeve's Law School at Litchfield.

As he believed that Stephens would make a good lawyer, he urged him to attend the law school in Connecticut. Stephens at first did not like the idea of leaving New York with its theatres, its clubs, and its balls, to go – at least for a year – into 'exile' in Connecticut: but 'leave' he did.

Litchfield, even now a stately Connecticut town, had been in 1722 an outpost for the north-west frontier. It lay on a high plateau above the Naugatuck Valley, just east of the Housatonic River on the main line of post coaches.

Stephens arrived in one of these great red, creaking four-horse coaches which made connection with the Hudson sloops at Poughkeepsie. Careering down the main street past the dignified colonial houses framed by giant elm trees, he saw that Litchfield was cosmopolitan despite its meager 6,000 population. Painted signs overhanging the red-bricked sidewalks announced an importer, a hatter, a bookbinder; and the *Gazeteer* listed the town as having '4 forges, 1 slitting mill, one nail factory . . . 1 paper mill, comb factories, hatters and grain'.

But it was not its modest commerciality that made Litchfield cosmopolitan but the students that it drew to its schools.

Tapping Reeve's Law School by the time of Stephens' arrival had managed in the half-century since its founding, to turn out two vice-presidents of the United States, sixteen senators, fifty members of Congress, two Supreme Court justices, ten governors, five cabinet members, and countless judges, lawyers and businessmen; even artists and writers.

The Law School was held in a small frame building adjacent to the home of Tapping Reeve. At first, in 1784, he had held classes in his home; but as his fame spread and more students arrived, he built America's first law school.

The law, as taught by Litchfield, was as comprehensive as its résumé implied. Lectures, six days a week, were given in the mornings, while the students took voluminous notes. The rest of the day was spent consulting the authorities. On Saturday afternoons the students were examined on the week's lectures, and on Monday – usually in the evening – occurred the high point of the week: the students held a moot court, in which they argued hypothetical cases.

In the study of the mental growth of the man who would one day discover the Maya culture, we have a series of Stephens' letters to his father.

Every Sunday he wrote to his father summarizing the week, choosing Sunday on 'a principle of expediency' so as not to interfere with church attendance.

He examined the Law, the school, and its mentors: 'One of the facts I think does me no small honour. I cannot account for my not having mentioned it before, since I can find no óther reason for my omission, I must attribute it to my modesty. I called attention to a fact which I think I may cover without fear of contradiction; *that I am the youngest student in the class.*'

The Law students were quartered with different families in town, at a cost of $45.00 the year – board cost $2.75 the week and fireplace wood $4.00 the cord. As for Stephens he wrote on 17 August, 1823:

> I am now situated in a room that I would not exchange for any in the place. The window at which I am now sitting commands a view of the larger and handsomer part of the village, while by merely turning my head, I can enjoy exclusively the beauties of the country, another window opening to one of the most picturesque landscapes in the neighbourhood.

On 20 September, 1823, Daniel Lord, the New York lawyer who had already given Stephens a clerkship, made him the offer which would begin his legal career which in turn would heighten his interest in politics and finally as a concatenation of cause and effect set him off on his travels. The offer was conveyed through his father Benjamin Stephens.

Stephens answered:

> If Mr. Lord could insure me the income he mentioned, this would be decisive of the question . . . When I see so many entering upon this profession which has already more than its share, so many of the finest talents, un-remitted application, and with every incentive to exertion, and hear so many complaints of the scanty pay the law allows it followers . . . there is comfort in the consideration of the fact, that many dull, stupid, ignoramusses etc.,

thrive and seem are able to live upon 'the fat of the land', and through a mortifying idea to hope to succeed because other blockheads do, yet this very humbling reflection brightens the prospects of one who believes sincerely in the 'glorious uncertainty of the law.'

On his eighteenth birthday, Stephens had his decision made for him. In bowing to his father's will to have him enter the office of Daniel Lord, Lawyer, he wrote: '. . . that in all family concerns, a Father is *Judge*, *Jury* and *Executioner*.'

In September 1824, John Lloyd Stephens, graduate of law and connected with one of the famous lawyers of the day, returned to New York, conveyed once again in one of those red, high-wheeled coaches.

In 1823, the Far West was still located east of the Mississippi. Although it was beginning to attract settlers much of the Ohio, Illinois, and Indiana territories were vast and vacant. One of John L. Stephens' aunts, Helena, had married a Quaker who had responded to the restlessness of the period and had migrated to Illinois territory.

A pitiful letter had come to the Stephens family from their Aunt Helena Ridgway telling of the death of her child.

'How shall I reveal to you my Dear sister my most unhappy moments . . . our sweet little Emma is gone, my grief is unutterable. . . .'

It was generally agreed that someone of the Stephens family should visit the Ridgways. Whereupon John Stephens, before he entered into his career as lawyer, elected to undertake the hazardous trip. His cousin, Charles Henrickson, also agreed; so it is to him, rather than Stephens, that we owe the chronicles of the first adventure.

By 26 September the cousins were in the Western reserve of Ohio. At Pittsburg they were immediately caught up in a riot about which Charles Henrickson wrote to his mother who already feared the worst.

Here the plains and hills were already swarming with pioneers; Marietta, Chillicothe, Cincinnati, were rapidly emerging as cities. Connestoga wagons crawled along the dirt-bound roads, and the rivers were lined with keelboats, flatboats, and broadhorns. The human stream carried along all manners of people: farmers, trappers, traders, German professors, Jewish peddlers, and now and then an elegant French émigré. Remembering this American growth gave Stephens a base for comparison, when later travelling in Russia:

> With us a few individuals cut down the trees of the forest, or settle themselves by the banks of a stream, where they happen to find some local advantages, and build houses suited to their necessities; others come and join them, and, by degrees, the little settlement becomes a large city. But here in Russia a gigantic government, endowed almost with creative powers, says: '*Let there be a city.*'

By 14 October, 1824 the two had reached Cincinnati. Charles Henrickson had kept up a running commentary: 'After starting in a keel boat (from Pittsburg) with five passengers besides John and myself we were one week going to Wheeling, West Virginia'. Arriving in Cincinnati they rode out to other cousins named Lloyd. But already Stephens was infecting his cousin in further travel down the Mississippi. This thoroughly alarmed his mother: 'Oh! My son I long to get a letter after you get to Illinois. . . . I hope you and your cousin John will have too much prudence to go to Natches for it is very Sickley there the Yellow Fevour rages. . . .'

By 24 November, after a 'very tedious passage' they arrived at Shaeneetown, in Illinois territory, and made their inquiries of the whereabouts of Caleb Ridgway. He was known as a Quaker of consequence for he appeared in the first 1820 census, listed as head of the family of 'five white males under twenty-one and two white females over twenty-one.'

Mounted, with a 'half-Indian breed,' as a guide, they made their way to Carmi which lay twenty miles from the mouth of the Little Wabash River. The land was sparsely settled; they rode for hours without seeing a single house, only an occasional Indian, who silently watched them ride by.

Carmi, Illinois, when they found it, was a post town with less than a square dozen of houses, although it lay, as the *Gazeteer* said, 'in lands of good quality.'

'It was about dusk when we arrived', Charles Henrickson wrote to his mother: 'and we decided not [to] let ourselves be known. Weed [the guide] went in and asked if we could stay there all night they informed us we could . . . Uncle Ridgway came home . . . we talked with him some time, none of them knew us, after keeping them in suspense for about an hour we made ourselves known to the great joy of all the family. Aunt Helena said she had not spent such a pleasant Evening since she had been in Illinois.'

After a few days with the Ridgways, they mounted again, reached St Louis by 4 December ('we will take a steamboat to New Orleans') and set off down the river, a journey Stephens would recall when he floated down the Nile except that by this time the steamer had been metamorphosed into a flat-bottomed boat: '. . . I remember it was the same on the Ohio and Mississippi. Several years since, when the water was low I started from Pittsburg in a flat-bottomed boat, to float down to New Orleans. There too we were in a habit of stopping along the banks of the river at night or in windy and foggy weather. . . .'

CHAPTER III

Mr Stephens' Tour

In 1827 Stephens journeyed to Albany in upper New York state and was admitted as a lawyer. At the age of twenty-one his name appeared in the *New York Directory: John Lloyd Stephens – Attorney at Law 52 Front Street.*

New York was rapidly becoming the empire state and a financial emporium. To keep pace with its sudden growth New York then as now continued to change its face. Philip Hone, the celebrated New York diarist wrote, 'The city is now undergoing its annual metamorphosis, houses are being pulled down, others altered. Pearl Street and Broadway in particular are almost impassible by the quantities of rubbish with which they are obstructed.'

The 'Greek Revival' relieved only somewhat the uniform solid red brick of the houses, which was the reigning style. Gaslight was being introduced under the impulse of commerce, bathtubs, heretofore never mentioned in polite society, were being installed within the houses and they were common enough for the Council in Philadelphia to ordinance against them on sanitary grounds. New York was exhibiting a changing culture, even though scavenger pigs still ran through the streets.

In 1828 Andrew Jackson became President. At that time a deep discontent lay over the land. For with the rise of industrialization there had been an influx of immigrants and a rise in slums and ghettoes. There were many voters who thought there had been 'a betrayal of the Jeffersonian principles of equal rights.' This attitude had elected Jackson. There followed an economic struggle between Andrew Jackson and the Bank of the United States; financial panic followed. One opinionated New Yorker elbowing his way through a mob gathered about a closed bank said: 'Public opinion means something more than the drilled voices of certain political friends of General Jackson who are pledged, body and soul, to support him at all events.'

Yet this was precisely what John Lloyd Stephens was doing. For the law which Stephens practiced from his office on Wall Street, now no longer held him: 'He never felt much ardour or zeal in the practise of law', a friend remembered. 'Instead his interest was directed towards politics.'

This enthusiasm for politics was to lead in a curious roundabout way to great discoveries, for his continued speaking engagements and 'politicking' caused Stephens to develop a streptococcic throat infection, and as the *coccaecae* did not yield to treatment, the family doctor advised a 'mild trip' to Europe. For America then was, like Europe, in the grip of the 'romantic agony.' People loved to seek out the ruins of lost and forgotten civilizations and sit among them to meditate on the transition of empires. So Stephens's 'mild trip' to Europe was well within the tune of the times.

In examining Stephens's career one must believe in the providence of accidents; Stephens became a world-traveler by accident; he became a writer by accident, and these two accidents produced the explorer, with the result that such a bevy of accidents led to one clear purpose – now no longer accidental: to the discovery of the Mayan civilization. Or was it merely the concatenation of cause and effect?

The 'mild European trip,' in search of health, took Stephens to the Continent, to Rome, to Naples (where he climbed Vesuvius 'for reasons of health') then on to Sicily (where he scaled Mount Etna for perhaps the same reason) and then to Greece in the wake of its revolution against the Turks. So with his head 'humming with Homer and Herodotus' he went to see Mycenae, saw 'the mute remains of its cyclopean walls,' and continued his mild European voyage toward the Levant. He was in the very narrow corner of this new and old world, duplicating the Hegira of Catherwood, going over the ground that he had covered just a few years previously.

The infection with the 'antique' was already taking hold of him and albeit he expressed himself literarily rather than artistically, still his experiences were preparing him for his future evaluation of the ruins that he was to see. It would also lead to his encounter with Catherwood.

In the month of April 1835, Stephens took ship for Smyrna, that is Izmir. But impatient at the slowness of the passage he had himself put ashore at Foggi, at the western end of the Gulf, rented a horse and rode on.

In three hours I was crossing the Caravan bridge – a bridge over the beautiful Melissus on the banks of which Homer was born and picking my way among caravans which for ages had continued to cross this bridge laden with all the riches of the East I entered the long-looked-for city of Smyrna.

On 16 April, 1835 John Lloyd Stephens, author, was born. It may have been, as he later said, that it was 'mere accident' that all his three 'letters', many pages in length, written to Fenno Hoffman, editor of the *American Magazine*, had been published 'without my knowledge';* however it seems that the 'mere accident' was contrived, for in his first 'letter' he wrote with Stephensian mockery: 'But you, my dear [Fenno], who know my *touching sensibilities* and who moreover have a tender regard for my character certainly will not publish me'.

Yet it must have been prearranged. The editor published the letter anonymously. Written 'by an American', it appeared under the title of 'Scenes in the Levant'.

There, under the Mussulman flag, pages of fairy-tale scenes flitted before Stephens' eyes; caravans led by turbaned

---

*'An account of my journey from Athens to Smyrna, given in a letter to friends at home, was published during my absence and without my knowledge in successive numbers of the *American Monthly Magazine*, and perhaps the favourable notice taken of it had some influence in inducing me to write a book' (Stephens' note).

Turks; camels plodding down narrow aisles of sun-splashed streets; women dressed in white, their veils effectually concealing every feature but bringing to 'bear only the artillery of their eyes' – Tartars, Greeks, Turks, and Franks – it was like the Scheherazade.

'I have just arrived at this place and I lived to tell it,' so he proceeded to write in the 'letter' that detailed his adventures from Athens to Smyrna. He wrote of Greece, Homer, and Scio, he painted verbal pictures of the land, and although at points he damned the Turks, he admitted they had 'exceedingly good points: chibouks, coffee and as many wives as they please.' He confessed that the ladies gave him no rest. 'I never saw so much beauty . . . such eyes large dark and rolling. And they walk too, as if conscious of their high pretensions . . . under enchanting turbans charged with the whole artillery of their charms. It is a perfectly unmasked battery; nothing can stand against it. I wonder the Sultan allows it'.

American trading communities had been in the Levant since colonial times and Stephens liked the free and easy way of the place. He found: 'Every Stranger, upon his arrival in Smyrna, is introduced to the Casino. I went there the first time to a concert. It is a large building, erected by a club of merchants, with a suite of rooms on the lower floor, billiards, cards, reading and sitting in the ball-room, and, from what I had seen in the streets, I expected an extraordinary display of beauty; but I was much disappointed. The company consisted only of the aristocracy or higher mercantile classes. A patent of nobility in Smyrna, as in our own city, is founded upon the time since the possessor gave up selling foods, or the number of consignments he receives in the course of a year.'

Stephens was also impressed with the scurrying of big business. 'Society in Smyrna is purely mercantile, and having been so long out of the way of it, [I] was actually grateful once more to hear men talking with all their souls about cotton, stocks, exchanges, and other topics of interest. . . .

I took up an American paper, and heard Boston, and New York, and Baltimore, and cotton, and opium, and freight, and quarter percent less bandied about, until I almost fancied myself at home.'

His real interests, however, continued to lean toward the antique and history. 'During one evening the young priest brought out an edition of Homer and I surprised *him* and *myself* by being able to translate a passage in the *Iliad*. I translated it into French and my companion explained it in modern Greek to the young priest'.

Stephens followed the Roman road to Ephesus and wandered among the ruins of one of the greatest cities of Asia. One can sense in his 'letter' the gradual cumulative effect that the pleasure of ruins was having upon him. In a *khan*, a Turkish tavern, he set about making himself comfortable. 'And here I spent half the night musing upon the strange concatenation of circumstances which had broken up the quiet [life of a] practicing attorney and set him a straggler from a busy money-getting land to meditate among the ruins of ancient cities, and sleep on a mud-floor with turbaned turks.'

Stephens then proceeded to Constantinople, 'in less time,' he said, 'than swift-footed Achilles could have traveled it'. He went by steamboat. 'Join me now in the race,' he wrote in his second letter. 'If your heart does not break at going by at the rate of eight to ten miles an hour, I will ship you over a piece of the most classic ground . . . in history.'

He sailed past the isles of Greece, shadowed by Mount Olympus, past Sigaeum, where Homeric battles were fought, into the Hellespont, where Leander swam for the love of Hero, and Lord Byron and Mr Ekenhead for fun. He constantly conversed with two Americans returning from a tour of Egypt. They spoke with such enthusiasm about the ruins that he was sorely tempted to try the Nile, but at that moment cholera was raging in Alexandria.

Constantinople was, like most of the Levantine cities, relatively new ground for an American. For it was only in 1800 that Commodore William Bainbridge, bearing the annual tribute, had put in to Constantinople, carrying for the first time the American flag into this Turkish world. Two years later a consul was appointed in the Levant, whence Turkish opium and Smyrna figs were exported to Boston. In 1831, only four years before Stephens' arrival, Commodore Porter had been raised to the rank of *chargé d'affaire*.

At this Constantinople Stephens had made arrangements with 'an ill-smelling Tartar' to ride with him through the Balkans to France, but at the last moment the departure of a Russian government vessel was announced, a miserable *pyrocaphe*, bound for the Black Sea and Odessa. So Stephens, following the theory of the causes and effects of accidents, gave up the Tartar. He went instead to Russia.

At Odessa, Stephens was immediately struck 'with the military aspect of things;' in front of the examining officers the passengers paraded, one at a time – Turks, Christians, Jews, Germans, Russians, Poles, Greeks, Illyrians, Moldavians. They were stripped of their clothes, fumigated and then examined* by the port doctor. They were also forced to pass through an involved *pratique*, including the declaration at customs of all books banned by the censors; Stephens did not declare his Byron, the author of *Childe Harold* had long been on the Russian list. For in a lyrical outburst he had lampooned 'that coxcomb Tsar, that autocrat of waltzes and

*'We were obliged to strip naked (but) the bodily examination was as delicate as the nature of the case would admit; for the doctor merely opened the door, looked in, and went out without taking his hand from the knob. It was none of my business, I know, and may be thought impertinent, but as he closed the door, I could not help calling him back to ask him whether he held the same inquisition upon the fair sex; to which he replied with a melancholy upturning of the eyes, that in the good old days of Russian barbarism this had been part of his duties, but that the march of improvements had invaded his rights and given this portion of his professional duties to a *sage femme*.'

war.' He was loath to part with Byron for he had been, as Stephens said, 'my companion in Italy, and Greece . . . so I put the book under my arm, threw my cloak over and walked out'.

Odessa – which had been a swamp until decreed a city by Empress Catherine – had been built in 1796. By 1835 it was a regal city; there was a promenade a mile in length, a palace for the governor, a casino, a theater where Stephens witnessed a performance of *The Barber of Seville*.

They bounded across Russia, dashing past miserable people who rushed at their appearance to do obeisance to what they believed must be a grand seigneur. They came into Kiev (Stephens was the first American ever to pass through it) and followed the river Dnieper on its sinuous course towards Moscow. Stephens was horrified by the abject misery of the serf.

Along the entire route there were neither inns, taverns, nor restaurants, and Stephens and his party, like Napoleon when he invaded Russia, had to 'trust, to make up the rest of their food by foraging'. The only succor they received was offered by Jews who were the wayside postmasters.

Moscow in 1835 presented a magnificent vista: six hundred churches – multiple-domed with gilded crosses, spires, and steeples – towering above the lesser buildings gave it an extraordinary appearance.

Installed in the Hotel Germania, and after a Turkish bath, Stephens toured Moscow. He was continuously amazed by its paradox; its mixture of barbarism and Parisian elegance. In his hotel, Stephens conversed with a French marquis attired in threadbare finery. He had taken part in Napoleon's invasion, was captured, and had remained in Moscow. The marquis insisted, between sips of brandy, that the only difference between Russian seigneurs and serfs was that one wore his shirt inside his trousers and the other outside. 'But my friend,' Stephens observed, 'spoke with the prejudice of twenty years of exile.'

The Frenchman earned his roubles by acting as a spy against foreigners. He confided to the American that he must watch not only his language but the content of his speech.

'It is almost impossible for an American,' Stephens wrote, 'to believe that even in Russia he incurs any risk in speaking what he thinks; he is apt to regard the stories of summary punishment for freedom of speech as bugbears of bygone things. In my own case, even when men looked cautiously around the room and then spoke in whispers I could not believe there was any danger. Still I had become prudent enough not to talk with any unnecessary indiscretion.'

The road from Moscow to St Petersburg – macadamized the whole way – was one of Europe's best. Inns, regulated by tariffs, were operated by the government. St Petersburg, the window that Peter had built so that the Russians might look upon Europe, was splendidly conceived with its palaces, its Hermitage, its memories of Peter and Catherine.

However, leaving St Petersburg was like entering it. On arrival Stephens had obtained a *carte de séjour*, without which no one could remain in the capital and he submitted to routine questions about age, destination, and so on, thoroughly satisfying the authorities that he 'had no intention of preaching democratic doctrines.' But just as one could not remain in St Petersburg without permission, neither could one leave without it. He had, according to law, to advertise his intention of departing in the *Government Gazette* on three successive days. Suspicion was directed toward him because he planned to cross Poland.

And for what purpose: pleasure? 'Who, in God's name,' said the exasperated police official, 'ever wanted to travel in Poland for pleasure?'

Stephens left for Warsaw in the company of a tall Pole, who, born in Belgium of French descent, possessed, he remembered, to a 'striking degree the compound *amor patriae* incident to the relationship in which he stood to these countries'.

Travel was done in a *kibitka*, a round-bottomed springless box, a cradle on four wheels. They bounced over the same road that Napoleon had followed two decades before in his advance on Moscow; they went over the immense distances along the execrable road past the Dvina River, into Minsk.

And beyond it, partially in ruins as the result of the latest revolution which had flared up, lay Warsaw. The Poles had begun this badly managed revolution on the night of 30 November, 1830.

The uprising was crushed.

Stephens, too, had his problems. He had not fully recovered from the illness that had sent him to Europe for a 'mild tour.' In Warsaw, he was so overcome by a malaise that he took to bed; from it wrote home:

> Warsaw, August 15, 1835
> I have reached this place to be put on my back by a Polish doctor. How long he will keep me here I do not know. He promises to set me going in a week; and, as he has plenty of patients without keeping me down, I have great confidence in him. Besides having weathered a Greek, an American, and a Russian, I think I shall be too much for a Pole.

So he escaped the doctor. In time he crossed the Vistula River, continued and passed over the border into Austria. Passing through Vienna, he went up the Danube into Germany, and then under the cloudy November skies he took the road to Paris.*

The preludes of winter had come to France as Stephens, travelling by *coche d'eau*, rolled past the files of poplars that lined the road. In Paris again, he walked with the satisfaction

---

*An account of this voyage was published under the title: *Incidents of Travel in Greece, Turkey, Russia and Poland* – his second book – by Harper and Brothers in 1838. There was a Dublin edition in 1838; British in 1841; and Swedish in 1841.

of a cosmopolitan entering his real milieu, the city. He had intended to return at once to America; in fact, he had written his father to expect him on the Le Havre packet in November 1835, but there was no passage. Emigrants crowding the ships to their gunwales were pouring into America; every ship leaving Le Havre was packed with them. All Europe in 1835 had an unsettled air – the people of Paris were rising against the Bourbons; Belgium and Holland were breaking apart, and Germany was in a state of flux. Everyone who could, fled. In Paris the emigrants sold their wagons and their horses at auction, and then bivouacked on the banks of the Seine, waiting their turn to move on to Le Havre.

Frustrated in this attempt to sail for home, Stephens spent his time among the bookstalls along the Seine, where booksellers offered beautifully illustrated folios at fancy prices. Ever since Stephens had trod the Homeric lands, he had been passionately interested in the antique, and he had carried with him Count Volney's rhapsodic elegies to *Ruins*.

All Americans, as Van Wyck Brooks explains, 'loved Volney's *Ruins* and as their cities multiplied, hopeful and busy and shining with fresh, bright paint, the more their imagination delighted in these desolate scenes of temples and tombs, lost in the deserts.' In one of these expensive folios on the ruins of empire, Stephens discovered some superbly beautiful lithographs 'of a most glorious ruin,' a city, buried in Stony Arabia, whose palaces had been cut out of the living rock. Its name was Petra.

Why did Stephens, once in Paris, decide to go to Petra by way of Egypt? We do not know. It was presumed that it was his perusal of Leon de Laborde's book *Voyage de l'Arabie Petrée*, recently published in Paris, that decided the issue, but apparently this Petra itinerary did not come up until he was well up the Nile, for while dining with some English gentlemen the subject of Petra was raised. 'It is to them,' Stephens wrote, 'that I am indebted for the first suggestion to me of the route to Petra.' Neither reason is suggested in books or letters – nothing – unless it lies in the providences of accidents. Whatever the cause, incident or accident, it was to be just one more of the concatenations of cause and effect. He would go to the Nile, to Egypt, and to Petra. This hegira was to change the course of his life.

It was also to begin the interest in American archaeology.

CHAPTER IV

The Grey Nile

John Lloyd Stephens was one of the three Americans to sign the United States consular book in Alexandria in the year 1836.* There had been, naturally, numerous Americans there before Stephens, notably John Ledyard of Connecticut.

Born in 1751, he had sailed with Captain Cook, went to Russia, and was then engaged by the African Society of London 'to Traverse from east to west . . . the widest part of Africa'. Upon arriving in Cairo in 1788, he promptly died.

Stephens then knew no more of Egypt than an intelligent reader might have learned from the material then available. And this was precious little.

Stephens's Nilitic adventure was done with his servant Paolo and his Arabic crew (and he remembered to keep the original contract in Arabic).

> For myself being along and not in very good health I had some heavy moments but I have no hesitation in saying that, with a friend, a good boat well fitted out with books, guns, plenty of time and a cook like Michael, a voyage on the Nile would exceed traveling within my experience.

*The list of American travelers who registered with John and George Gliddon, the first U.S. consuls at Alexandria and Cairo 1836 (based on John Gliddon's Appendix to *The American in Egypt*) were:
1836
John Lloyd Stephens
New York
James Augustus Dorr
Boston
Richard K. Haight
New York

At the age of twenty-four Alexander the Great had founded the city bearing his illustrious name. He had been welcomed to Egypt as a young general in 332 B.C. and a conquering demiurge and, finding a wind-free harbor where Greek ships could enter and carry away the produce of the Nile, he himself designed the city and called it Alexandria.

A century after its founding it was peopled with a million inhabitants, the most populous city in the ancient world, and the most industrious.

'Some,' said the ancient geographer, Strabo, 'blow glass, others make papyrus sheets, others weave linen – every man practices a craft.'

It was still a magnificent city of libraries, baths, and immense buildings when, centuries later, it was captured by the Saracens. 'We found it,' reported a general to the Caliph Omar, 'with four thousand palaces, four thousand baths, four hundred theaters, twelve thousand shops – and forty thousand tributary Jews.'

The influence of time and man, both iconoclasts, had completely changed Alexandria. After centuries of deterioration Egypt, for a brief historical moment, saw General Napoleon Bonaparte. And then he, too, went away, leaving behind him a trail of wreckage.

The latest catastrophe was the cholera epidemic in 1834 that despoiled the city of fifty thousand of its inhabitants.

So when Stephens – his face covered with a handkerchief – went through the narrow streets of Alexandria in December 1835, he was overwhelmed by beggars squatting in the shadows of overhanging *mushrabiyas*, exhibiting their sores and begging for alms. He had expected to see, as he walked along the sun-drenched lanes, fabulous bazaars offering the wealth of the Orient. What he saw left him unimpressed:

'. . . Why, I do not believe that the contents of all the bazaars of the largest towns in Egypt were worth as much as the stock of an ordinary dealer in dry goods on Broadway.'

So he made his way to the American Consulate, and there

met the man who was to give his Egyptian travels direction and content.

George Gliddon: British-born like his father, succeeded him as the first American consular agent in Egypt. Although his vocation was the care and feeding of American tourists (along with consular invoices), his consuming passion was Egyptian archaeology; his pamphlet, *Appeal to the Antiquarians in the Destruction of Monuments* in 1841 marked the genesis of American archaeological interest in Egypt.

The American invasion of Egypt began in 1832 when the Nile was discovered as a winter resort for convalescents and a haven for the wealthy. Still, Egypt in 1835 was scarcely a tourist's paradise; it offered, in truth, no more security for the traveler than the western wilderness of America, and for that reason, it was suggested to Stephens – after he had seen the marvels of Alexandria – that they repair to Cairo, have audience with Mehemet Ali, and secure for his person, if possible, a firman from the Pasha of Egypt.

'I was not ambitious,' Stephens confessed, 'for a tête-á-tête with his highness, and merely wanted to see him as one of the lions of the country'. Still he went, mounted on a superb horse, richly caparisoned and preceded by a janizary, in the manner of a Turkish gentleman of quality.

Mehemet Ali, a grand vizier come to life from the Arabian Nights, was surrounded by a eunuch-guarded harem, a company of wives, and a regiment of children, which he continued to beget in spite of his seventy-six years. In a marble hall of a palace built by Saladin, cooled by tinkling fountains surrounded by scarlet ottomans, Mehemet Ali, with his full white beard, sat in silken robes, and bejeweled turban, looking precisely what he was not – a kindly patriarch.

European powers, contending among themselves for the mastery of the Mediterranean and the gateway to India, found their perfidy matched by Mehemet Ali; even Talleyrand, that master of obliquity, paid him heavy compliment. As for the British, they were usually furious with him. At one time Lord Palmerston threatened to 'chuck him into the Nile,' yet Mehemet survived all threats and all attempted assassinations. He died as seldom does the tyrant, in his bed at eighty years of age, gently mad, surrounded by the army of descendants that was his family.

Mehemet Ali received John Lloyd Stephens with marked attention; a water pipe was given to him, coffee was brought, jet black and sugared in the Turkish fashion. After chatting discursively on this and that, Stephens suggested that the Pasha might continue his good works by introducing a steamboat from Alexandria to Cairo.

Said Stephens:

He took the pipe from his mouth again, and in the tone of 'Let there be light' said that he had ordered a couple . . . considering that a steamboat was an appropriate weapon in the hands of the American. . . . I told him that I had seen . . . in a European paper a project to run steamboats from New York to Liverpool in twelve or fourteen days. . . . He then asked the rate of the speed of the steamboats on our rivers . . . remembering an old crazy five or six miles an hour boat that I had seen in Alexandria, I was afraid to tell the truth.

Mehemet Ali was far from being so naive as he appeared to Stephens. As the creator of modern Egypt, his first gesture as dictator was to give back to Cairo its former grandeur, for Cairo was one of the great centers of Islamic culture. The university was housed in the ancient Al Azhur Mosque where until the Pasha had appeared only the subtleties of medieval logic had been taught.

European experts had been brought to Cairo, the curriculum was developed, with students and officers trained by Europeans. Costi, an Italian, taught drawing and mathematics; a Frenchman, Colonel Sève, who had fought with distinction at Waterloo, established a modern army.

A printing press had been set up at Bulaq in Cairo's suburbs, where seventy-three oriental works had already been printed.

Americans had been known – and respected – in the Mediterranean ever since, in 1804, Captain William Eaton at the head of eight Marines, thirty-eight Greeks, and a motley assortment of Arabs, captured Derna. The short war with Tripoli had further enhanced the reputation of the Americans, and many were urged to settle in Egypt.

R. B. Jones, later United States Consul in Egypt, took service in the Pasha's navy; another American, George Bethune English, took part in an expedition up the Nile to Dongola, the published account became the first original American contribution to Egyptian literature. Later, American naval architects were employed at Alexandria building the fleet of Mehemet Ali, used to suppress the Greeks, the same people that other Americans were trying to succor.

So John Lloyd Stephens was to Mehemet Ali no *rara avis*. But he welcomed him to Egypt, expressed his wish, in Allah's name, that he would enjoy himself, and forthwith gave Stephens his firman as a talisman for his expedition up the Nile.

On 1 January, 1836, 'with a fair wind and the star-spangled banner made for [him] by an Arab tailor,' Stephens started up the Nile. He had hired a *falookha* and a captain and a crew to sail it, sealing the bargain with a contract in Arabic* which neither he nor the captain understood. For the rest he had only a copy of the *Modern Traveller*, Volney's *Ruins*, and an Italian dictionary – and Paolo Nuozzo.

Stephens had first met him in Constantinople and, finding him without employment, hired him for his hegira to Egypt. Multilingual and somewhat arrogant, making enemies wherever he went, Paolo was nevertheless a man experienced in Arabian travel. Stephens owed his life to him in many instances.

*This contract is still extant.

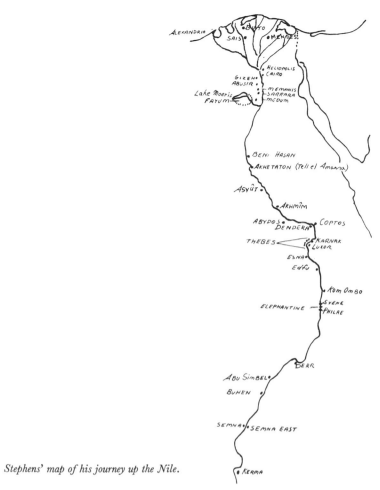

19. *Stephens' map of his journey up the Nile.*

20. *Catherwood's watercolour of the Temple of Dendera, visited by Stephens in 1836.*

> Paolo Nuozzo . . . was a man about thirty-five years old; stout, square built, intelligent; a passionate admirer of ruins of the Nile; honest and faithful as the sun, and one of the greatest cowards that luninary ever shone upon. He called himself my dragoman, and I remember, wrote himself such in the convent of Mt. Sinai and the temple of Petra. . . . He spoke French, Italian, Maltese, Greek, Turkish, and Arabic.

They inched past Memphis and going up the Nile passed the pyramids of Gizeh. The wind was contrary and the weather cold, so cold that Stephens was delighted to join the swarthy natives at Minch in a steaming Turkish bath.

> My white skin made me a marked object among the swarthy figures lying around me; and half a dozen of the operatives, lank, bony fellows, and perfectly naked, came up and claimed me. . . . I had been shampooed at Smyrna, Constantinople and Cairo, but who thought I would have been carried to seventh heaven at the little town of Minyeh?

All through the month of January he continued to ascend the dark thread of the Nile, stopping here and there to examine ruins, enter a pyramid, and otherwise fill his journal with his observations.

'Sunday, January 18. At eight o'clock in the morning we arrived at Ghenneh [Qena], where, leaving my boat and crew to make a few additions to our stock, Paul and I crossed over in a sort of ferryboat to Dendera.

'The Temple of Dendera is one of the finest specimens of the arts in Egypt, and the best preserved of any on the Nile. It stands about a mile from the river, on the edge of the desert, and, coming up, may be seen at a great distance. I shall not attempt any description of this beautiful temple; its great dimensions, its magnificent propylon or gateway,

21. *The great Temple of Amun at Karnak.*

portico, and columns; the sculptured figures on the walls; the spirit of the devices, and their admirable execution; the winged globe and the sacred vulture, the hawk and the ibis, Isis, Osiris, and Horus, gods, goddesses, priests, and women; harps, altars, and people clapping their hands, and the whole interior covered with hieroglyphics and paintings, in some places, after a lapse of more than two thousand years, in colors fresh as if but the work of yesterday.

'*It was the first temple I had seen in Egypt;* and, although I ought not perhaps to say so, I was disappointed. . . . The temple is more than half buried in the sand. For many years it has formed the nucleus of a village. The Arabs have built their huts within and around it'.

On the twentieth the wind was light yet favourable. Part of the time the men were on shore towing Stephens' boat with rope cables; he was approaching, he said, 'the most interesting spot on the Nile.'

A thousand miles up the Nile, they came upon the ruins of Thebes. In the moonlight, with the stars reflected in the water, Stephens walked among the rows of battered statuary of the Colossi that led to the great ruined palace of King Amenem-het.

A new feeling possessed him now as he threaded a way through the disconcerting chaos of carved granite.

Where he might have been expected to lapse into some sort of Volneysque meditation on 'ruins' in the turgid language of the period, he remained silent and contemplative. The spell was working. After Thebes, he walked over to adjacent Luxor and passed among the Great Temples of Amun, which had been erected in 2100 B.C. to honour Queen Hatshepsut. Here Stephens felt a surging interest in unravelling time lost civilizations.

'The ancient city' Stephens observed, 'was twenty-three miles in circumference. The valley of the Nile was not large enough to contain it, and its extremities rested upon the bases of the mountains of Arabia and Africa. The whole of this great extent is more or less strewed with ruins, broken columns, and avenues of sphinxes, colossal figures, obelisks, pyramidal gateways, porticos, blocks of polished granite and stones of extraordinary magnitude, while above them . . . in all the nakedness of desolation, the colossal skeletons of giant temples are standing in the unwatered sands, in solitude and silence. They are neither gray nor blackened; there is no lichen, no moss, no rank grass or mantling ivy to robe them and conceal their deformities. Like the bones of man, they seem to whiten under the sun of the desert. The sand of Africa has been their most fearful enemy; blown upon them for more than three thousand years, it has buried the largest monuments, and, in some instances, almost entire temples . . .

'The temple of Luxor stands near the bank of the river, built there as is supposed, for the convenience of the Egyptian boatmen. Before the magnificent gateway of this temple, until within a few years, stood two lofty obelisks, each a single block of red granite, more than eighty feet high, covered with sculpture and hieroglyphics fresh as if but yesterday from the hands of the sculptor. One of them has been lately taken down by the French, and at this moment rears its daring summit to the skies in the center of admiring Paris; the other is yet standing on the spot where it was first erected. . . .'

But great and magnificent as was the temple of Luxor, it served but as a portal to the greater Karnak. Standing nearly two miles from Luxor, the whole road to it was lined with rows of sphinxes, each of a solid block of granite. At this end they are broken, and, for the most part, buried under the sand and heaps of rubbish. But, approaching Karnak, they stand entire, still and solemn as when the ancient Egyptians passed between them to worship in the great temple of Ammon. Four grand propylons terminate this avenue of sphinxes, and, passing through the last, the scene which presents itself defies description.

Before continuing up the Nile, Stephens crossed over

23.   *George Holton's photograph of the obelisk at Luxor and (inset) Catherwood's drawing.*

The Gateway at Karnak.

from Karnak to look at the famous Colossi of Memnon. Standing near the ruined temples of Medinet Habu, seventy-feet high, were the two statues of the seated Amen-hotep III.

Stephens gazed up at its worn face, its scars and bruises: 'and my heart warmed to it. It told of exposure, for unknown ages, to the rude assaults of the elements, and the ruder assaults of men. I climbed upon the pedestal; upon the still hardy legs of the Memnon. I pored over a thousand inscriptions in Greek and Latin and a thousand names of strangers from distant lands, who had come like me to do homage to the mighty monuments of Thebes . . .'

If Stephens studied the modern graffiti closely he would have seen the name of *'F. Catherwood Archt'*; for only two years before, in 1833, Catherwood had been there.

If so, this was the first encounter of the two, Stephens and Catherwood. The New Yorker would find 'Catherwood' over and over again until they finally met in the flesh.

After this Stephens made his way up the Nile, its colour now turning from a slate grey to a light blue, to the Rock of Chains, 'GeBel-es-silsila' which Stephen spells outrageously as 'Hadjar Silsily', where that narrowest part of the Nile, the mountains of Africa to the west and Arabia to the east seem to be marching to meet each other.

Coming to the Island of Elephantine and the little town of Aswan, the site of the present day great dam, Stephens claimed to find 'little to detain me.'

It was however better built than most of the towns on the Nile, 'and has its street of bazaars; the slave-bazaars being by far the best supplied of any. In one of the little *caftorias* opposite the slave market, a Turk . . . that marked him as a man of rank, attracted my particular attention. He was almost the last of the Mamelukes, but yesterday the lords of Egypt; one of the few who escaped the general massacre of his race, and one of the very few permitted to drag out the remnant of their days in the pacha's dominions.'

In ancient times Elephantine had been ruled over by

66

Khnum, the ram-god Prince of the cataract region. The eastern quarries at Aswan, which had provided the grey and red granite for sculptors and architects for centuries, were subject to control from Elephantine. As the gateway to Nubia it had, under the Egyptians, a fortress, customs post and the villas of the very rich. Under Persian rule the large Jewish garrison colony built there a temple to Jahweh. Stephens found it all incredibly beautiful.

Eight miles above Aswan was the island of Philae – the island whose death caused the first dam to be built and was so movingly lamented by Pierre Loti. In Stephens' time it had not yet been submerged.

> The temple of Philae is a magnificent ruin, four hundred and thirty-five feet in length and one hundred and five in width. It stands at the south-west corner of the island, close upon the bank of the river, and the approach to it is by a grand colonnade, extending two hundred and forty feet along the edge of the river to the grand propylon.

Buildings in Philae had been dedicated to Hathor, the Goddess of distant places. The greatest of the temples – and the same which Frederick Catherwood drew in 1833 – was dedicated to Isis, wife of Osiris. The emperor Trajan also had erected one of its temples. It was at Philae that paganism resisted Christianity most obstinately. The Egyptian temples long closed brought pagan pilgrims to Philae where they carved on the walls of the sanctuaries hymns and prayers to the great Isis: the last being dated A.D. 473. There among the profusion of names, Stephens discovered that of his old school friend, 'Cornelius Bradford, U.S. of America,' written with his own hand.

'I did not know that he had been here, although I knew he had been many years from home, and I had read in a newspaper that he had died in Palestine. A thousand recollections crowded upon me, of joys departed, never to return, and made me sad. I wrote my name under his and left the temple'.

Stephens found the sable-skinned Nubians of the greatest interest as they walked under the hot sun naked except for a fringe of leather six inches in width that encircled their loins. A negroid race, early Christianized, who had formed a powerful tribe in Upper Egypt, the Nubians had been conquered by the Arabs, and were converted to Mohammedanism; now under the alchemy of change they were living in a neo-arcadia, their economy regulated to date-gathering on the banks of the Nile.

How Pierre Loti would have loved the Aswan of Stephens' day! There was no dam to regulate the flow of the Nile, no flood water to bury the Temple of Isis at Philae, no flesh-tortured reformers to clothe the ebony nakedness of the voluptuous Nubians. He would have written tantalizingly of the smooth skin, the large jet-black eyes in unceasing movement, the high, pouting breasts, exquisitely moulded; the Nubians would have joined Loti's other exotic heroines – Azyade, Rarahu, Fatou-Gaye, and all the rest – whom he has allowed the world to taste in intoxication, to delirium, even to stupor.

But Stephens was not Pierre Loti. He made an effort to keep his observations on a scientific plane: 'The Nubian is tall, thin, sinewy and graceful, possessing what would be called in civilized life an uncommon degree of gentility; his face is rather dark, though far removed from African blackness, his features are long and aquiline. . . .'

After bargaining for and obtaining one of the large heavy clubs, made from the palm tree, which every Nubian carries (and which Stephens himself carried throughout the rest of his journey) he turned to another piece of negotiation: 'I began to bargain for the costume of a Nubian lady, and, to use an expressive phrase, though in this case not literally true, I bought it off her back . . . She was not more than sixteen, with a sweet mild face, and a figure that the finest lady might be proud to exhibit: every limb charmingly rounded. It would have been a burning shame to put such a figure into frock and petticoat, though I thought nothing of seeing women all but naked, that at first I did feel somewhat delicate in attempting to buy the few inches that constituted the young girl's only wardrobe. Paul [Paolo Nuozza] had no such scruples, and I found, too, that, as in the road to vice, *'ce n'est que le premièr pas qui coûte.'* In short, I bought it, and have it with me'.

With that John Lloyd Stephens, attorney-at-law, knelt down and carefully unhinged the naked Nubian's breechclout.

CHAPTER V

Arabia Petraea

On 14 March, 1836, John Lloyd Stephens was metamorphosed into 'Abdel Hassis,' 'the slave of God.' For his
personal *équipage* he . . . provided himself 'with the under-
pretending and respectable costume of a Cairo merchant,
a long red silk gown, yellow striped handkerchief rolled
around it as a turban; white trousers, large red shoes, yellow
slippers, blue sash, a pair of large Turkish pistols,' and adopted
the Arab name. It is so costumed that Stephens appears in
an illustration in his book *Arabia Petraea*, preserving his
anonymity as – 'a Merchant of Cairo.'

Stephens had the good fortune to meet Adolphe Linant,*
the co-author of a celebrated book on Petra in which he
described the route Stephens proposed.

Linant told Stephens how his party had travelled with a
large retinue of camels and horses, with great display, so as to
overawe the Bedouins. Their expedition had been the second
to Petra since its rediscovery in 1812. For a thousand years
that city had lain in Stony Arabia, forgotten in the annals of
man and known only to the Bedouins. Yet once, in Roman
times, it had been one of the greatest cities of the East.

In 1806 Ulrich Seetzen, a German Orientalist traveling
as an Arab, had heard a Bedouin say: 'O! how I weep when
I behold the ruins of Petra.' Excited by its prospects, he had
tried to enter the lost city, but his disguise was penetrated
and he was murdered.

Johann Ludwig Burckhardt, who finally discovered it,
had spent two years in preparation, studying Arabic, learning
the Koran by rote, and with Teutonic thoroughness even

*Leon de Laborde and Maurice-Adolphe Linant, *Voyage de L'Arabia Petrée*,
Paris, 1830; London, 1838. Stephens thought so highly of the work that he
pirated all the illustrations of this book for his own.

25.   The Sik Gorge at Petra and the Temple of El Khaznáh. Photograph by George Holton.

having himself circumcised, for a foreskin was as dangerous as the Bible in Arabia; then under the pretence of being an Arabian beggar called Ibrahim Ibn Abdallah, who had vowed to slaughter a goat in honour of Aaron, he made his entrance into it in 1812. This Petra was Stephens' goal.

Cairo's seasoned travelers pointed out to him the dangers of his itinerary, for beyond the Nile, the firman of Mehemet Ali was so much paper, but with an experienced camel driver and his faithful sevant Paolo dressed as an Arab, Stephens mounted a vault-ribbed camel and disappeared into the desert.

He wrote home, 'I am about to cross a dreary waste of land, to pitch my tent wherever the setting sun might find me, and . . . to have for my wandering footsteps of children of Israel . . . to visit Mount Sinai, and then to the long-lost city of Petra, the capital of Arabia Petraea'.

With his small caravan of five camels he took the Hajd road to Mecca, passed through Suez and followed the route along the shores of the Red Sea. As most travelers, they soon lacked water, and in two days they were in utter want.

Rivers were floating through my imagination when we saw a single palm tree shading a fountain . . . and without much respect of persons, we all threw ourselves upon the fountain.

If any of my friends at home could have seen me then, they would have laughed to see me scrambling among a party of Arabs for a place around a fountain, all prostrate on the ground, with our heads together, for a moment raising them to look gravely at each other while we paused for breath, and then burying our noses again in the delicious water; and yet, when my thirst was satisfied, and I had time to look at it, I thought it lucky that I had not seen it before. It was not a fountain, but merely a deposit of water in a hollow sandstone rock; the surface was green, and the bottom muddy. Such as it was, however, we filled our skins and returned to the main track.

Herman Melville remembered that episode when he saw Stephens 'that wonderful Arabian Traveller' in church, 'for I very well remembered,' Melville wrote in *Redburn*, 'staring at the man myself . . . who had been in Stony Arabia and passed through strange adventures there, all of which with my own eyes I had read in the book which he wrote, an arid-looking book in a pale yellow cover.

' "See what big eyes he has," whispered my aunt; "They got so big because when he was almost dead with famishing in the desert, he all at once caught sight of a date tree, with ripe fruit hanging on it."

'Upon this I stared at him until I thought his eyes were really of an uncommon size, and stuck out from his head like lobster – I am sure my own eyes must have been magnified as I stared.'

For days the caravan moved between parallel ranges of mountains, **receding in some places**, and then again converging. At midday on the fourth day they came to a narrow and rugged defile, bounded on each side with precipitous granite rocks more than a thousand feet high. They entered at the very bottom of this defile, moving for a time along the dry bed of a torrent, now obstructed with sand and stones, the whole scene wild with sublimity. The camels stumbled among the rocky fragments so much that they dismounted, and passed through the wild defile on foot. At the other end they came suddenly upon a plain table of ground, and before them towered Mount Sinai in awful grandeur, so huge and dark that it seemed close. 'The moon had risen', Stephens remembered.

The moon had risen, but her light could not penetrate the deep defile through which I was toiling slowly on to the foot of Sinai. From about half way up it shone with a pale

and solemn lustre, while below all was in the deepest
shade, and a dark spot on the side of the mountain,
seeming perfectly black in contrast with the light above
it, marked the situation of the convent.

The convent was a very large building, and the high stone
walls surrounding it, with turrets at the corners, gave it the
appearance of a fortress.

They began to shout for admission, first singly, and then
all together, in French, English, and Arabic.

'We made,' he wrote, 'almost noise enough to wake the
dead; and it was not until we had discharged two volleys
of firearms that we succeeded in rousing any of the slumbering
inmates. On one side were two or three little slits or portholes,
and a monk, with a long white beard and a lighted taper in
his hand, cautiously thrust out his head at one of them,
and demanded our business. This was soon told; we were
strangers and Christians, and wanted admission; and had a
letter from the Greek patriarch at Cairo. The head disappeared from the loophole, and soon after I saw its owner
slowly open the little door, and let down a rope for the
patriarch's letter. He read it by the feeble glimmer of his
lamp, and then again appeared at the window, and bade us
welcome. The rope was again let down; I tied it around my
arms; and after dangling in the air for a brief space, swinging
to and fro against the walls, found myself clasped in the
arms of a burly, long-bearded monk, who hauled me in,
kissed me on both cheeks, our long beards rubbing together
in friendly union, and, untwisting the rope, set me upon my
feet, and passed me over to his associates.

'By this time nearly all the monks had assembled, and all
pressed forward to welcome me. They shook my hand, took
me in their arms, kissed my face; and if I had been their
dearest friend just escaped from the jaws of death . . . I could
have spared the kissing.

'Twice the rope descended and brought up my tent,

baggage, and the third time it brought up Paul, hung round with guns, pistols, and swords, like a traveling battery. The rope was wound up by a windlass, half a dozen monks, in long black frocks with white stripes, turning it with all their might. The monks had been roused from sleep, and some of them were hardly yet awake; the superior was the last who came. . . .

'The superior was a Greek by birth, and though it was forty years since he had first come to the convent at Sinai, and twenty years since he entered it for the last time, he was still a Greek in heart. His relations with his native land were kept up by the occasional visits of pilgrims. He had heard of their bloody struggle for liberty, and of what America had done for her in her hour of need, and he told me that, next to his own country, he loved mine; and by his kindness to me as an individual, he sought to repay, in part, his country's debt of gratitude. In my wanderings in Greece, I had invariably found the warmest feelings towards my country.'

The following day, Stephens set his heart upon the ascent of Mount Sinai, for his was a sentimental age and this sacred mountain loomed large in his interest.

After an exhausting climb, he wrote:

I stand now upon the very peak of Sinai. I have stood upon the summit of the giant Etna, and looked over the clouds floating beneath it, upon the bold scenery of Sicily, and the distant mountains of Calabria; upon the top of Vesuvius, and looked down upon the waves of lava, and the ruined and half-recovered cities at its floor; but they are nothing compared with the terrific solitudes and bleak majesty of Sinai. An observing traveller has well called it 'a perfect sea of desolation.' Not a tree, or shrub, or blade of grass is to be seen . . .

Later Stephens came to the Rock of Horeb, the stone which Moses struck with his rod, 'and caused the waters to gush out.' The stone, twelve feet high, had on one side eight or ten deep gashes from one to three feet long, and from one to two inches wide, out of which water was trickling. Three names were written on the Rock; one German, the second of an Englishman, and the third of his boyhood friend, Cornelius Bradford the same he had seen on the rocks of the Cataracts of the Nile.

'So again,' Stephens wrote, 'I wrote my name under his . . .'

Leaving the convent, where he had undergone the monkish bearded kisses of farewell, he changed his course from the old Roman track to Gaza and turning east instead took the route to Aqaba. A narrow opening in the mountain defile set him on his way.

'It was a day such as can only be seen in the mountainous desert of Arabia, presenting a clearness and purity in the atmosphere, and a gentle freshness in the air. . . .

'We continued for several hours along the valley, which was closely bounded on either side by mountains, not high, but bare, cracked, and crumbling into fragments.'

Towards evening the travelers could see Aqaba distinctly, though still on the opposite side of the gulf, and still at a formidable distance. Night was coming on fast: Stephens was extremely anxious to sleep within the fortress that night and, fearful that 'a stranger would not be admitted after dark' he sent Paul on ahead with his compliments to the governor and the modest request that he would keep the gates open till his arrival.

In the classical period Aqaba had been the *entrepôt* of the spice riches of the Far East. Trade ships arriving at the Gulf of Aqaba on the Red Sea brought produce from Arabia Deserta, Arabia Felix, Ceylon, India, and beyond, and for centuries caravans were funneled through it to Petra. Cinnamon came from Ceylon, as did cloves; nutmeg and mace came from Malaya. Ginger root came from the wild parts of India. Pepper was a Roman passion.

Pearls came from the coast of India; the best were from Ceylon. 'I swear before the gods,' said a returning Roman trader, 'that the bottom of the sea seems to be covered with them.' Coral – also highly valued by Roman jewellers – covered the bottom of the Red Sea, giving the sea its colour and its name. Diamonds were found in the gravel of Indian rivers and were a trade item; the Romans called them 'adamantes,' the invincible stones, since there were no tools that would cut them. India also traded in sapphires. And there were jade, crystals, rose-quartz, carnelian, jasper, agate, onyx, and beryls. Then, too, there were the slave trade and the ivory trade. The Romans had a passion for ivory; seats for judges were made of ivory and Caracalla's horses fed out of ivory mangers.

All this luxury trade was carried by ships to the port of Aqaba. It was also reached from Egypt through the desert region known to the Romans as Saracei.

At this Aqaba, masquerading as Abdel Hassis, the merchant of Cairo, Stephens arrived as he said 'deadly ill,' and took refuge in the fortress. Of it he wrote:

This little fortress is seldom visited by travellers, and it is worth a brief description.* It stands at the extremity of the eastern or Elanitic branch of the Red Sea, at the foot of the sandstone mountains, near the shore, and almost buried in a grove of palm-trees, the only living things in that region of barren sands. It is the last stopping-place of the caravan of pilgrims on its way to Mecca . . . the arrival of a traveller is of exceedingly rare occurrence, and seldom does even the wandering Bedouin stop within its walls; no ship rides in its harbour, and not even a solitary fishing-boat breaks the stillness of the water at its feet.

*This fourteenth-century fort – now restored and reoccupied – has the coat-of-arms of the Hashemite family above the main entrance.

The arrival of Stephens brought the whole population of the fortress (that is the Bedouins living under the palm trees outside), to gather around and gaze at him. The great caravan of pilgrims for Mecca had left only three days before; and except upon the departure and return of this caravan, years would pass by without a stranger ever appearing here.

Here Stephens met El Alouin, the Sheikh in whose suzerainity the ruins of Petra lay, and whom he had met before in Cairo. Now they haggled over the terms for El Alouin's services in conducting him into his domain. Unable to come to terms, Stephens cast aside his legal training and agreed to hire the Sheikh at an undetermined price.

The Sheikh, like Stephens, was on horseback. He wore a red silk gown and over it a voluminous cloak of scarlet cloth, a red tarboosh with a shawl rolled round it, long red boots, and a sash. He carried pistols, a sword, and a spear about twelve feet long. The rest of the party were armed with swords and matchlock guns and wore the common Bedouin dress.

The way road that they followed was once a Roman road, originally largely paved, along the great Wadi-el-Butu. It was built, as the surviving Roman milestones stated, by the Legio IX Hispana. The road itself had long since disappeared and now the way was as primeval as before the advent of the Romans.

From this port the engineers of the Legio IX Hispana built the great arterial road that was to run from Aqaba through Amman-Philadelphia, then on to Bostra, Damascus, and finally to Palmyra in the Syrian desert.

One hundred miles northward, the road having passed through desert, a lateral road – still marked with milestones – led to the city of Petra.

Stephens tried some light talk with the Sheikh. 'I asked some casual questions about the road; but I might better have held my peace, for it seemed that I could not well have hit upon a subject more displeasing'.

Each day had the general features of the day before, the same, eternal barrenness and desolation. But at one o'clock on the third day they were at the foot of the mountains of Seir; and towering above all the rest, surmounted by a circular dome, like the tombs of the sheikhs in Egypt, was the bare and rugged summit of Mount Hor, the burial place of Aaron, visible in every direction at a great distance from below, and on both sides the great range of mountains.

'It was a beautiful afternoon,' Stephens recalled; 'gazelles were playing in the valleys, and partridges running wild up the sides of the mountains: we pitched our tent partly over a carpet of grass.'

During the 150-mile ride the Sheikh tried this and that to make Stephens reveal the amount of money that he carried, and every step of the way he increased his clamour for bakshish. Near the entrance of Petra the leader, by a clever stratagem, told Stephens they would have to choose between fighting their way in or buying an entrance, and so relieved our 'Abdel Hassis' of five hundred piasters for 'bribes.'

The Sik was the entrance to Petra. An earth convulsion had cleft the rocks, creating a two-hundred-foot high chasm; into this narrow-necked gorge Stephens entered, paced by the red-robed Sheikh. It was so narrow that no more than six horsemen abreast could ride through it.

After a quarter of a mile, following the bewitching walls of the cleft, the Sik suddenly ended, and through the narrow slit Stephens could see a temple carved out of the side of the living rock, marble white and moon red, its façade dazzling.

In the shadows Stephens rhapsodized upon this El Khaznah, 'a temple, delicate and limpid, carved like a cameo from a solid mountain wall.'

Columns of the Corinthian order held up a richly carved façade which towered a hundred feet high, all cut out of the mountain.

Paolo, who had lived among the ruins of Baalbek and Crete, involuntarily cried out when he saw this architectural miracle. The effect on Stephens was equally profound. One glimpse of El Khaznah and he was an archaeologist.

> The first view of that superb façade must produce an effect which would never pass away. Even [after I] returned to the pursuits and thought-engrossing incidents of a life in the busiest city of the world, often in situations as widely different as light and darkness, I still see before me the façade of that temple.

Stephens' wonder grew with each advancing step.

Once the tomb of kings, El Khaznah was now only the nightstalls of the nomad, and blackened with herdsmen's fires. On either side of the central hall, north and south, were additional rock chambers; they, like the other, were solid, plain, undecorated. On the back wall Stephens found the names of some English travellers -- Leigh, Bankee, Irby and Mangles, who had paid 1500 piasters to gain entrance to Petra in 1818. Below them were the names of León, Marquis LaBorde, and Stephens' friend Maurice-Adolphe Linant. Stephens was the first American to visit Petra. 'I confess that I felt what, I trust, was not an inexcusable pride, in writing upon the innermost wall of that temple, the name of an American citizen.'*

Beyond the Temple of Isis, the wadi led to a trapezoidal-shaped canyon, one mile in width, the heart of Petra. At the edge, where the rock wall rose precipitously, a vast crescent-shaped Roman amphitheatre had been carved, as the rest, out of solid rock.

'The whole theater,' Stephens noted, 'is at this day in such a state of preservation, that if the tenants of the tombs

---

Incidents of Travel in Egypt, Arabia Petraea and the Holy Land published anonymously as by a Gentleman. Harpers & Brothers (New York 1837). New edition under the same title published by the University of Oklahoma Press (Norman Okla, 1970) with a life of the author, notes and introduction by Victor Wolfgang von Hagen.

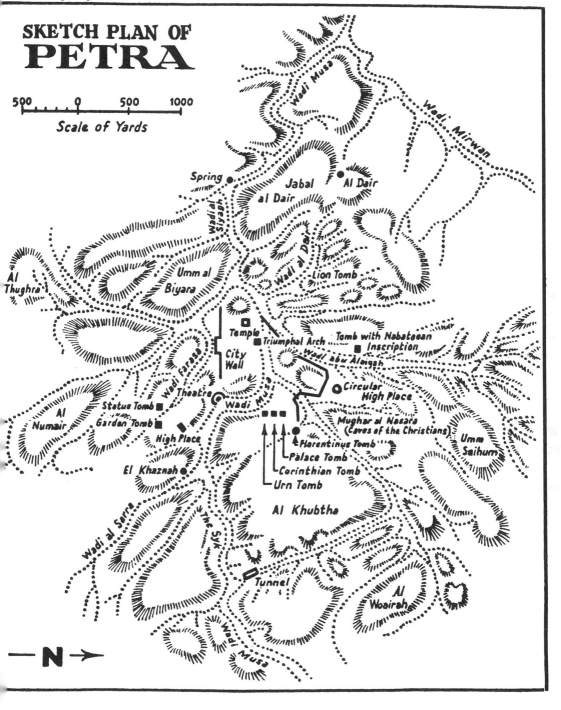

SKETCH PLAN OF
PETRA

500   0   500   1000

Scale of Yards

Wadi Musa

Wadi Mirwan

Spring

Jabal al Dair

Al Dair

Wadi al Siyagh

Wadi al Dair

Al Thughra

Umm al Biyara

Lion Tomb

Temple

Triumphal Arch

Tomb with Nabataean Inscription

Wadi abu Aleigah

City Wall

Wadi Farasa

Theatre

Wadi Musa

Circular High Place

Al Numair

Statue Tomb

Garden Tomb

Wadi Musa

High Place

Mughar al Nasara (Caves of the Christians)

Umm Saihun

El Khaznah

Florentinus Tomb

Palace Tomb

Corinthian Tomb

Urn Tomb

Wadi al Sorra

The Syk

Al Khubtha

Tunnel

Al Woairah

Wadi Musa

→ N →

around could once more rise into life, they might take their old places on its seats.' Stephens wandered from tomb to tomb. He climbed the Urn Temple, etched with a Greek inscription; he crawled into the El Khubata, the largest monument in Petra, and, like the Temple of Isis, bare within. He saw where the ancients had stripped away a whole sandstone mountain to build another temple, El Dair, severely classical in style.

Stephens was lost for words. In his journal he sought for the adjectives that would describe the mere colouring of the rock temples. In the morning they were like great rainbows, flashing out vermilion, saffron, and streaked with white

27. *Map of Petra sketched by Leon de Laboede in 1829.*

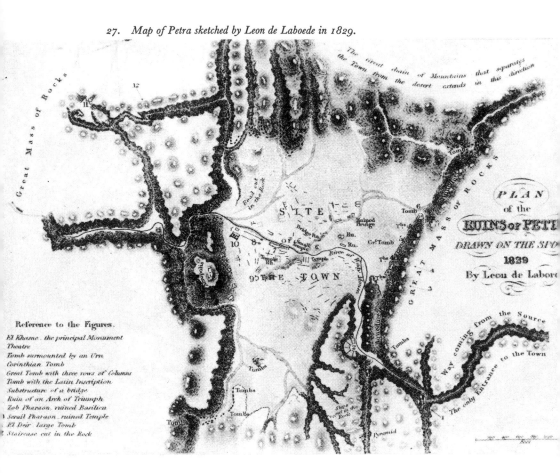

and crimson; at dusk, when the stone was enveloped in its last shadows, it was rose red, shot blue with porphyry, a perfect quilt of swirling ribbons marked like watered silk. 'Match me such marvel,' sang the poet of Petra:

Match me such a marvel save in Eastern clime,

A rose-red city, half as old as time.

In the flat, mile-square valley were the ruins of a temple, an isolated column, some remains of a bridge, a triumphal arch and part of a pavement thought to be the main road. Potsherds were scattered everywhere.

At the end of the valley, the mountain closed once more into another Sik-like chasm; from this cul-de-sac, the out-road led to Arabia Felix. Through these canyon portals trade poured for a thousand years. Its history was alive and pulsating, especially to an American.

Petra's architecture was so much part of its mountainscape that it seemed more the work of nature than of man, yet it was actually the ancient Nabataeans who had carved the city. In this corner of Arabia Petraea the Nabataeans became merchants, traders, mercenaries, and carriers of trade from Arabia Felix. Their accretions increased their prestige until, by the first century B.C., they were one of the most important powers in the East, and Petra was their capital.

The territory of the Nabataeans spread to Damascus in the north, and south to the shores of the Red Sea. They began as fighting nomads, revolted against the Assyrians in the sixth century B.C., and filled the geographical vacuum left by the Jews when they were taken to their Babylon captivity.

The Nabataeans seized, occupied, and then fortified the mountain fastnesses of Petra. Since the earliest times they had been carrying on a spice trade with Central Arabia.

Under the kingship of Aretas III, in 60 B.C., the Nabataeans came into collision with the Romans. In A.D. 106 Trajan annexed Petra; later, Hadrian renamed it 'Hadriana.'

Stephens made his way to the Holy Land over an old land route which had once been a Roman road track. He rode through the utterly desolate Land of Edom, a formidable land passage, even now.

His narration, *A Journey Through Idumea*, was used by Herman Melville. When he wrote his *Encantadas*** he spoke of 'a desolation which exalts them above Idumea' and again 'like split Syrian gourds left withering in the sun' and finally the desert's 'emphatic uninhabitableness.'

His route to Palestine led through the dreaded and utterly desolate Land of Edom, which lay under a biblical curse and through which no one, at least no foreigner, apparently had ever passed before. Yet aside from a strenuous monetary argument with his guides, Stephens came through unscathed, and rather proud of his achievement:

> I am the only person, except the wandering Arabs, who ever did pass through the doomed and forbidden Edom, beholding with his own eyes the fearful fulfilment of the terrible denunciations of an offended God.
>
> We pursued the route which I had originally contemplated, through the land of Idumea. In regard to this part of my journey I wish to be particularly understood. Three different parties, at different times and under different circumstances, after an interval of twenty years from its discovery by Burckhardt, had entered the city of Petra, but not one of them had passed through the land of Idumea.

Stephens' caravan followed the Roman route to the first formal road stop, known to the Romans as 'Thamaro' (Chirbet umm Eksir.)

Stephens observed: 'The valley continued the same as

*Herman Melville, *The Encantadas* or *Enchanted Isles*, with an introduction, critical epilogue, and bibliographical notes by Victor Wolfgang von Hagen, The Grabhorn Press, San Francisco, March 1940. Limited to 550 copies.

before, hillocks, thorn-bushes, gullies, the dry beds of streams and furnishing all the way incontestable evidence that it had once been covered with the waters of a river.' Had Stephens been a geologist, 'every step *would have* opened a new page in the Nature's book; carrying him back to the time when all was chaos, and darkness covered the face of the earth'. The impression it conveyed to him was a confused mass of matter settling into 'form and substance,' the earth covered with a mighty deluge, the waters retiring, and leaving bare the mountains above him, and a rolling river at his feet.

Stephens noted there were two ancient roads where he now wandered, but since he does not mention the names, either Arab or Roman, it's not certain altogether on which one he voyaged. Since he mentions the Gaza road he must have been at Moleatha where there are remains of a fort.

Here 'was a road leading to the ancient city of Gaza, a regular caravan route for four thousand years, now and yet so perfect in the wildness of nature, and so undistinguish-able . . .'

About three hours farther on, and half a mile on the right they came to a quadrangular arch with a dome; and near it was a low stone building also arched, with a small temple; this was the Roman east Anaea (now Ghuven). For about a mile, in different places on each side of the desert track, was a galaxy of villas formed around the fortress. At Chermula (Kurmul) there were mounds of crumbling ruins.

Directly on the caravan track there were two remarkable wells, of the very best Roman workmanship, about fifty feet deep, 'lined with large stones, as firm and perfect as on the day in which they were laid. The uppermost layer, round the top of the well, which was on a level with the pavement, was of marble, and had many grooves cut in it, apparently worn by the continued use of ropes in drawing water. Around each of the wells were circular ranges of columns, which, when the city existed, and the inhabitants

85

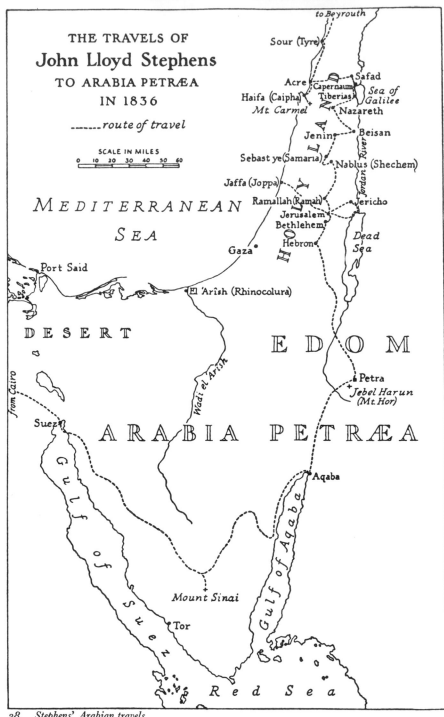

THE TRAVELS OF
John Lloyd Stephens
TO ARABIA PETRÆA
IN 1836

------ route of travel

SCALE IN MILES
0 10 20 30 40 50 60

to Beyrouth

Sour (Tyre)

Acre
Haifa (Caipha)
Mt. Carmel
Capernaum
Tiberias
Safad
Sea of Galilee
Nazareth

MEDITERRANEAN SEA

Jenin
Beisan
Sebast ye (Samaria)
Nablus (Shechem)
Jaffa (Joppa)
Ramallah (Ramah)
Jericho
Jerusalem
Bethlehem
Hebron
Dead Sea

HOLY LAND

Jordan River

Gaza

Port Said

El 'Arîsh (Rhinocolura)

DESERT

EDOM

Petra
Jebel Harun
(Mt. Hor)

from Cairo

Wadi el Arish

Suez

ARABIA PETRÆA

Aqaba

Gulf of Suez

Gulf of Aqaba

Mount Sinai

Tor

Red Sea

28.   *Stephens' Arabian travels.*

came there to drink, might and probably did support a roof similar to those now seen over the fountains in Constantinople. There were no remains of such a roof.'

Stephens believed, and it could well be true, that 'he was the first traveller [in modern times] who has ever seen these ruins.' One can only regret with Stephens that he 'did not have the ability to add to the scanty stock of knowledge already possessed by the geographers.' For Hebron (Al Khalil) which lay between the Dead Sea and the Mediterranean had been one of the largest Roman cities at the desert's edge; still to be seen was a fortress and Roman milestones on the road.

Hebron, one of the oldest cities of Canaan, was, in Stephens' time – 1836 – a small Arab town, containing seven or eight hundred Arab families. The inhabitants, he found, were the wildest, most lawless, and desperate people in the Holy Land; 'and it is a singular fact,' Stephens wrote, 'that they sustain now the same mutinous character with the rebels of ancient days . . .'

Stephens moved his caravan north, entering the Vale of Eschcol, where he remembered it was here that Moses had sent out spies who found grapes growing so heavily that each bunch had to be held at the end of a pole; he passed the Caves of Machpelah, passed through Bethlehem and into Jerusalem, where he arrived on 12 March, 1836. Here he waited upon the Turkish governor.

'At the moment of my entry,' Stephens recalled, 'the Governor was breathing on a brilliant diamond, and I noticed on his finger an uncommonly beautiful emerald. He received me with great politeness; and when I handed him the Pasha's firman, with a delicacy and courtesy I never saw surpassed, he returned it to me unopened and unread, telling me that my dress and appearance were sufficient recommendation to the best services in his power. I stood before the governor in a red tarboosh, with a long black silk tassel, boots splashed with mud, a red sash, a pair of large Turkish pistols, sword, and my Nubian club in my hand; and the only decided mark of aristocracy about me was my beard, which, though not so long as the governor's, far exceeded it in brilliancy of complexion.*

'From the place where I sat, the Mosque of Omar was the only object that relieved the general dullness of the city, and all the rest was dark, monotonous, and gloomy. . . . All was as still as death; and the only sign of life that I could see was the straggling figure of a Mussulman, with his slippers in his hand, stealing up the long courtyard to the threshold of the mosque. The Mosque of Omar, like the great mosque at Mecca, the birthplace of the Prophet, is regarded with far more veneration than even that of St. Sophia, or any other edifice of the Mohammedan worship; and to this day the Koran or the sword is the doom of any bold intruder within its sacred precincts. At the northern extremity of the mosque is the Golden Gate, for many years closed, and flanked with a tower, in which a Mussulman soldier is constantly on guard; for the Turks believe that, by that gate, the Christians will one day enter and obtain possession of the city – city of mystery and wonder.'

Stephens was unaware then and learned only later in London that only two years before Frederick Catherwood† had made complete plans of the Mosque of El-Aqsa.

'When the Arabs swept into the Jordan Valley, overwhelming the armies of Heraclitus, all Palestine fell. The Arabs entered Jerusalem in A.D. 640. Behind the ancient city wall – the lower courses of which belonged to the period of Herod the Great – the Arabs, with the aid of Greek Christian architects and workmen, erected the magnificent Dome of

*Stephens' beard was a fiery red.

†Frederick Catherwood first became known to Stephens in Palestine, when he found in a bookseller's shop a Plan of Jerusalem published 1 August, 1835 at 21 Charles Sq., Hoxton, London by F. Catherwood. 'I was fortunate,' wrote Stephens, 'to find a lithographic map by Mr. Catherwood. . . . and which I found a better guide to all the interesting localities than any other I could procure in Jerusalem.'

the Rock. This and the adjoining Mosque of El-Aqsa were built in A.D. 691 by the Umaiyad prince Abd el-Malik'.

Stephens had one more task before he left Jerusalem – to visit the grave of his school-friend under whose name he had placed his own all along the way. He found the grave of Cornelius Bradford near Mount Zion. He had died in 1830 at twenty-five years of age in a convent, having been converted to Catholicism on the narrow fringe of death: an elaborate tombstone inscribed in Latin marked his grave.

This young American had been a merry fellow, well known in Parisian society, and a particular pet of the family of General Lafayette, who had recommended him to Martin Van Buren as a treaty negotiator with the Turks. Lafayette's suggestion was politely turned down, but Bradford was appointed U.S. consul at Lyons in 1829.

After six months he applied for leave to come home to America; this being granted, he unaccountably turned up several months later in the East. Stephens had traced Bradford's path by the places where he had scratched his name on antiquities. 'Years had rolled away since I bade him farewell in the streets of our native New York city. I had heard of him in the gay circles of Paris as about to wed with one of the proudest names in France; again, as a wanderer in the East, and then as dead in Palestine . . .'*

After making a brief tour of the Dead Sea on which he made experiments in floating, Stephens obtained a map of it, through the agency of an Irishman, named Costigan. It was one of the first known maps since Roman times.†

Stephens then stepped back into conventional clothing

*For at least a generation Bradford's grave was a stopping place on tours of Jerusalem given to American travelers by the American missionaries. Their interest was partly professional, for they shared Stephens's indignation at Bradford's apparent conversion under duress.

†This published map of the Dead Sea in Stephens's book, *Incidents of Travel in Arabia Petraea*, was done a year before two Englishmen Messrs. Moon and Bebe made an estimation of its altitude based on the boiling point of water: they determined the Dead Sea was 600 feet below sea-level. Before that few, except Stephens, realized that the Dead Sea, although only fifty miles from the Mediterranean, was below sea-level (actually it is 1,300 feet).

and moved on to Sidon seeking a vessel to carry him to France or London. While there he decided to call upon Lady Hester Stanhope, that white-robed Sibyl of Lebanon who had been the mistress of the William Pitt home when he was Prime Minister. Granted a large pension on his death, she wandered, in queenly fashion throughout the Levant. In 1814 she settled on Mount Lebanon, adopted eastern culture, interfered in Turkish-Arabian politics, maintained a wonderful ascendancy over the tribes about her, rose to be a prophetess and became in time a monument which every traveler in her realm thought it his duty to visit.

So on his arrival at Sidon Stephens drove to the Arab Consular agent to consult him on the protocol.

He told me that I must send a note to her ladyship, requesting permission to present myself, and wait her pleasure for an answer; that sometimes she was rather capricious. The state of my health would not permit my waiting anywhere upon an uncertainty. I was but one day from Beiruit, where I looked for rest and medical attendance; but I did not like to go past, and I made application perhaps with more regard to my own convenience and feelings than the respect due to those of the lady, and demanded an immediate answer.

I have since read Mon. de La Martine's account of his visit to her ladyship, by which it appears that her ladyship had regard to the phraseology of a note. Mine, as near as I can recollect it, was as follows: 'Mr. S., a young American, on the point of leaving the Holy Land, would regret exceedingly being obliged to do so without first having paid his respects to the Lady Esther [sic] Stanhope. If the Lady Esther [sic] Stanhope will allow him that honour, Mr. S. will present himself *to-morrow*, at any hour her ladyship will name.' If the reader will compare this note with the letter of M. de La Martine, he will amost wonder that my poor messenger, demanding, too, an immediate answer, was not kicked out of doors. My horses were at the door, either for Beirut or her ladyship's residence; and when obliged to turn away from the latter. Her ladyship was exceedingly lucky, by-the-way, in not having received me; for that night I broke down at Beirut; my travels in the West were abruptly terminated; and, after lying ten days under the attendance of an old Italian quack, with a blue frock coat and great frog buttons. He frightened me half to death every time he approached my bedside.

So Stephens returned to Alexandria, and loitering there long enough to gather his effects, and, after traveling adventurously half way around the world for 'reasons of health,' set sail to England which then was on the shortest route to New York City. He arrived in the autumn of 1836.

CHAPTER VI

The Meeting

Stephens drank in the sights and sounds of London as he had once drunk in the fetid waters of Idumea. The press of the crowds, the well-dressed women issuing from elegant carriages, the splendid shops, many lighted with the newly arrived gaslight, acted as an intoxicant on his impressionable nature.

He found himself received with marked attention at the American Consulate by Colonel Thomas Aspinwall, who acted in dual capacity as Consul and as literary representative. A capable, friendly man, his appearance was no less dignified by an empty sleeve, for he had lost an arm in the War of 1812 whereat he gained his military title as well as his sinecure as American Consul. Since he was only partially beholden to his government, the rest was private business; and his was the representation of American authors in England.

Stephens saw the copies of the *American Monthly Magazine* and himself in print there, in 'A Journey through Idumea'.

His guise of 'an American gentleman' was soon penetrated and he was treated as a new literary lion.

Apart from the fashionable dinners, which he continuously attended, he made the tour of London. He looked in at Tattersall's auctions, rambled through the Mall, gazed in rapture at the celebrated Elgin marbles at the British Museum, then going on successive nights along the Corinthian path, he breathed in the odors of London after dark.

In his way, he came upon Leicester Square. In front of Burford's Panorama was emblazened *The ruins of Jerusalem.*

How did I meet Mr. Catherwood? Why, in the simplest way in the world. While in the Holy Land, I was so fortunate to find in 1836, in the hands of a missionary, a lithographic map made from Mr. Catherwood's drawing; I found this a better guide to all the interesting localities than anything else I could procure in Jerusalem . . .

Stephens visited and viewed the Panorama and there met F. Catherwood, Archt., as he styled himself on his calling cards. From this chance meeting – another one in the series of accidents – of a New York lawyer and a London-born architect was to develop through the next years, one of the most romantic – and productive – episodes in archae-ological history. It was also to bring about the discovery of the Maya civilization and mark the beginnings of American archaeology.

Neither Stephens nor Catherwood recorded the next step in their relationship, but it was obvious enough. Stephens viewed the immense panorama of Jerusalem.

A circular mural, it was illuminated by gaslight, then highly combustible, and was eventually destroyed. All we know of it is a pamphlet advertising it: '*Description of a View*

29. *New York from Governor's Island, 1844, from a lithograph by Catherwood.*

of the City of Jerusalem painted from Drawings . . . by Frederick
Catherwood with a woodcut of the mural.'

Later in the year the panorama was moved to New York
City, where it was boosted as: 'A painting of the largest
class, 10,000 square feet from drawings by Mr. Catherwood
brilliantly illuminated every evening by upwards of 200
gaslights.'

The New York to which Stephens returned in 1836 in
order to write *Arabia Petraea* had visibly changed since he had
left it, two years before, to go upon his Ulysseian wandering.
Much of New York City was a blackened shell. The fire that
had gutted it broke out on a winter's night in 1835, somewhere
in the vicinity of Maiden Lane, and made a flaming advance
since the freezing conditions put the firefighting equipment
out of action.

Yet New York City, undeterred by fire or politics, was
growing out of its traditional bounds; the new census placed
the population at over two hundred thousand, and the city
limits were stretching beyond the City Hall.

Martin Van Buren, the newly-elected President, entered
office with an impressive mandate from the people.

He inherited Andrew Jackson's office and immediately
on taking over he also inherited the financial crash.

Inflation as a concomitant of Jackson's policies had been
gaining steadily since 1834; by 1837 paper money had grown
far beyond the proportion of specie. There were crop failures
and speculation. Credit was tightened. Gold fled the country,
and America was in the grip of the worst depression it had
ever known. By May 1837 eight hundred banks had suspended
payment, freezing $120,000,000 in deposits. In a short six
months, one-third of the population of New York City was
unemployed.

But Stephens would have been oblivious to the financial
chaos, for he was immersed in setting down his impressions
of his travels in Egypt and Arabia Petraea. The reception of

the fragment of his travel story, the published 'letter', was so enthusiastic that he was urged to write the whole of it.

The manner of his first venture into authorship was detailed many years later by one who must surely have been in on its beginnings:

> John L. Stephens, a clever enterprising New York lawyer, and author, made his entry into the world of literature in a rather whimsical fashion. He had been, many years ago, in Eastern Europe, upon I know not what business. After his return to New York, he happened one day to be in the publishing house of Harper Bros. when the senior member of the firm, Mayor Harper, fell into conversation with him about literature – that is, the sort of books he sold most of, which was his special interest in the matter.
>
> 'Travels sell about the best of anything we get hold of,' said he. 'They don't always go with a rush, like a novel by a celebrated author, but they sell longer, and in the end, pay better. By the way, you've been to Europe; why not write us a book of travels?'
>
> 'Never thought of such a thing', said the lawyer, 'I traveled in out-of-the-way places and went very fast. I made no notes and should have very little to write about.'
>
> 'That's no matter,' said the publisher, 'you went through and saw the signs. We have got plenty of books about those countries. You just pick out as many as you want, and I will send them home for you; you can dish up something.'
>
> 'He did dish up three volumes of very amusing travels and in due time, three more, and the Harpers paid him some twenty-five thousand dollars as his portion of the enterprise.'*

The book was not precisely 'dished up.' *Incidents of Travel in Arabia Petraea*, published in two small volumes, consisted

*Thomas Low Nichols, *Forty Years of American Life*, 1829–1861, New York, 1937, pp. 211–212.

of 180,000 words written in less than a year and was, despite its light touch and its droll and casual style, based on considerable research. Stephens did not pad out the book with learned intrusions that would spoil the flow of the narrative so that his infrequent excursus into history was highly readable.

Edgar Allen Poe's review of *Arabia Petraea* (he was the only critic who had anything intelligent to say about the mechanics of writing) highly praised it and so sent it on its way. A century later, the late Van Wyck Brooks, an eminent literary critic, singled out Stephens as 'the greatest of American travel writers.'

In itself the success of *Arabia Petraea* was unusual. Authorship then was considered mostly as a diversion of amateurs and a gratification of idleness. Moreover, Stephens was warned that the fact that he had written a book might be injurious to his law practice, since he might be considered frivolous; hence the fact that the author in the first edition is listed as J.L.S.

Those Americans who did write received little for their efforts. Emerson obtained nothing from his own publications; in 1828, Nathaniel Hawthorne published, at his own expense; Edgar Allan Poe never solved the problem of living by his writings; as for Thoreau, he did not seem to need money for the type of life he lived.

It was axiomatic then in publishing circles that it would be deleterious to publish an American author. 'Why should they anyway?' questioned the English critic, Sydney Smith. 'Why should Americans write books when a six weeks' passage brings them in their own language our sense, our science and genius in bales and hogheads . . . In the four quarters of the Globe, whoever has read an American book?'

But people *did* read *Arabia Petraea*. The irascible Sydney Smith found 'not a wearisome page in the whole work . . . excellent, unaffected with a flavour of freshness and perhaps something of the carelessness of conversation . . .'

So within two years *Arabia Petraea* had sold 21,000 copies, and Stephens was $25,000 richer – a fabulous sum for authorship in 1837 and even now a very respectable one. More important than the influence of the book – it was in print until 1881 – was that it provided the financial background for the discovery of the Maya.

By that time, in 1836, Frederick Catherwood had arrived in New York.

What brought or who brought Catherwood to New York? Presumably Stephens. New York City had been devastated by the recent fire and had to be rebuilt. The city was pushing itself uptown. There was a need for architects.

Of this part of Catherwood's career there is a definite record. In the New York of 1836, Frederick Catherwood encountered little difficulty in finding employment in his profession as much of lower Manhattan was in a building frenzy. A business card, still preserved, announces:

F. CATHERWOOD,

Architect,

NO. 4 WALL-STREET,

NEW-YORK.

Later Catherwood went into partnership with another architect, Frederick Diaper, and circulars sent throughout the city announced:

The Subscribers [Catherwood & Diaper] respectfully inform their friends that they have entered into arrangements to carry on together the profession of Architects and Surveyors in the City of New York. Their office for the present is at No. 94 Greenwich Street.

Their claims to public favor are:

Mr. Catherwood, Fellow of the Institute of British Architects and F.R.A.S., has in the course of his studies as an Architect visited Italy, Greece, Egypt, France, Germany, England &c. in which countries he has measured and drawn many of the principal remains of ancient magnificence as well as the more important and striking modern edifices. His studies have been pursued during between 7 and 8 years with the greatest perseverance and zeal.

Mr. Diaper was a pupil of Sir Robert Smirke one of the principal Architects to the English Government and has consequently had the most favorable opportunities of seeing and assisting in the construction and superintendence of the great works that have been recently executed and that are now in progress in the English Capitol. The Subscribers are willing to design and superintend the erection of Public Buildings, Houses in Town or Country, Ornamental villas, and the laying out grounds—and to undertake all that appertains to the Science of Architecture and Land Surveying.

Catherwood & Diaper

After some difficult months, Catherwood began to prosper and went to England to collect his wife and sons. He brought back as well many of the panoramas he had painted for Robert Burford.

He took a house at 488 Houston Street, and leased a piece of ground from John Jacob Astor on Broadway at Prince Street, in front of Niblo's Garden.

There, in 1838, he erected his own panorama, and soon New Yorkers were entering night and day to see 'The Splendid Panorama of Jerusalem'. It was a profitable enterprise and was greatly assisted by Stephens, who in his eighth edition of *Arabia Petraea* (September 1838) highly praised the show and suggested that all New Yorkers view it.

The effect of the cumulative publicity was reflected in the numbers of people who crowded the panoramas for the constantly changing programs. ('He has under his control,' wrote Stephens, 'large panoramas of Jerusalem, Thebes, Damascus, Baalbec, Algiers, Carthage and Athens.') It was this financial success that finally released Catherwood from the gnawing problem of turning his talents to profit. He could now shift his thoughts (with Stephens) toward the problems of the mysterious cultures in Central America.

John Russell Bartlett wrote in his unpublished journal:

I claim to have first suggested [the ruins in Central America] to Stephens . . . One day in my office I said to him. Why do you not undertake the exploration of Yucatán and Central America? I invited him to come to my house where I showed him [Jean-Frédéric] Waldeck's work on Yucatán, a beautiful work in folio containing views of some of the ruined edifices in that country which I had just imported from Paris. . . . There is a field that is quite unexplored where there are numerous objects of interest in ruined cities, temples and other works of art. Mr. Stephens said he never heard of these remains but he would be glad to know more about them.

Mr. Stephens called at once upon me and examined the book. At the same time, I showed him several other books on the countries in question and pointed out to him in other works references to the ancient remains in Yucatán and Central America. Mr. Stephens was greatly interested in what I showed him and took some of the book home for a more careful examination.*

*John R. Bartlett, born in Providence, Rhode Island, in 1805 (on the identical day that Stephens was born), came from an old Massachusetts family, which installed him, after graduation from college, in the banking house of Cyrus

In 1837, in conjunction with Charles Welford, Bartlett established the firm of Bartlett & Welford, booksellers and publishers, on the ground floor of John Jacob Astor's famed Astor House, which had risen from the ashes of the fire of 1835 and imposed itself, a huge pile of Grecian pediment, across from the City Hall.

Around it gyrated the fashionable world; Broadway was its promenade, ladies dressed in coal-scuttle bonnets and short-waisted, tight-fitting spencers walked beside their gentlemen in the full tide of a romantic period which still lived by candlelight. Elegant barouches with spanking horses bowled along the cobblestoned street. Mounted gentlemen pranced the streets, riding their horses on a snaffle, ignoring the horse-drawn omnibuses with high-sounding names that conveyed their passengers within the limited area which was then New York. One began and ended at the Astor House, for there were the fashionable shops.

And there the history of the Maya began.

Butler. A founder member of the Providence Athenaeum, he was more interested in books than in dollars.

His greatest contribution to bibliography was his *catalogue raisonné* of the library of John Carter Brown: *Bibliotheca Americana*, in the *Library of John Carter Brown*, 1865–1870, 4 vols. Bartlett died in 1886. His résumé of the advances of anthropology, *The Progress of Ethnology*, may still be read with profit.

PART 2

THE FIRST JOURNEY

CHAPTER VII

The Mysterious Maya

Stephens was astounded by what he now read. He had been absorbed for weeks in reading descriptions of the ruins that were supposed to exist in the jungles of Central America, beginning with the adventures of Capitán del Rió, who discovered the ruins called Palenque in southern Mexico, in his *Descriptions of the Ruins of an Ancient City.*

Reading the book again now, Stephens was convinced that, shadowy and inchoate as the descriptions were, some sort of high culture had once existed in tropical America. This was confirmed by yet another book, a huge folio volume written from the accounts of Capitán Guillelmo Dupaix, an officer of the Mexican Army, who had also explored the Palenque ruins. In the same volume, *Antiquités Méxicaines,* another ruined city called Uxmal was said to exist in the State of Yucatán. The author of this article was Lorenzo de Zavala, who had been born in Yucatán and had seen these ruins with his own eyes. When Minister to Paris, he contributed a *Notice sur les monuments antiques d'Ushmal, dans la province de Yucatán* to the work on Mexican antiquities. And only lately there had appeared in one of the learned American journals the first notices of yet another ruined city called Copán, which, as Stephens said: 'Instead of electrifying the public, either from want of interest in the subject, or some other cause . . . *little notice* was taken of it.'

So three names were engraved in Stephens' mind: Copán – Palenque – Uxmal. Although he could find none of these sites on the existing maps, it was obvious to him that although hundreds of miles apart, these ruined cities represented a widely spread culture.

In 1839 all these vague ruins were covered by the generic

103

30.   The back of an idol at Copán, from a lithograph by Catherwood.

31. *The Huasteca depicted in* Antiquités Méxicaines, *published in 1834.*

32. *Palenque depicted in* Antiquités Méxicaines, *published in 1834.*

term 'Mexican,' and their very existence was treated with great scepticism by world scholars.

'The first light thrown upon the subject,' Stephens reflected, 'was by the great Alexander von Humboldt, who visited that country at a time when . . . it was almost as much closed against strangers as China is now. . . . At that time the monuments of the country were not a leading object of research; but Humboldt collected from various sources information and drawings, particularly of Mitla . . . Xoxichalco . . . and the great pyramid of Temple of Cholula he visited himself. . . . Unfortunately, of the great cities beyond the vale of Mexico, buried in forests, ruined, desolate and without a name, Humboldt never heard, or, at least . . . never visited. It is but lately that accounts of their existence reached Europe and our own country. These accounts, however vague and unsatisfactory, had roused our curiosity.'

The acceptance of an 'Indian civilization' demanded, to a North American living in 1839, an entire reorientation, for to him an Indian was one of those barbaric, half-naked, tepee-dwellers against whom wars were constantly waged, rude subhuman people who hunted with the stealth of animals, the artisans of buffalo robes, arrow-heads, and spears, and little else. Nor did one ever think of calling the other indigenous inhabitants of the continent 'civilized.' In accepted opinion, they were like their North American counterparts – savages. Few thought that throughout the table-lands of Mexico, in the tangled scrub jungles of the Yucatán, covered by jungle verdure, there stood ruins of temples, acropolises, and stone causeways of a civilization as great in extent as Egypt's.

The names of Hernán Cortés, Pizarro, Bernal Díaz del Castillo were but synonyms for rapine; 'Aztec,' 'Maya,' 'Toltec', and 'Inca' were in no dictionary, and in few histories. These civilizations were not only dead, for dead implied having once lived, but even to the world immersed in searching out the antique, absolutely unknown.

This blanket of oblivion that covered these civilizations had, in part, been woven on the loom of the well-known William Robertson (1721–1793), the famed Scottish historian and churchman whose *History of the Discovery and Settlement of America* was widely praised and equally widely read, and who had settled for himself and for his readers the definitive position of American culture:

'Neither the Mexicans nor Peruvians [were] entitled to rank with those nations which merit the name of civilized.' As for the palaces ascribed to them by the Spanish conquistadores, Robertson dismisses those cities as:

> More fit to be the habitation of men just emerging from barbarity than the residence of a polished people. . . . Nor does the fabric of their temples and other public edifices appear to have been such as entitled them to high praises . . . these structures convey no high idea of progress in art and ingenuity. . . . If the buildings corresponding to such descriptions had ever existed in the Mexican cities, it is probable that some remains of them would still be visible . . . it seems altogether incredible that in a period so short even vestige of this boasted elegance and grandeur should have disappeared. . . . The Spanish accounts appear highly embellished.

Yet if the vestiges of ruined stone cities did exist in tropical America – for one could no longer deny the evidence of these publications – and they were not built by the Indians, who built them? The antiquarians all tried to speak at once: they were built by the Egyptians, the Norsemen, the Chinese, the Mongols who came with elephants, the Romans, the Phoenicians, the Carthaginians, the lost tribes of Israel.

It was an old controversy and one that had raged in the academies, in the priories, and in the council rooms, where, on occasion, blood had been spilled in arguing out a favorite hypothesis.

For after America was declared to be a new continent, and its explorers confronted with a heretofore unknown race of people, the Church found itself in a dilemma. If the flood had destroyed the world's population, as detailed in Genesis, leaving only Noah and his chosen family to repopulate it, whence came the American Indians?

Noting the faces of the Indians, some Spaniards believed they were looking at Semitic faces and, remembering the well-known skill of the Phoenicians in oceanic travel, the theory was advanced that the Indians were descendants of the lost Tribes of Israel. This fancy was to endure for four hundred years and into our own century, for the doctrines of the Mormon Church are based upon it. Gregoric Garciá, writing in 1607 in his *Origin of Indians of the New World*, made the Biblical Orpir, Perú; Joktan (of The Book of Genesis) became the Yucatán of the Mayas. Another fraile Padre Durán, wandering among the thousands of Indians that constituted Mexico, wrote:

> . . . the supposition is confirmed. These natives are of the Ten Tribes of Israel that Salmanassar, king of the Assyrians, made prisoners and carried to Assyria in the time of Hoshea, king of Israel.

The Dutch soon entered the controversy. The learned Huig de Groot – the famous Hugo Grotius of international law – muddied the anthropological waters by writing that the Indians of North America were Scandinavian; the Peruvians, Chinese; and the Brazilians, African. He was immediately answered by his countryman, Johannes de Laet, who, stirred to rage over such logic, wrote that anyone except a dunderpate could see that the American Indians were Scythians.

By this time the Londoners of Cromwellian England were also involved in the anthropological battle. One Thomas Thorowgood had heard from a rabbi in Holland of an

Antonio Montesinos who was entertained by a community of Jews in Peru, Indians who practiced the circumcisional rites; this and other apocrypha he wrote into his pamphlet, *Jewes in America*. But he was soon challenged by another writer whose tract was engagingly titled: *Americans no Jewes*.*

By the beginning of the eighteenth century it was universally accepted in America that the Indian was the descendant of the Lost Tribes of Israel. William Penn, when he had seen the Indians, said: 'I imagined myself in the Jewish Quarter of London.'

Centuries of repetition had hardened it into an accepted anthropological fact. Even as Stephens was studying these works of questionable erudition, there were arriving in America from London copies of *The Antiquities of Mexico*, huge folios that offered 'scientific proof' – from archaeology itself – that the Indians were Jews.

The Antiquities of Mexico, in nine volumes (published at £30 the folio), was written by Edward King, third Earl of Kingstone, Lord Kingsborough, who was born in 1795.

As an Oxford undergraduate he was suddenly precipitated into American antiquities by examining in the Bodleian Library an original Aztec hieroglyphic tribute chart – the Codex Mendoza. His imagination was fired and his lordly purse opened.

The publication of these massive tomes lost him his fortune and eventually his life, for he died in a Dublin debtors' prison as a result of his failure to meet the cost of the handmade paper on which they were printed.

The illustrated material within the nine volumes was historically important, for Kingsborough had gathered the whole of the then known collection of Mexican codices in Europe and had them lithographed and then hand colored. He elucidated this valuable illustrative material with a written text, a potpourri of Greek, Hebrew, Latin, and Sanskrit interspersed with occasional English words.

*Written by Harmon L'Estrange, 1652.

The work took a form which was to Kingsborough's mind logic, but to his reader the essence of confusion. Anyone whose patience was able to withstand these millions of words, could learn, in sum, that America had been peopled by the Lost Tribes of Israel.

So that it was a simple bibliographic fact that in 1839 there was no literature available to the American reader on the ancient American civilization other than those recently published works which Stephens had read.

The immediate result of his literary success was that it provided the financial means for the search and discovery of the Mayas.

Of a certainty Stephens talked at considerable length with Frederick Catherwood about the Central American trip.

John R. Bartlett records in his journal:

Fortunately [for Stephens] Mr. Frederick Catherwood . . . with whom he was on intimate terms, was then in New York. Mr. Catherwood had great enthusiasm in anything pertaining to architecture, and was an ardent lover of the picturesque and of archaeological researches. Mr. Stephens made him a favorable offer to accompany him to Central America, which offer he at once accepted.

On 17 September, 1839, Stephens drew up a contract. An absorbing historical document and vitally important in the literary history of the Mayas. It ran:

Memorandum of an agreement made this day (September 9, 1839) between John L. Stephens and Frederick Catherwood. Frederick Catherwood agrees to accompany the said Stephens on his journey to Central America, and to continue and remain with the said Stephens until the said Stephens shall finish his official duties with the government of Central America, and then to accompany the said Stephens on a tour through the provinces of

Chiapas and Yucatán, and that he, the said Catherwood, will throughout the said tour exercise his skill as an artist and make drawings of the ruins of Palenque, Uxmal, Copán and such other ruined cities, places, scenes and monuments as may be considered desirable by the said Stephens, and that he will keep and preserve the said drawings to be engraved or otherwise made use of by the said Stephens for the sole use and benefit of the said Stephens, until released from his obligation by the said Stephens; and that he will not publish directly or indirectly the said drawings, nor any narration of the incidents of his journey, nor any description of places or persons, and that he will not in any way interfere with the right of the said Stephens to the absolute and exclusive use of all the information drawings and material collected on the said journey. And in consideration of the above, the said Stephens agrees to pay the traveling expenses of the said Catherwood from the time of his departure from New York until his return thereto and the said Stephens stipulates that the said Catherwood shall make and realize out of the materials collected on the said journey and at the disposal of the said Stephens the sum of one thousand and five hundred dollars within one year after the return of the said Stephens and Catherwood to the said city – and in case said sum shall not be so realized the said Stephens agrees to pay the same in cash – or else in lieu of the said sum of $1500 the said Stephens will deliver for Mr. Catherwood's benefit an introductive lecture or two lectures in one, two or three courses of lectures on the antiquities of Central America, and whether the said Stephens shall deliver the said lecture or lectures or not shall be agreed upon and determined by and between the said Stephens and Catherwood after their return to this city.

And the said Stephens further agrees that he will make provision for the payment of twenty-five dollars per week to Mrs. Catherwood and family during the absence of said Catherwood; it being understood that all the money which shall so be paid to Mrs. Catherwood and family shall be deducted from the above-said sum of $1500 or otherwise taken into the amount of a final settlement as so much money paid to the said Catherwood.

New York – September 1839.

Received two hundred dollars on account of the above sum of fifteen hundred. F.C.*

Then death made John L. Stephens a diplomat. Preparations for their expedition had been almost completed, passage on a vessel sailing to Central America had been arranged, when, as Bartlett explains:

Mr. William Leggett, of New York, our Minister in Central America, died, Mr. Stephens, whose politics [that is of Democratic party] were the same as Mr. Van Buren's, applied to the President for the vacant place. He was supported by a large number of prominent men in New York and his name being at the time very much before the country by his interesting books of travel in the East, he was appointed to the vacant mission. We had several interviews on the proposed visit to Central America and Mr. Stephens determined that as soon as he had presented his credentials and attended the diplomatic duties with which he was charged, he would undertake the exploration of Yucatán and the Mayas.

Stephens received these instructions on 13 August, 1839 from the Secretary of State, John Forsyth.

Sir: this department having occasion to send a confidential agent to Central America on business connected with our

*The author extends his gratitude to the Directors of the Bancroft Library University of California, Berkeley, for their kindness in allowing him access to this and other of the J. L. Stephens papers.

late diplomatic mission to the country, the President has selected you for the performance of the duty and the time has now arrived when you are expected to enter upon the discharge of it.

The instructions were clear even though no one knew whether a Central American government still existed, or if it did, the location of its present capital, or the name of either its president or its minister of foreign affairs.

Stephens' duties as outlined seem uncomplicated; he was to close the legation, ship back its official papers, find the seat of government, present his credentials, and secure the ratification of a trade treaty. So, in anticipation of his ministerial duties, Stephens went to a tailor on Broadway and had fashioned for himself a blue diplomat's coat, embroidered with a flow of golden braid and golden buttons. Frederick Catherwood, for his part, purchased reams of drawing paper, a mold of sepia colors and brushes, a new camera lucida and surveying and meteorological equipment. Then, turning over the management of his Panorama to his partner George Jackson, the bookseller, he embraced Mrs. Catherwood and his two sons and impatiently awaited the settlement of Mr. Stephens' 'diplomatic matters.'

On the third day of October, 1839, accompanied by a few friends, Stephens and Catherwood went to the North River.

They found their ship, the British brig *Mary Ann* with its anchor apeak and its sails loose, ready to sail. Whaling ships, Pacific bound, were putting out to sea on the ebb-tide.

Stephens recorded:

It was seven o'clock in the morning; the streets and wharfs were still; the Battery was desolate, and at that moment of leaving it on a voyage of uncertain duration, New York seemed more beautiful than I had ever known it before.

As the *Mary Ann* put out to sea, Stephens opened a letter that had been delivered just before sailing. It was from the widow of the late diplomat Charles G. DeWitt. She referred to all the other diplomats who had died in Central America and then sounded an ominous note: 'May you be more fortunate than any of your predecessors have been.'

CHAPTER VIII

Copán and the Way Thither

Belize looked enchanting from the sea. A thin row of white houses stretched along the shore, framed between masses of coconut palm fronds, and to Stephens and Catherwood for an unthinking moment it looked, as they rowed ashore in a mahogany dugout, like a Venice or an Alexandria. When they landed, sinking to their boot-tops in the muddy streets and had their nostrils assaulted by the heavy odor of human refuse, Belize exhibited its true character; it was an untidy, shabby, tropical port – the postern of Middle America. It was also the only way into Central America. North America had not yet acquired California; the Pacific route was impossible so that unless one wanted to ride through the whole of Mexico, Belize was the only possible route.

Although it had been settled since 1670, Belize gave no indication of it; most of the city seemed newly fashioned, like the settlements that Stephens had seen in the Illinois wilderness.

The port settlement, intersected by the Belize River, contained most of its principal buildings on its western side. There were two avenues, Front and Back Streets; along these, scavenger hogs were taking mud baths in the undried holes.

All the houses were raised on stilts, airily balconied, tastefully planted with tropical flowers, scarlet hibiscus and flaming crotons gave life to the mud, counterbalancing as it were, the stench of the port.

At the extreme end of Front Street were the Government House, the Barracks, Parade Ground, the Parsonage, the Free School, and the Burial Ground – in order of their importance.

Back of the settlement stood a forest of cohune palms alternating with savannahs of reddish, sandy soil that supported pitch pine, and tall, toughly succulent savannah grass on which the town cattle browsed.

Back of this again was a solid phalanx of jungle, an obstacle as effective as the Great Wall of China. With no land communications with the interior, Belize hung on the jagged littoral, a brief oasis in the chaos of disorder that was then Central America.

Of the settlement's six thousand population, listed in the Honduras Almanac, four thousand were Negro. 'They were a fine-looking race,' Stephens observed, 'tall, straight, and athletic, with skins black, smooth, and glossy as velvet, and well dressed, and the women with large red earrings and necklaces.'

Coming from a land of tightly corseted women who wrapped their bodies cocoon-like in swatches of petticoats, making the ankle the most exciting part of the anatomy, Stephens 'could not help remarking that the frock was their only article of dress, and that it was the fashion of these sable ladies to drop this considerably from off the right shoulder, and to carry the skirt in the left hand, and raise it to any height necessary for the crossing puddles.'

Breakfast found the explorers seated with an assortment of peoples and colors: a white British officer in brilliant red coat, two neatly dressed mulattoes; as for Stephens, he was sandwiched between two colored gentlemen.

> Some of my countrymen would have hesitated about taking it, but I did not; both were well dressed, well educated, and polite.

In Belize there was no rigid demarcation between white and black as in the United States, as Stephens found:

> Before I had an hour in Belize, I learned that the great work of practical amalgamation, the subject of so much angry controversy at home [he was writing in 1839],

had been going on quietly for generations; colour was considered mere matter of taste; and that some of the most respectable inhabitants had black wives and mongrel children, whom they educated with as much care, and made money for with as much zeal, as if their skins were perfectly white. I hardly knew whether to be shocked or amused at this condition of society.

The Negro had long been in Belize. Negro slaves captured from the seventeenth-century Spanish *asientos* were brought to Belize to work mahogany even when Belize was still occupied by the Mopán tribes of the Maya. These were either absorbed or annihilated by the more aggressive Negro.

The tropics being the Negroes' milieu, they outreproduced their white masters, so that they soon became, as they are today, the dominant race not only of British Honduras but of the whole of the Caribbean. On 31 August, 1839, just before Stephens's arrival, the nominal yoke of slavery (though their slavery was casual) was removed by the act of general abolition.

For two centuries Belize hung precariously on the fringe of the Gulf of Honduras, hidden behind the defenses of razor-sharp coral cays. It became in the power politics of its day the pitiful residue of the ill-conceived plans of Oliver Cromwell.

The Western Design had been conceived for one swift, telling blow – to be struck at all the vulnerable ports of the Spanish Empire in America: Panama, Porto Bello, Cartagena, Jamaica, and Cuba – by which the Lord Protector hoped all America would be wrested from Spain. But the scheme had miscarried, though from it the British developed a political wedge: the commercial invasion of Jamaica, hard on Cuba, and Belize in Central America.

These footholds were the Achilles' heel of Spain. Jamaica, captured in 1655, became the piratical exchange of the Main; Belize its continental branch. When piracy was suppressed by William III, the buccaneers broke up into small groups, scattering themselves on the Atlantic coast of Central America. They abandoned freebooting and turned to logging – fustic for dye, mahogany for fine wood – and so Belize become the new piratical capital.

His Catholic Majesty, King Philip V of Spain, soon learned that by suppression of official piracy his ambassadors had done him no service, for now these privateers – the most dangerous of the British fauna – were entrenched along the entire Caribbean, from Belize to Nicaragua, and not only did they carry off his botanical treasures, but when the rains came and they were unable to log, they thought nothing of running down the King's caravels, carrying off his royal fifth, and dumping his loyal subjects without ceremony into the barracuda-infested Caribbean.

These irritations led to wars, one hundred and fifty years of brutal engagements which kept the whole continent on edge. At length, in 1783, Spain was ready for compromise; she acknowledged British rights on the Atlantic coast of Central America and gave them logging rights, official sanction to cut mahogany, dye-woods, and *lignum vitae*. It was expressly stipulated, however, that the King of Spain yielded, thereby, no rights beyond these.

Aldous Huxley was to ask his fellow Englishmen:

Why do we bother to keep this strange little fragment of Empire? Certainly not from motives of self-interest. Hardly one Englishman in fifty thousand derives any profit from the Britishness of British Honduras. . . . To the overwhelming majority of British voters, taken as individuals, it is probably a matter of indifference whether British Honduras remains within the Empire or not.

Back of British Honduras lay mysterious Central America, a triangle of violent geography, roughly seven hundred miles long, a land of graceful Spanish cities centuries old, skirted by jungles, filled with fiercely disposed Indians.

The land was mountainous, tumbled and indented; it had no central mountain range, and was covered only by a thin earthcrust that burst out volcanically with threatening regularity.

Central America was without a natural system of communication, such as existed in the high plateau of the Andes: it lacked geographical unity.

The high, jungle-topped mountains sent their flooding streams to coalesce into tempestous rivers – rivers which did not admit of easy navigation.

Even the name for this 177,000 square miles of volcano-infested land was an anachronism: 'Central' America was not a geographical description, but a political term invented in 1823, to cover a republic which included Guatemala, Salvador, Honduras, Nicaragua, and Costa Rica.

Central America remained for centuries the focal point of foreign intrigue, for here, if it was to be constructed at all, was the proposed location of a canal passage to the Pacific.

The British, at the moment of Stephens's visit, had the most effective foothold, and the policy at that moment was directed by the colonies' superintendent.

Stephens paid Colonel MacDonald a visit of state in a style reminiscent of his visit to Mehemet Ali in Cairo. But this time, instead of riding a richly saddled horse, he went in a native pitpan, a forty-foot-long Indian dugout, fashioned from a single mahogany log powered by eight black soldiers who as they paddled chanted the half-forgotten tribal songs of Africa.

Colonel MacDonald met them on the steps of the government house, 'One of a race that is fast passing away,' Stephens observed 'and with whom an American seldom meets.'

MacDonald was a professional soldier, Empire-style, handsome and expansive. He had fought twenty years in the

Napoleonic Wars and seen action in the Peninsular War and at Waterloo; his tunic was rainbowed with medals. He also had connections; Sir John MacDonald, his brother, was Adjutant-General of England; his cousin was a marshal of France. His attitude reflected his genealogy. His conversation was full of hyperbole: 'like reading a page of history,' Stephens thought.

He toasted the Queen, the health of Mr Van Buren, President of the United States and the successful journey of the explorers, all this in the hearty manner of the empire builder.

Stephens, although 'unused to taking the President and the people upon my shoulders,' responded to the toast, so the official dinner went on its brilliant way.

The American Secretary of State at the moment would have been glad to know more about the plans of Colonel MacDonald, for His Excellency was about to seize the Bay Islands in the Caribbean, and planned other little imperialistic expansions that would upset what balance of power still existed in Central America.

When they took their leave, MacDonald put his arm through that of Stephens and in an easy spirit of camaraderie told him that he was about to enter a distracted country (a euphemism for the confused slaughter that was going on in the hinterlands), that if danger ever threatened, he was to gather all the Europeans together, run up the British flag and send for Colonel MacDonald.

But the Colonel did not intend that Stephens and Catherwood should get to the mysterious city of Palenque first, and may have hinted as much since Stephens later became aware of the duplicity.

He planned to send, without official Foreign Office approval of the expenses of the trip, two men of the colony to forestall Stephens.

Patrick Walker, who arrived at Belize in April 1837, was listed by the leader of the colony as 'one of the most exemplary young men I have ever met.' He had assumed one post after another until by January 1839 he was appointed member of the general staff of the Prince Regent's Royal Honduras Militia, as 'Inspector and Keeper of Arms, Clothing, and Accoutrements.'

He was given the rank of major, taking on the additional task of serving as aide-de-camp to the commander.

In June, he became both the advocate for the Crown in The Settlement and the magistrate of the Bay of Honduras, 'thereby compounding the complexity of his legal duties, but saving space in the courtroom; one chair sufficed to seat the clerk, magistrate, Crown advocate and one of the judges.'

When Stephens met him he said: 'Mr. Walker as "Secretary of government," held such a list of offices as would make the greatest pluralist among us [Americans] feel insignificant.'

The local Press had it:

> From the talented pen of Mr. Walker we expect to have a solution [of Palenque] of which we have heard so many extraordinary reports.

Lt John Caddy of the Royal artillery was to be the 'recording artist'; he was born in Quebec in 1801, trained at the Royal Military College as engineer and canoneer, studied art betimes, was stationed for many years in the West Indies and had finally arrived at Belize in April 1837.

Said the Belize *Daily Bugle:*

> We trust that Lieutenant Caddy's graphic pencil . . . will give facsimile copies of the hieroglyphics. . . .

And so Walker and Caddy departed on 13 November, 1839.

Caddy kept a journal, and comparing his 'Incidents of Travel' one sees why Stephens was so highly esteemed as a writer.

A typical Caddy entry:

With ears that swept away the morning dew; Crock-knee'd, and dew lapp'd, like Thessalian bulls whose deep bass voice roused us from our soundest slumbers on several occasions – José declared he never barked unless he snift Tigers, and whenever this was the case, the whole of the 'Perros' came barking and cringing among the people in the hut – we were told that it frequently occurs that the Tiger will watch his opportunity – when sleep has overtaken the weary traveller and he swings in his hammock suspended between two trees, wrapped in his Chimarro with his faithful dog crouching under his – and seize his prey in an instant.

Walker and Caddy arrived at Palenque with considerable difficulty, and made their investigations, such as they were. Caddy sketched the monuments but in comparison with the expert architectural drawings of Catherwood they were puerile.

Returning after one hundred and forty-four days, Patrick Walker's conclusion was the general view of the time: the origin of Palenque was not cisatlantic. The Empire of Mexico at the time of its conquest by the Spaniards was

Inhabited by an unskilful and feeble race, incapable of great designs or the ability to execute any work of magnitude and art – ignorant also of the use of letters its traditions for previous generations had been preserved by means of paintings of a peculiar description, we may infer from this circumstance and from the presence of regular letters and tablets in the ruins, the great space which must have intervened betwixt the time when a language expressed in written characters prevailed and that which obtained by means of figurative emblems. And until we obtain a knowledge of those characters, *which are most decidedly*

Asiatic, we must share with the humblest peasant that ever trod its streets, one common fate in the gulph of oblivion, where lie entombed so many records which frail humanity sought to render perpetual.

Lt John Caddy when presenting his illustrations in London stated that he supposed 'these ruins to be of Egypto-Indian origin.'

The Foreign Office refused to reimburse them for their journey as they 'had no previous sanction from the Treasury for the motive was merely that we might not be outstript in this case in scientific zeal by the Americans.' The excursion of Walker and Caddy sank in the stream of time.*

Stephens and Catherwood, for the moment unaware of all this, took leave of Belize on an old ship, the *Vera Paz*, which plied among the atolls and cays of the Caribbean.

As the ship moved away from Belize, to Stephens's surprise a salute of thirteen guns was given. 'You will ask, Stephens wrote, 'how I bore all these honours. I had visited many cities, but it was the first time that flags and cannons announced to the world that I was going away. . . . Verily, thought I, if these are the fruits of official appointments, it is not strange that men are found willing to accept them.'

After stopping at Punta Gorda, a Carib village, the wood-burning *Vera Paz*, befouling the porcelain blue tropic sky with huge wreaths of smoke, rattled into the crescent shaped bay where the Rio Dulce debouched its waters into Lake Isabel. Ghostly herons flew along the shore, iguanas clung to the sides of trees, indifferent to the roaring monster that broke the jungle peace. 'Could this be the portal to a land of volcanoes and earthquakes, torn and distracted by civil war?' Stephens asked.

The narrow walls of the river passage recalled to him his entrance into Petra, only the steamboat seemed to mar the

*David M. Pendergast, *Palenque. The Walker—Caddy Expedition to the Ancient Maya City 1839–1840*. Univ. of Oklahoma Press, 1967.

romantic illusion. The age of steam had hardly begun, and already John L. Stephens was apostrophizing its shattering of romance. 'Steam boats have destroyed some of the most pleasing illusions of my life. I was hurried to Hellespont, past Sestos and Abydos, and the Plain of Troy under the clatter of a steam-engine; and it struck at the root of all the romance connected with the adventures of Columbus to follow in his track, accompanied by the clamor of some panting monster.'

The Rio Dulce continued its narrow passage for nine miles, then opened into a lake, there reflecting the cloudless sky, Lago Isabel seemed like the polished surface of an emerald. At the end of the lake – the harbour and entrepôt of violence and chaos – was the port of Isabel. Among the coconut palms and bananas were scattered the palm-thatched huts of its inhabitants. There was only one frame building, the commercial establishment of Ampudio Y Pulleiro, whose main occupation was to collect the cargo which arrived on the *Vera Paz* and engage muleteers to carry it over Mico Mountain Trail, the principal route into the heart of Central America. The muleteers, ragged and mud splattered, lay sleeping on stinking, sweat-permeated mule blankets, about which swarmed stingless bees slaking their thirst on the inexudate, while the mules, noisily crunching sugar cane, were trying to console themselves for the return trip.

They were as well provided as they could be under the circumstances for the expedition to find a government and the 'mysterious cities.' Catherwood, from long experience, knew what his work would demand: surveying equipment, reams of drawing paper, a camera lucida – the same that he had used in the Old World, pencils, pens, brushes and a large supply of sepia ink (which was his favorite medium). Stephens had naturally less to carry. He provided them with folding beds (which were soon discarded for native hammocks). The deaths of his all diplomatic predecessors had made him bring along mosquito nets. In addition to his diplomatic coat and his credentials with the large State seal of the United States, in case these did not give them sufficient protection, he brought a brace of pistols; to this they each added a long wide-bladed machete (Stephens called it a Jungle knife) and for Stephens himself, a large cargo of tobacco cheroots. They thought themselves with all this properly equipped to carry out their widely differing programs.

Stephens called upon the commandant.

A soldier, 'a *minus habeans* of about fourteen years, with a bell-crowned straw hat falling over his eyes like an extinguisher upon a candle,' stood at the door as sentinel.

His Excellency, Don Juan Peñol, commandant of the port, shirt hanging out of his trousers, could give Stephens no assurance that his passport would be respected. The Carrera faction in Guatemala might recognize it, but the troops of General Morazán, his adversary, definitely would not. Stephens was given the impression that there were three contending parties in the scrambled politics of Central America: Morazán, Carrera, and Ferrara. Carrera, an Indian, and Ferrara, a mulatto – 'though not fighting for any common purpose, they sympathized in opposition to General Morazán.'

Altogether the commandant's picture of the country was like something out of Dante's tableaux of horrors, and had the discovery of ruins not been their principal object in these travels rather than making logic out of the chaos of government, they would have made a *volte face* then and there.

Their object now was to get to the Maya ruins of Copán as quickly as possible. Death hung around the place.

Catherwood called upon a Thomas Rush, the engineer of the *Vera Paz*, an Englishman of Herculean frame, six feet four, stout in proportion, who had been struck down by malaria. He wanted, in his nightly bout with the 'ague' to have a fellow countryman about.

Stephens remembered that a predecessor in office, the

Minister to Central America Mr James Shannon, had died in Isabel and set out to locate his grave. On a knoll in the forest, back of the village, under the shadows of the epiphytic plants, was the improperly inscribed grave of the late *chargé d'affaires*. Considering it a 'gloomy burial-place for a country-man,' and fighting the depression of spirit that the place gave him, Stephens ordered that a fence be built around the grave and a coconut tree placed as a marker.

At daylight the next day they began the ascent of Mico Mountain. The mules had been arranged the night before by Augustin, whom they had picked up in Belize, a young cut-throat with a machete scar across his face. He was born on the Island of Santo Domingo, sired by a French father. At first they thought him 'not very sharp,' but as they continued, they found he possessed a Machiavellian shrewd-ness. As he spoke French, it became the expedition's *lingua franca*.

Augustin, who had been over the Mico trail before, knew what was required. They mounted their mules and set off into the gloomy jungle, alive with the call of parrots. Stephens and Catherwood were armed with a brace of pistols; Augustin, carried pistols and a sword, while the principal muleteer, who guided the Indians and the pack mules, carried, unsheathed, a murderous-looking machete. On his shoeless feet a pair of enormous spurs jingled like the fetters of a convict.

Shafts of morning light filtered through the leaves like the sun breaking through the stained-glass windows of a cathedral. But the road was a quagmire. Soon they were lost, engulfed. Ahead white Morpho butterflies floated and about them was the bleating of unseen treefrogs giving the darkened jungle aisles a melancholy note. The roots of giant matapalo trees and mahoganies, awash from the black earth, broke across the road, making hurdles for the mules. Stephens, holding on to the saddle pommel, had all he could do to save himself from being unseated.

For five long hours we were dragged through mudholes, squeezed in gulleys, knocked against trees, and tumbled over roots; every step required care and great physical exertion; . . . I felt that our inglorious epitaph might be, *'tossed over the head of a mule, brained by a trunk of a mahogany-tree, and buried in the mud of Mico Mountain.'*

Later Frederick Catherwood, who had borne all these discomforts without a word of complaint, was violently thrown from his saddle when his mule failed to clear an exposed root and struck his back with great violence against a tree. He lay half-buried in the mud, and for a moment there was not a sound from him; then, without moving from the mudhole where he lay, he said: 'If I had known of this cursed Mico Mountain before I agreed to come, you would have come alone to Central America.'

Was it possible that this was the great 'highroad' to Guatemala City? Was this the road over which all traffic passed to feed the wants of the largest of the Central American states? The muleteers insisted that almost all the merchandise from Europe came by this route. Augustin said that the reason for its condition was that it was traversed by so many mules, to which Stephens replied that in most other countries that alone would have been considered sufficient reason for making it better.

During the whole of the first part of the day the party encountered no other living person. Then suddenly at a turn in the path, they came upon a tall, dark-complexioned man in a wide-brimmed panama. Over his shoulders he had tossed a Guatemalan poncho, and in his hand was an unsheathed machete.

He had a brace of pistols sticking out of his belt and knife-sharp spurs like a fighting cock, on his splattered boots.

To their utter amazement, he doffed his panama and spoke to them in the cultured tones of an English gentleman. He had lost his guides, his mule had fallen twice, and his nerves were frayed raw. He asked for a drink of brandy. With his feet buried in the mud of Mico Mountain, he told them that he had come from Guatemala City, where he had been trying for two years to negotiate a bank charter.

Said Stephens:

> Fresh as I was from America and the land of banks, I almost thought he intended a fling at me, but he did not look like one in a humour for jesting; and, for the benefit of those who will regard it as an evidence of incipient improvement, I am able to state that he had the charter secured . . . and was then on his way to England to sell the stock.

The second day found Stephens and Catherwood on the road to Gualán. Geography had metamorphosed the thick turmoil of the lowland jungles into sun-filled highlands. Purple-hued mountains filled with pine trees succeeded each other; elfish, fantastic peaks; some bare, some verdured; they reached into the clouds like a scene from fabled Walpurgis. Instead of jungle, they now had enormous candelabra cacti, mile upon mile of strange, dully green cacti holding their spiny arms stiffly aloft. Cacti were succeeded by pine, and pine by thickets of mimosa, covered with fluffy pale yellow balls which filled the evening air with an intoxicating odor.

The enchanting hiatus of distance, the green hillsides filled with pine trees and grazing cattle, reminded Catherwood of the pencillings of George Morland and gave a faint feeling of rural England.

They crossed the Rio Motagua that afternoon and found themselves in the village of Encuentros, the first habitation they had seen since they had left Belize.

Stephens was forcibly struck by the natural simplicity of the people, their fundamental dignity. The courtesy of their women was like that of some well-bred chatelaine. They asked him to dismount and placed their homes – even though only covered with palm thatch – at his disposal. The every act of kindness seemed to come from an instinctive sense of personal pride.

Food was scarce and, when available, monotonous. Yet there were always corn tortillas which Stephens was at pains to describe. These corn cakes, black beans fried in grease savoured with garlic, with an occasional piece of meat, washed down with jet black coffee flavoured with native brown sugar, was the regime for all the day's meals.

They continued to follow the Rio Motagua – called the *camino real* – passing Gualán, through pine and oak regions, after which they entered Zacapa, the largest settlement they had encountered in Guatemala.

The streets were roughly cobblestoned, the houses, coming to the edge of the street in the Spanish manner, were neatly whitewashed. The main plaza, planted with scarlet hibiscus and palm trees, was dominated by a large church, decorated with a Moorish façade. Stephens and Catherwood, directed to the finest house in Zacapa, knocked at a gargantuan gate and were admitted by a French-speaking Santo Domingo Negro.

With easy grace the servant said that although his master was not in, the gentlemen must be pleased to consider this their home.

Said Stephens in his droll manner:

So we had candles lighted and made ourselves at home. I was sitting at a table writing, when we heard the tramp of mules outside, and a gentleman entered, took off his sword and spurs, and laid his pistols upon the table. Supposing him to be a traveler like ourselves, we asked him to take a seat; and when supper was served, invited him to join us. It was not till bed time that we found we were doing the honours to one of the masters of the house. He must have thought us a bit cool, but I flatter myself he had no reason to complain of any want of attention.

They reached Chiquimula the following day. After crossing the deep barranncas which cicatrized the land, the first object that met Stephens's eyes was a young lady standing in a doorway who smiled at them as they rode by. Her face was of uncommon interest – her eyes were like dark pools and the eyebrows finely penciled. Stephens instantly marked her house as their lodging. He suggested it, and she accepted with graceful courtesy. As yet, Stephens did not know whether she should be addressed as Senora or Senorita:

> But unhappily we found that a man whom we supposed her father, was her husband, and a ten-year-old boy whom we supposed to be her brother turned out to be her child. '*Es mio*,' she said, smiling enchantingly, laying her hand upon his head. But it was so long since I had seen a woman who was at all attractive, and her face was so interesting, her manners were so good, her voice so sweet, the Spanish words rolled so beautifully from her lips, and her frock was tied so close behind, that in spite of the ten-year-old boy and the cigar which she smoked, I clung to my first impressions.

Their direction was now westward along the branch of the Rio Motagua, the ancient river road to Copán. It was a quiet country, there were patchworks of corn and bananas and an occasional plantation of cochineal. Mountains intervened; an interminable wilderness of peaks and quiescent volcanoes lay around them and tall and gloomy mountain peaks had their verdure-covered tops buried in the clouds. An occasional naked child would peer out from a white-washed adobe house, only to be snatched in quickly. They passed churches, primitive types of Hispanic-Moorish architecture which appeared in every little village.

At the town of Comatán, they came to the seventh church in as many hours. Its whitewashed façade supported eight rococo pillars, displaying its four saints, properly placed in niches. The bells hung silent; an iron cross, eroded and ancient, crowned the top and fought with the plants growing out of its roof. The grass in the plaza fronting the church was green and unscarred even by a mule path. Back of it lay scattered red-tiled houses. In front of the church lay the village cabildo, an adobe structure forty feet long, roofed with tile.

Stephens took off the chain of the iron door, and they entered a large, empty room. A table was the only item of furniture.

Augustin was sent out to forage for food, and returned with one egg.

Later on the Alcalde of Comatán called upon them carrying his wand of office, a silver-headed cane. As was the custom, he asked their business. Stephens displayed his official passport, which the Alcalde was unable to read, and he departed with his retinue.

The explorers, tired by the long journey, had to be content with the one egg, stale bread, and chocolate for their supper. They arranged their sleeping quarters, lighted some pine slivers for light, and settled in their hammocks. In the wreaths of smoke from their cigars, they speculated on the fabled ruins of Copán, which they would reach tomorrow.

Suddenly there was a shuffling of feet outside. The door burst open. Into the room suddenly made ablaze with sputtering pine torches, poured a horde of men, all armed – alcaldes, alguacils, soldiers, Indians, Mestizos. A young officer with a glazed hat and a sword demanded to see their passport.

Augustin gave it to him, explaining in an aside the official character of the endorsements.

The toothless Indian alcalde, poking his wrinkled face over the officer's shoulder, ventured that he had seen a passport before, but that it was printed on a small piece of paper, not larger than his hand, whereas that which he held before him was as large as a quarto sheet.

The conversation grew heated. The officer said that the party could not proceed on their journey to Copán, that they would remain prisoners in Comatán until more information came from General Cascara at Chiquimula.

Stephens was adamant. Rather than lose time, they would abandon the journey to Copán. The officer said that 'the Senores would neither go forward nor backward'. He then demanded the passport.

Stephens refused. It had been given to him, he said, by his government for his protection, and he would not surrender it.

Frederick Catherwood was now aroused. It was not the custom for Englishmen to be set upon by the uncivilized, nor to take such effrontery supinely. He made a learned exposition of the law of nations; he touched upon the sacrosanct quality of ambassadors; he passed down the ages, dwelt upon diplomatic immunity; he ended with a threat that this miserable coxcomb would bring down upon him the wrath of the Estados Unidos del Norte.

Through all this the officer never realized the supercilious look on his face. Stephens, remembering his difficulties with the Sheikh in Arabia Petrae, and recalling that it is sometimes good to be in a passion, deliberately replaced his passport in his breast pocket, folded his arms across his chest, and said: 'If you want it, you will have to get it by force.'

The soldiers raised their muskets, cocked them, pointed them within three feet of Stephens's head. Had Stephens known how little value was placed on human life in that period, he would have yielded. But Augustin, always bellicose and appearing more so with the pine torches reflecting on his scarred face, shouted in French: 'Give me the order to fire, Monsieur; one round will scatter them.'

At that moment another officer, older and slightly permeated with reason, entered the room.

The soldiers lowered their rifles. At Catherwood's request

the newly arrived officer read the passport aloud. It was agreed that a courier, at their expense, should be dispatched to General Cascara.

Stephens wrote the letter, Catherwood translated it into Italian and signed the note 'Secretary.' Having no official seal, Stephens took from his pocket a newly minted American half-dollar and impressed it in the wax.

Guards were posted at the door of what was now their cell; and, exhausted by the ordeal, the travelers dropped into their hammocks.

At midnight the door burst open again. Once more the same routine. There was a repetition of the confusion. This time the explorers, pistols cocked for action, thirsted for battle.

There was no need. They were told that they were now free to continue to Copán.

It was an unfavorable introduction to American archaeology, and the incident long rankled with Stephens. He wrote a letter of protest to John Forsyth, Secretary of State: 'I regret to be obliged to say that on my way . . . I was arrested and imprisoned. I made a complaint to the Government of this State.'

CHAPTER IX

The Rise of The Maya

Of time-mythed Copán, on the edge of the tropical Rio Copán, Stephens wrote, 'Soon we came to the bank of a river, and saw directly opposite a stone wall, perhaps a hundred feet high, with furze growing out of the top, running north and south along the river, in some places fallen, but in others entire. It had more the character of a structure than any we had ever seen, ascribed to the aborigines of America. . . .'

For one thousand years Copán had lain there, covered by trees, embraced by roots of the strangler ficus, engulfed by the detritus of the centuries, centuries which gradually covered up one of the greatest archaic civilizations the world has ever known. Now monkeys were the only tenants of Copán.

Stephens and Catherwood entered, through a maze of tropical undergrowth, the Eastern Court of the acropolis of Copán. From invisible stations in the tree tops, cicadas quietly raised their rhythmic song. Long-armed black spider monkeys scolded and chattered as they watched the invasion of their sanctuary.

Stephens noted cut stones meticulously set which formed some kind of amphitheater, and in the distance at the top of Cyclopean steps was the ruin of a temple enveloped in the pallid tentacles of a strangler fig tree. On a broken stairway stone jaguars reared up on their hind legs. Above them a huge stone head, the symbol of the corn god, was fighting to retain its place with a tree which, scorning the need for earth, had grown out of the interstices of the stone stairway. They, who had seen the remains of the classical civilizations, were able to gauge from a decorated stone and a ruined plaza the significance of their discovery.

Stephens made instant judgment:

33. *Catherwood drawing of the Ma[y]* *of the Harvest, Yum Kax.*

34. *Catherwood's impression of th[e]* *'idol' at Copán.*

'America, say historians, was peopled by savages, but savages never carved these stones. . . .'

They climbed over more pyramids and descended into a veritable jungle growing in the principal plaza. There, through the darkened stands of huge buttressed trees, they discerned the white shadows of huge, intricately carved monoliths, some still standing erect, disdaining the jungle that usurped their place in the sun.

Stephens came upon a colossal stone figure:

About fourteen feet high and three feet on each side, sculptured in very bold relief. . . . The front was a figure of a man curiously and richly dressed, and the face, evidently a portrait, solemn, stern, and well-fitted to excite terror. The back was of a different design, unlike anything we had ever seen before, and the sides were covered with glyphs . . . before it, at a distance of three feet, was a large block of stone, also sculptured with figures and emblematical devices, which we called an altar. The sight of this unexpected monument put at rest at once and forever, in our minds, all uncertainty in regard to the character of American antiquities. . . . With an interest perhaps stronger than we had ever felt in wandering among the ruins of Egypt, we followed our guide . . . to fourteen monuments of the same character and appearance, some with more elegant designs, and some in workmanship equal to the finest monuments of the Egyptians.

Who had built these stone structures? What race or what people in America had reached so great a height of culture as to be able to create such sculptures?

For Stephens and Catherwood the whole history of the monuments, and indeed of Copán itself, was one huge blank. Even now a century of archaeological investigation has answered the question only partially. Thus the importance of this first discovery can only be placed in its proper perspective by an excursus into time.

When the Maya poured into the compact eight-mile-long valley which was Copán, it was perhaps uninhabited. If man had been there before them, he had disappeared and left nothing of himself.

The widely spread Maya tribes themselves had come out of a period of great wandering. The entire span of their existence, as a tribe, had been a ceaseless migration. So remote in time were these first migrations that even their time-obsessed astrologers had been unable to preserve the confused memory of events; for who among the Maya could remember the cold that once covered his world, that epoch of eternal winter when the earth was whirling ice-bound through interplanetary space?

The Ice Age was ending and a new world was forming. The glacial ice that had held the world in frigid embrace was melting and pouring brawling streams into the oceans.

Plants that had survived pushed their pallid heads out of the tundra, spores of seeds wafted on the streams of warmer air current, found root, and under this slow climatic change rank luxuriance gradually usurped the place of the ice.

Over the face of this strange new green earth, where myriads of animal forms had appeared and disappeared, after aeons of evolutionary progress, man, real man, appeared.

He is not outside the pale of world memory. Three hundred centuries ago he was making zoomorphic engravings on the walls of caves, creditable intaglios of bison, mammoths, deer, wolves.

In body, this man was a completely formed type not materially different from modern man; he had wit, ornament, a technique of living; he had custom.

The massive herds of mammals that roamed the earth soon made the acquaintance of this tool-using primate.

Man wandered around the Mediterranean and crossed it, and he appeared along the sand wilderness of the Nile; he was present in the sylvan lands of India, Java, China and throughout the whole of Eurasia. Finally he broke into outer Mongolia and northern Siberia.

Slow century followed slow century and the metamorphoses of time were transforming this primitive man: the descendants of Pithecanthropos were becoming a 'race.'

These Siberian dwellers, with their coarse, black hair, beardless faces, flat noses and high cheekbones were indexed by an epicanthic fold of the eyes. They were already using stone celts for tools.

Then some of them mutated from their Siberian world and moved into an utterly new one; two hundred centuries ago, these men with the mongoloid eyes, following the northern paths of migrating mammals, were making the first invasion of the Americas.

Primitive man came to America over its roof: the land masses of Alaska and Siberia are even now only fifty miles apart and below it are the Aleutian Islands, a geological residue of volcanic action (which still continues) that once united the two continents. Once this was a land bridge chain, a connecting link between continents, and over them for countless epochs herds of camels, tapirs, and elephants had migrated.

The Ice Age in the North was still the dominant element when ancient man came to America. We know of his presence; he has left his bones commingled in fossilized death with those of extinct animals.

Throughout the centuries following their Siberian migration, these proto-Americans moved down the unglaciated Alaskan corridor into the cast land theaters of America.

By 9,000 B.C. this man had penetrated the most remote corners of the hemisphere, from ice-bound north to ice-bound south, eventually covering America's entire 135 degrees of latitude.

Man settled on the shores of frozen or tropical waters at altitudes varying from sea level to several thousand feet. He lived in forests, on grassy plains, in deserts; here starved, there in plenty; here with a night of six months' duration, there with a night twelve hours long; here among health-giving winds, there cursed with disease. Out of all this, ancient man in America, even though greatly varying in his cultural attainments, was emerging into a new creature – *Homo Americanus.*

In 5000 B.C. this American did not much differ in his cultural accomplishments from primitive man elsewhere. While man was cultivating millet and barley in Mesopotamia and laying down the agricultural base upon which civilization was to flower, the American was selecting the wild plants which would become his maize, potatoes, tomatoes, beans, and squash, on which he would hypothecate his own civilization.

In only one respect – and this an important one, for American cultural history – did he differ from Eurasian man. America went through no Iron Age; man here never quit his Neolithic horizon. His tool (despite the Inca invention of bronze), remained the tool of the Pithecanthropi – the stone-celt.

By the time the Egyptians had reached their cultural apogee and erected the Temple of Amon in 2100 B.C., many other cultures had come and gone. The legendary Cadmus had left the alphabet, and the glory that was to be Greece was yet contained in societies of primitive Hellenes.

In America, at the same time, the period of great wandering had come to an end. Vast spaces of the American earth were man-filled. Out of these cysts of geography, human cultures came into being. In the hyperborean regions, the Eskimo, flat of face and rotund of body, still lived in the environments of the Ice Age; on the North American plains, tall, keen eyed tepee-dwellers regulated their lives to the biology of the roving bison; further south where the caress of the sun was longer, the Indian, becoming partly sedentary, cultivated his plants and under the shelter of rock caves erected crudely constructed pueblos. At the other extreme of America, the antipodal south, giant Fuegians, their naked bodies wrapped in guanaco skins, walked the frozen tundra, leaving the imprint of their widely spreading feet – 'patagoes' – on the land of fire.

In the luxuriant jungles of that same South America, naked Indians with filed teeth hunted man and beast. West of these dwelling places of the Amazon and the Orinoco was the evening land of the Andes. There in the high, cold antiplano, a huge-chested people were developing a great civilization. Around a frigid Andean lake called Titicaca, an Aymara-speaking race had, by the year 1000 B.C., laid down the agricultural patterns that would become the monolithic civilization of Tiahuanacu.

Below the Aymara and around them, there were other tribes speaking related languages. In time one of these would become 'Incas' and weld all the other Andean tribes into an empire.

North of the Incas were the Quitus; north of them the territory of such tribes as the Chibcha, whose strange customs already included the piercing of the nasal septum for the insertion of golden ornaments. They were to create the myth of El Dorado.

Between these two geographic monsters, North and South America, lay Middle America and Mexico, their land still rent by volcanic outbursts. This was to be the scene of the greatest civilization of ancient America, the Maya.

Most of Mexico had a homogeneous culture. Whether it was Totonac, Toltec, Zapotec, Otomi, Huasteca, or Maya, tribe was developed from family; animal diet was supplemented by a rude splash and burn agriculture – plots of ground were burned and seeds were inserted in holes made by a fire-hardened stick. Agriculture revolved around maize as the staple. Society was then purely human. There were

35. *Maya sculpture of a bat at Copán.*

36. *A bull frog carved out of a basaltic outcrop near Copán.*

I. *Catherwood's copies of details of Egyptian painting.*

II. *Catherwood's reconstruction of an Egyptian Temple.*

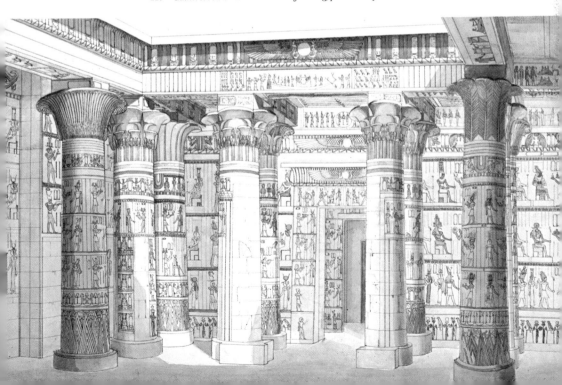

III. *Catherwood's coloured lithograph of the House of the Governor, Uxmal.*

no draft animals, the denominator of speed was man's foot. Dress was the breechclout and men walked in sandaled feet. Women wore a short-petticoated cincture of woven cotton cloth; bare breasts matched bare feet.

In all these tribes society was organized on cognate kinship; the unit was the clan, and each clan had a totemic name. Together these clans became a tribe, bound not only by the holding of land, but by the ties of blood.

Equally homogeneous was their religion. Belief was animistic; everything in their world, was animate and possessed of 'soul,' everything was alive, sentient, willful. Gods, whether good and evil, had to be propitiated, and art, when it evolved, was dedicated to the metaphysics of this theology.

The tides of cultural inheritance ebbed and flowed among all tribes of Mexico and Middle America until that which had been the exclusive cultural property of one tribal kin became the cultural currency of all. There was no visible or weighable intrusion of anything from either Europe or Asia; within itself and by itself America created its own world.

Then out of this mosaic of archaic cultures sometime after 2000 B.C., one tribe, the Maya, sprang forward in this struggle and for 2,500 years it never fully relinquished its cultural dominance. The Maya were, in great measure, to be the apotheosis of American Indian culture, creating a solar calendar, glyphic writing, fabulous temples of carved stone, and a system of agriculture.

A hundred centuries ago, a relatively recent event in the geological time-scale, a convulsion of nature pushed out of the Caribbean a huge mass of limestone composed of fossil marine animals; this peninsula, converted by time's alembic, became the strangely featured peninsula of Yucatán. The relation of the Maya to their limestone habitat was, in a sense, symbiotic, for limestone when burned became their cement; when crushed into a fine powder caustic it softened the corn kernels for maize-tortillas; when split and fashioned, it became their building material. And even more life-sustaining, the porous limestone worn by erosion opened here and there about the land into *dzonotes* (cenotes) gigantic water cisterns.

Sometime around 2000 B.C.,* the proto-Maya were in possession of this tropical globe; before A.D. 300 they were already possessed of glyphic writing and a 365-day calendar, based on acute astronomical observations, a calendar bound

*Dr E. Wyllys Andrews who had spent fully two decades continuously in the field, most notably excavating the ruins of Dzibilchaltun in Northern Yucatán who authored numerous excellent reports and analytical papers – but most unfortunately for us all, no book – visited me in Rome in Summer 1970 after the Burg Wartenstein Symposium.

We sat, drank and picnicked among the ruins of Ostia Antica, the *quondam* port of ancient Rome and there, between laughter and martinis, he talked of Maya origins, the subject of his lecture. His summing up of a lifetime given to archaeological field work in the Northern Maya area was this:

After he had reviewed all the techniques that have been used to augment our knowledge of the Maya Stratigraphy, Radioactive Isotopes, Geomagnetism, Thermoluminescence, Hieroglyphics, dates and dating, his conclusions are: 'The first humans in Meso-America were nomadic hunters who appeared about 11000 B.C. in the terminal Pleistocene . . . Although widely spread in Meso-America, remains of these Paleo-Indians have not been found in the Maya Lowlands . . .'

'Between 7000 and 2000 B.C. Meso-American man slowly supplemented his hunting economy by gathering wild foods and finally by growing his own. . . . The Formative [culture] developed in the period roughly between 2000 B.C. to A.D. 0. . . . The Formative [cultures] which mark the first known occupation of the Maya Lowlands are relatively late . . . According to the extant C^{14}[Carbon fourteen] datings, the earliest of these . . . is at Dzibilchaltun in Northern Yucatán with a base date of 975 B.C. $\pm$ 340. Structure 60 at Dzibilchaltun begun in this period was constantly reworked and inhabited for almost 3,000 years.

'*The rise of the Maya*. The sudden emergence of a syndrome of cultural innovations, appearing about the birth of Christ and foreshadowed by manifestations at the end of the Formative led rapidly to the flowering of Maya culture. These achievements include the corbelled vault, a remarkable progress in mathematics, astronomy and the calendar . . . the refinement of hieroglyphic writing . . .

'Many people for several centuries have been tempted to attribute this impressive cultural surge to some outside stimulus. Near-Eastern influences, including Egyptian, would simply have been too late. I can see sporadic groups, traders, adventurers, or castaways, making their way to the New World in quite ancient times. But if they actually had done so, I feel strongly that their impact on indigenous cultures would have been close to nil.'

E. Wyllys Andrews IV *Emergent Civilization in Mesoamerica as compared to Parallel Developments in the Old World*. Burg Wartenstein Symposium No 47 (July 4–13, 1970). Wenner-Gren Foundation, New York up with a religious ritual. Tribal communities formed about the giant wells and here they planted their fields.

Maize ('ixim' in Maya) was life. Everything in Maya life began and ended with the planting of the maize-field, for man no longer fought against nature, but for it. In his world, the Maya sought to alter nature, not to plunder it, and with this feeling the earth became more than soil, it became the earth-mother.

'O, god, be patient with me,' the Maya murmured when sowing. 'I am about to do that which my fathers and my fathers' fathers have done before me.'

A profound affinity was set up between spawning and begetting, between harvest and death. The priests who read the stars and made the permutations of the calendar, filling in the marching adjunct of the stars, became the first chieftains. Under their directions, temples were raised to the gods; and under their hypnosis of religious ecstasy, Maya art had its genesis.

In El Petén, in the humid, wet regions of Guatemala, the Maya built Uaxactún, their first known religious center; a pyramidal structure of rubble coated with a thick layer of plaster and flanked by broad buttresses into which grotesque masks were carved. This was the beginning of the culture of Maya cities. The Maya political system was theocratic and its *halach uinic* – its 'higher men' – were hereditary. Maya society was divided into classes: slave, commoner, and noble. Religion and state were one and inseparable. Everything was god-directed.

At Uaxactún, the Mayas began to build truncated pyramids, with temples at their summits, buildings, faced with stucco, ornamented with portraits of their gods. Within the plazas, the priests erected huge monoliths, on which were carved hieratic glyphs. One stela, older than all the rest, which spoke of time, is dated 11 April, A.D. 328.

At about that time Constantine was being converted to Christianity.

The heart of the religious center was the pyramidal temple. Leading from it, in geometric squares, were narrow streets frowned upon by oval-shaped dwellings calcimined into brilliant whiteness; these were the dwellings of the 'highly esteemed'.

The homes of the people, the simple artisan farmer and soldier, lay on the periphery until their houses were swallowed up by the shadows of the uncleared jungle. Throughout all this region there was a sudden cultural floresence. Tribal communities multiplied and spread out over the Yucatán; cities rose of embellished stone – Xmakabatun, Xultun, and Nakun. But of all these Tikal was the greatest.

Lying twenty miles south-west of the first known Maya city, Tikal was founded one hundred years after Uaxactún (its first stela is dated A.D. 292); of all Maya cities it endured the longest – five hundred years. The temples, towering with supreme arrogance on the two-hundred-foot pyramids, had roof combs, intricately carved, protruding above the highest trees of the Petén jungle.

During five centuries the Maya laid out this city-state with an ordered maze of quadrangular plazas and filled it with a wealth of hieroglyphic carvings.

Few of the world's archaic peoples lavished so much industry on a religious center. Stone causeways spanned the cicatrized earth for miles upon miles, flanking out on all sides of Tikal.

The Maya possessed a city culture; as Spengler has suggested: 'All great cultures are town cultures.'

Maya history was bound up with its primary classes, the priesthood and the nobility, and these classes were the motivating soul of the city. The simple Maya Indian was without history. He was, in most instances, unable to read the glyphs which the priest set down on his folding charts, nor could he understand the necromancy of the stars. He felt but did not know the involved ritual of the appeasement of the gods. Yet this simple Indian was the builder of these magnificent stone monuments, the creator of an art which now has taken its place beside the best in the world.

Around the Petén, these religious centers (today only muted necropolises embraced by the jungle) could at the end of a few short centuries be counted in the hundreds. For as the technique of stone-carving was mastered there were ceaseless cultural mutations, colonies extending the sway of 'empire' – Empire not in the political sense (since the Maya-speaking tribes were autonomous) but in the cultural sense.

The cultural growth of Copán, like that of all cities, was a gradual process. It began with temples set on small truncated pyramids filled with rubble, faced with carved stone. Time-markers were erected.

The earlier monuments exhibit the sculptor's struggle to master the volcanic stuff out of which they were carved.

So far as the glyphical record is known, Copán began in A.D. 436. The main acropolis was built, a complicated maze of courts, plazas, pyramids, and stairways, during the three and one-half centuries of the occupancy.

Throughout its cultural growth, Copán's pyramids were altered, improved, heightened, and embellished; a great plaza was laid out, eight hundred feet in length, faced with tier upon tier of stone seats, capable of seating most of the population of the city-state of Copán. Within this immensity, huge monoliths of stone were erected, carved, and dedicated, first every twenty years, then every ten, and then in full triumph over their material, every five years. These stelae, carved with incredible profusion of floral, animal, and religious motifs, are as densely alive as the jungle itself. They offer proof that great art is the product of the struggle for the mastery of the materials and that the decline of art comes when that mastery is won.

Then without prelude, disaster.

Copán raised its last monument and by A.D. 810, was giving off its death rattle; and then: the great silence. So far as its glyphic history is concerned, Copán comes to an end.

'A people is like a man,' writes Elie Faure: 'When he has disappeared nothing is left of him unless he had taken the precaution to leave his imprint on the stones of the road.'

The huge pyramids, the embellished figures in the sacred temples, the tall, awesome monoliths that stared upon the empty plaza were soon reclaimed by the jungle.

In the fertile earth, sun-loving balsas and cecropias sprang up, their shadings gave impetus to the seeds of other huge trees, wild-fig seeds, imprisoned in bird feces, were dropped within the darkened interstices of the palaces, and these, germinating in the warm tropical air, took root and grew. Within a century the huge, snakelike roots of the strangler Ficus had entangled the palaces of the Maya. Other trees grew up, shaded, and then enveloped the ruins.

Within a hundred years Copán was blotted out of human memory.

And there, so far as archaeological history is concerned, Copán lay for a thousand years, waiting for its discoverers. These, when they came, were in the persons of John Lloyd Stephens, New Yorker, and Frederick Catherwood, Londoner.

CHAPTER X

Copán: The New Ground

'We are abruptly entering upon new ground', Stephens said.

He and Catherwood were fully aware that they stood at the threshold of an unknown world. For if the ruins of Copán were a reality then so must be Palenque and the other mystery cities of which there had been more than rumors. But it was not merely an archaeological site they were discovering, but an entire civilization. They moved around the ruins, passing into the Eastern courtyard, examining there, the figure of a jaguar, admiring here a colossal head. They climbed over stone seats that recalled some of the tumbled Roman ruins. A feeling of grandeur, of the immensity of human endeavor came over them, possessed them, and was never to leave them. Stephens, lawyer by profession, diplomat through expediency, traveler by inclination, and archaeologist by choice, and Frederick Catherwood, architect and archaeologist, were discovering a whole civilization, as yet without a published history, a civilization so obscure that it was even without a name.

It was Stephens and Catherwood who were the ones who were to transmit these discoveries by well-written, well-illustrated volumes, which have already aroused five generations of incipient archaeologists.

In all this flowering chaos, where were they to start? First they must have a place to stay, for the weather was unsettled; then to clear the ground they must have workmen.

So they went back to the village of Copán, a few miles distant from the ruins, and there they were unceremoniously rebuffed. They collided with Don Gregorio.

Don Gregorio did not like Mr Stephens, nor did he like Mr Catherwood, who spoke Spanish with an Italian accent, nor Augustin's habit of talking to them in French.

37. *A plan of Copán drawn by Catherwood.*

East

A Square Altar sculptured on the four sides and top
B Statue erect.
C Statue and Altar.
D   do.   do.
E   do.   Fallen do. with many fragments on side of Pyramid.
F Colossal Head.
G Remains of sculptured figures.
H Colossal Head.
I Sepulchre and under-ground passage leading to the River.
J Remains of 2 circular Towers with Stairs.
K Statue and Altar, (Fallen.)
L Statue and Altar, (Erect.)
M   do.   do.   do.
N   do.   do.   do.
O   do.   do.   (Fallen.)
P   do.   do.   (Erect.)

Q Statue and Altar, (Erect.)
R   do.   do.   (Fallen.)
S Statue of Female with Altar, (Erect.)
T Beautiful Fragment, partly buried.
U Court Yard, with steps on three sides.
V Entrance with remains of Shafts of Columns.
W Pyramidal Building, Steps 10 ft. wide, and 6 ft. high
X Area, overgrown with Trees.
Y YYYYY Remains of Walls.
Z ZZZZZZ Remains of Pyramidal Buildings.

The dotted line shows the boundaries of the survey.

Indian Rubber, Mahogany, Cedar, and other large trees are
    dispersed over the Ruins.

PLAN
OF
COPAN

Scale of English Feet.

RIVER COPAN

F. Catherwood.   West.   No. 5.

38. *Modern ground plan of Copán by Dr. S. Morley.*

In the village of Copán, with its six miserable thatched huts, he was a man to be reckoned with.

Who was this Don Gregorio? He was a man, said Stephens, 'about fifty, had large black whiskers, and a beard of several days' growth; and, from the behavior of all around, it was easy to see . . . a domestic tyrant.'

He performed none of the graces of the *posada*; no chair was offered, no invitation to the travelers to make this their home; his whole manner – and one which at once infected the legion of women and children that surrounded him – was that he did not want them at Copán, for he thought that looking for 'idols' was merely a ruse to cover political activities. In effect, his manner was to deny them freedom of access to the ruins.

Stephens, hardly of the temperament to accept such behavior without a violent reaction, was working himself up to a proper rage when Catherwood stopped him by saying:

'If we had an open quarrel with him, after all our trouble we would be prevented from seeing the ruins.'

Catherwood, who had eight years of experience in dealing with the natives of the Mediterranean, had acquired a diplomatic mask; so 'with a great effort,' as Stephens expressed himself, 'I resolved to smother my indignation until I could pour it out with safety.'

Now Don Gregorio relaxed sufficiently to offer them use of the sapling uprights that formed the house, on which to stretch their hammocks. It was a very small section, Stephens remembered, affording 'so little room that my body described an inverted parabola, with my heels as high as my head. It was vexatious and ridiculous; or, in the words of the English tourist in *Fra Diavolo*, it was "shocking! positively shocking!" '

As if Don Gregorio had not already provided difficulty enough for archaeology, there now appeared a new snag: the owner of the ruins of Copán himself, a middle-aged man, cleanly dressed in cotton shirt and pantaloons, José María

Asebedo told them that the 'idols' were his property. Further, that no one could enter his land without his permission; whereupon he exhibited his title papers. In his best legal manner, Stephens thrust his thumbs into the upper pockets of his long shooting frock, rocked back on his heels and studied José María's title deeds, 'as attentively as if I meditated an action in ejectment.'

Señor Asebedo showed intelligent interest; particularly as his wife was ill, and he wanted something from the Catherwood's pharmacopoeia for her 'ague.'

So the travelers quit Don Gregorio's hovel, crossed the river, and took up residence at José María's.

They passed the first night agreeably enough, lying in their hammocks listening to the fall of rain on the corn-husk roof and smoking 'cigars of Copán tobacco, the most famed in Central America, of José María's own growing and his wife's own making'.

Their host was an intelligent man, although his face, his appearance, and the troglodytic dwelling loudly denied it; he could 'read and write, bleed, and draw teeth.'

Wreathed in tobacco smoke, naked except for a pair of pants (for his wet clothes were drying over the fire), Stephens lay back in his hammock 'brooding over the title-deeds' of Copán. He finally told Catherwood (who lay awake wondering how he might record the Copán monuments) that he had in mind a gigantic operation. ('Hide your heads, ye speculators in building lots!') To buy Copán!

> To remove the monuments of a by-gone people from the desolate region in which they were buried, set them up [in New York City] and found an institution, to be the nucleus of a great national museum of American antiquities!

But could the 'idols' be removed? Was the river deep enough to float down the idols? Stephens asked his host.

From the darkness came the answer – 'The Rio Copán is filled with rapids.'

Stephens then turned back to his archaeological reveries. 'Other ruins might be discovered even more interesting and accessible . . . with visions of glory and indistinct fancies of receiving the thanks of the corporation [of New York] flitting before my eyes, I . . . fell asleep.'

In the morning, Catherwood left to limn the ruins while Stephens remained to fight for the title deeds of Don José María. He explained that he would like to hire a crew of men, build a hut for them in which to live, and bring spades, crowbars, and ladders in order to excavate the ruins; this he could not do unless he held the title; so in short, how much would Don José María take for the whole ruin of Copán with all its idols?

José María was tempted. For when would he have another chance to sell so unprofitable a piece of real estate, encumbered as it was with acres of stone idols, too large to be removed or to be broken up?

The matter would have been easily settled had it not been for Don Gregorio lurking in the background. Hearing of the negotiations, he wanted to know if Don José was aware that these mysterious men had been arrested in Comatán. Was he going to risk his neck by selling land to those who might well be the enemies of the republic?

Now the befuddled José María was newly distressed; torn between *amor patria* and a chance to convert unproductive property into money, he was a picture of frustrated dejection

Stephens produced his passport with the flaming red seal of the United States; shades of suspicion still lingered.

Stephens made a final gesture. He opened his traveling trunk and donned his diplomatic coat with its profusion of large golden buttons. 'I had on,' Stephens later recalled, 'a Panama hat, soaked with rain and spotted with mud, a check shirt, white pantaloons, yellow up to the knees with mud, and was about as outré as the negro king who received a company of British officers on the coast of Africa in a cocked hat and military coat, without anything to hide his inexpressibles.' José María could not withstand the buttons on the coat, and the household stood in awe as Stephens, with the best diplomatic hauteur, paced the mud floor. They thought themselves in the presence of some *illustre;* one more look at the golden buttons, and José María succumbed: he agreed to sell the ruins of Copán.

'You are perhaps curious to know,' says Stephens, 'how old ruins sell in Central America. Like other articles of trade, they are regulated by the quantity in market, and the demand . . . I paid fifty dollars for Copán. There was never any difficulty about price. I offered that sum, for which Don José María thought me only a fool; if I had offered more, he would probably have considered me something worse.'*

17 November 1839 is a memorable date in the history of American archaeology, for on that day the first systematic work on the Maya civilization was begun. Under the dark shadows of rain clouds, the new owner of Copán, as befitting his station (he felt, he said, more like the cicerone of the Pitti Palace), left for the ruins, paced by two retainers. First the site was measured; Catherwood worked the surveyor's theodolite, while Stephens cut the stations, using the same tape reel that Catherwood had used to map the ruins of Thebes. Bruno, one of the workers, whose eyes had the same staring vacancy as the Copán sculptures, felled the trees, while Francisco, whose placidity masked the incipient taste of an antiquarian, put his straw hat on a pole as a guide point for Catherwood's observations; by the second day, the two Copánecos were 'thoroughly in the spirit of it.'

*In the Stephens Papers at Bancroft Library, University of California, Berkeley, California, there are the original letters over the transaction for Stephens' purchase of Copán and later the ruins of Quirigua. The letter is addressed to Sr. Esterreny (i.e. Stephens), Minister of the United States in Central America, and dated 5 August, 1840.

Out of these operations Catherwood made a most creditable map, accurate when one considers that the whole site was embraced by dense jungle, and even though, in the printing of the map, the cardinal points were reversed 180 degrees, making Catherwood's north, south.

The denseness of the jungle concealed the great extent of the ruins, but their discoveries, disclosed in the delightful style of Stephens and the dramatically accurate drawings of Catherwood, were to stimulate others to study the ruins of Copán, though not for a half-century would anyone follow them there.

Alfred P. Maudslay, a discerning English amateur, went out in 1882–1883 'merely as a journey of curiosity . . . with no intention of making a study of American archaeology.' Stephens's books had led him to Copán.

Under the hands of Maudslay, Copán began to reveal some of its secrets. He was followed by an expedition of the Peabody Museum of Harvard, and this in turn yielded to the practiced hands of the archaeologists of the Carnegie Institution. A century after Stephens, Copán had taken on something of its ancient form.

Copán, a complex of three main courts, is composed of several pyramids, with flattened tops, on which in times past were rectangular temples. In the Eastern Court – considered the most sacred part of the acropolis – there are tiers of stone seats, not unlike those in a classical coliseum, having on one side an extended platform beside which are two large stone jaguars, with spots sculptured in intaglio fashioned in a fanciful mood, rising on their hind legs: of these Stephens found only fragments.

Above the courtyard is a gigantic head of the Maya Lord of the Harvest, Yum Kax, which Catherwood so faithfully rendered. At the end of the courtyard (buried when Stephens was there and uncovered a half-century later by Maudslay) was a temple enlivened by an entrance by all odds the most unique in Maya art. Crouching sculptured human figures form caryatids to the ornamental doorway, holding above their heads a great wealth of sculpture.

Stone stairways lead from these courtyards 125 feet down to another section, now called The Court of the Hieroglyphic Stairway (which in Stephens, time was buried under a mountain of debris, although he discovered some of the sculptured figures which ornamented it). It is one of the most magnificent remains of an American people, a stairway rising to almost 75 feet in height, at an angle of sixty degrees, the 63 treads of which are composed of 2,500 separate hieroglyphics so arranged as to be read in lines, rather than as usual in columns. It was built or completed in A.D. 756 and was one of the last monuments of Copán. And doubtless, one of the major undertakings of the Maya civilization. Even though much of the text still remains untranslated, the late Dr S. G. Morley regarded it as 'an epitome of the principal events which befell one of the greatest cities during the greatest period of Maya civilization.'

39. The Serpent God at Copán.

By 1839 the encroachments of the jungle had erased much of its architectural form; yet Catherwood's trained architect's eye was able to detect the main elements of its structure.

It was obvious to him that here, as in Egypt, architecture was dominantly religious and that the working relation between priest and sculptor-architect was very close. Architecture seemed to be but a form of Maya sculpture. Catherwood did not know then that the Maya had no idea of the true arch, or that their architects lacked the knowledge of bonding corners and did not know the formula by which to lay off a right angle. He was unable until later to make a comparative judgment of this civilization with that of Egypt or Mesopotamia until the technological limitations of the Maya were known.

North of the Stairway Court was the Sacred Ball Court. There during the times of the city's occupancy men played at a game much resembling basketball and called by the Maya *pot-a-tok.*

Beyond this, the acropolis dissolved into the Great Plaza, flanked on all three of its sides with tiers of stone seats. Within this plaza stood the huge slabs of carved limestone – the famous stela of Copán.

Since there were no structures to draw, Catherwood turned to the 'idols,' those which Stephens and his two helpers had uncovered. For the first time in a thousand years light fell upon these strange monolithic slabs (called stelae after their Greek prototypes) in the Great Plaza. These sculptures, generally twelve feet in height and three and one-half feet in breadth, stood solitary in the jungle, detached from the fallen buildings. They made a profound impression on their discoverers. Fashioned in something of the likeness of a human being, they were carved in high relief, the clothing and headdresses incredibly ornate; the sides and backs covered with glyphs. Eleven of these had been found. Stephens being impressed with 'the development of the antiquarian taste of my helpers . . . Francisco found the feet and legs of a statue and Bruno a part of the body to match and the effect was electric upon both.'

When Stephens came upon Catherwood sketching an idol, he expected to find him excited over his discoveries. Instead, 'his mood was black.' For Maya art, as all pre-historic, American art, flowering in isolation, developed, as Mr Pál Kelemen has written

A completely individual ideal of beauty, untouched by historical influences such as co-operated throughout the Eastern hemisphere.

Maya art was unique. Its symmetry, its art-patterns were not those of the outside world; Catherwood, as Stephens reported, 'found difficulty in drawing. He made several attempts, both with the camera lucida and without it, but he failed to satisfy himself . . . The "idol" seemed to dry his art; two monkeys on a tree on one side appeared to be laughing at him, and I felt discouraged and despondent.'

The tropical luxuriance of design was confusing; the Maya artist seemed to have a fear of empty space, and the *horri vacui* was filled with people, reptiles, flowers, bird plumes, which flowed in and out of the principal design, oozing about like ectoplasm. Yet so complete was his mastery over his material that the sculptor treated a thirty-ton stone as carelessly as an oriental craftsman might a piece of ivory.

Catherwood tore up many of his first drawings, but gradually as the day wore on, he began to feel the spirit that pervaded Maya art. He passed laboriously from idol to idol drawing each one with extraordinary verity. In the century since he first drew them, few reproductions have surpassed his accuracy; none have ever eclipsed their beauty.

It was the glyphs which drew Stephens into speculation. What did they really mean? Stephens could 'hardly doubt that its history was graven on its monuments,' and he dreamed of another Champollion-like discovery, a Maya Rosetta stone,

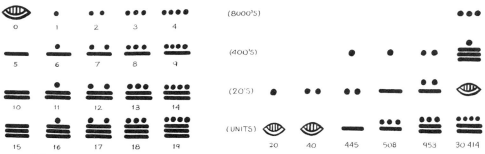

40. *Maya numerical notation.*

CATHERWOOD D.   ANDERSON S.

41. *Catherwood's exact copy from an altar at Copán compared with (below) a page from the Dresden Codex, showing the similarity of the glyphs.*

which would provide the key to these curious symbols of ancient American history which he was certain lay hidden in these 'carved stones.' For over a century, it was deemed as certain that the glyphs spoke only of time, not of history: it was the view of almost all – this author among them – that all the corpus of dated monuments were merely one vast monument to the Maya's extraordinary preoccupation with time.

Stephens' feeling that these dated and decorated stelae spoke of history began to take positive form only in 1958 when Heinrich Berlin, in a constant working over of the 'Emblem Glyph' wrote that the names of the cities themselves were recognizable (the names by which they are now known not being the original ones) and that glyphs bore the names of the dynasties that had erected them and perhaps even the names of the chieftains, and doubtless – as Stephens believed – the histories of the cities themselves.

Tatiana Proskouriakoff, known for her superb drawings of Maya sites, all based on a thorough ground knowledge of Maya architecture, used her not inconsiderable talents in analyzing 35 dates: with the monuments of *Piedras Negras* (on the Usumacinta river, 75 miles south-west of the ruins of Palenque, she found that each group covered a span no longer than a Maya's lifetime. By stylistic analysis and by associating individual glyphs, she found that these corresponded to the birthday, of the person who had erected a given stone stela.

She found that by her system, she could read of marriages, glyph signs of personal names, perhaps even titles – for the Mayas set great store by them – and since the Maya were like all others war-like, the names of military victories. The shade of John Lloyd Stephens can now be satisfied.

But above all, the Maya were time-possessed. Monoliths were raised every *katun*, 7,200 days or 20 years. At Copán these dated monoliths appeared every ten years; then, as the mastery grew, every five years. In the twilight of the Mayan gods, close to the end of their occupancy of the valley, the time fetish spread to the whole of the architecture: there was not an altar, a step, a doorjamb, a cornice, a lintel that did not have carved in calculi-form-shaped writing the date on which the work was either initiated or completed.

Few people in history have been so preoccupied with the flux of time as the Maya. The Greeks, it is true, mourned the transience of youth, marking the intervals of the Olympiads, yet even Hipparchus' 304-year period was accepted as a unit of time only by those philosophers who speculated on the infinite; beyond that the Greeks would not go.

In timeless Egypt, Hecataeus, 'thinking to put himself on the very edge of eternity, traced his descendants to a god in the person of his sixteenth ancestor.' Yet in America, the Maya priest-astronomers had calculated recurring cycles of millions of days! Did the Maya find time so unbearable, that each day must have a symbol, each month its god? Man everywhere has in some measure studded the calendar round with festivals to break up the constant flow of time, but this obsession of the Maya . . . The archaeologist deciphering these dates can follow the gradual growth of Copán; through these he can witness the slow evolution of the acropolis, like the unrolling pages of history. Even in the studied silence of the Maya themselves, one can see the architectural progress of Copán between A.D. 460 and 810.

After A.D. 900 'something happened.' They built no more. Everywhere in the 'Old Empire,' within that cultural triangle of Copán, Tikal, and Palenque, activity ceased. There is no hint of it in the architecture. The technique of the sculptures does not deteriorate, nor seemingly, does the Maya civilization. For not long before the end at Copán, the Maya erected their greatest monument, the Hieroglyphic Stairway, the most magnificent architectural achievement in all Indian America. Then that 'something' happened, after three hundred and fifty years of occupancy. The Maya slowly left the valley of Copán.

42. *Catherwood's original lithograph showing a stela and altar at Copán.*

Stephens and Catherwood naturally knew nothing of this, not even the word 'Maya'. Nor had they any idea of the extent of this civilization at Copán. Yet they sensed it, and showed much discernment.

In the Western Court, where excavation a century later was to uncover amazing huge-headed sculptures in the full-round, Stephens stumbled across a square stone altar, which 'presents as curious a subject of speculation as any monument in Copán.'

It was an altar, a single rectangular block of stone, 1.42 meters square, seventy-four centimeters high, resting on four roughly spherical supports, containing sixteen carved human figures, four to each side, sitting cross-legged on glyphs. On top, the altar was divided into thirty-six glyphs which, Stephens, said 'beyond doubt, record some event in history of the mysterious people who once inhabited the city.' Catherwood must immediately stop drawing a stone in the court and come to copy this extraordinary altar. What excited Stephens' interest were the carved figures, for they held in their hands rolls of paper, which were the Maya's books, and these they seemed to carry as sceptres.

Stephens' belief that the altar recorded a conference, was confirmed a century later. It commemorated a congress of priest-astronomers meeting in the city; and the sculptor gave great prominence to the Maya date, 6 *Caban*, 10 *Mol* (A.D. 765) emphasizing this symbol again on the top of the altar. It was in that great epoch, or close to it, that the decline sent the Old Maya Empire spinning into oblivion.

Stephens showed great sagacity in speculating upon the importance of this altar; and Catherwood did five full drawings of it.

They were to discover something else about the altar. When they returned to America, and compared its glyphs with the reproduction of a curious polychromic manuscript – called the Dresden Codex – written in the eleventh century, which Alexander von Humboldt had published, and placed these two, manuscript and sculpture, together, it was deduced – quite correctly – that the people who had written the one, had carved the other.*

They stayed thirteen days at Copán, from November 17th until November 30th. Catherwood had already completed several of his sepia drawings and wanted to do more but Stephens could stay no longer, for he had to perform 'a desperate chase after a government.' Should he remain too long, he feared that among the ruins of Copán he 'might wreck his own political fortunes and bring reproach upon his political friends.' He called a council at the base of one of the idols and while the eyes of the stone figure stared down upon them, it was decided that Frederick Catherwood was to remain behind alone, and continue to copy the sculptures, while John Lloyd Stephens, minister rather extraordinary, was to ride off to Guatemala City in search of the Central American government. After that, they would meet again in Guatemala, and God willing, go off in search of other ruins.

*Prescott, writing to Stephens, 2 August, 1841: 'I had long come to the conclusion that [the Dresden Codex] is not Aztec. No one knows from what part of America it came into Germany, and its appearance precisely answers to the description given by Peter Martyr of papyri from Yucatán. From this quarter of some part of Central America, I imagine it came.' Prescott, *Correspondence*, p. 242.

CHAPTER XI

Diplomacy: Ends and Means

Stephens rode into Guatemala City with his clothes mud-spattered and his rear end saddle-galled. The streets were deserted as if a plague had swept away the population, the shutters of all of the one-storied houses were drawn tight; the capital city of La República was as silent as a tomb.

'Perhaps,' Stephens reflected, 'no diplomatist ever made a more unpretending entry into a capital.'

He found with difficulty the house of Mr Hall, the British Vice-Consul, which like the others was sealed as tightly as an Egyptian pyramid. Augustin's knocking brought out a head and Stephens shouted his name and business and eventually, after much rattling of bolts, the British Consul, terribly agitated, opened the great doors just wide enough for Stephens and Augustin, with their mules, to slide in.

Rafael Carrera's unpaid soldiers, he explained, were in revolt; only the previous day they had exacted a 'loan' from Mr Hall's French neighbor to meet their salaries.

They had declared the British standard a *'bandera de guerra,'* and fired on it, and Mr Hall had struck his colors. (Stephens wondered why he did not run them up again and send for Colonel MacDonald in Belize to come with his gallants and lay about him.)

Yet Stephens found the city of Guatemala enchanting. Even at five thousand feet altitude it had a tropical feel with a diaphanous air, and the gardens of its one-storied houses were canopied with glowing bougainvillaea.

As was usual among Spanish colonial cities, the center was the principal plaza, where on its four sides stood symbols of power: the old vice-regal palace, residence of the capitán-general under the Crown, the *cabildo*, which disposed of city affairs; on the third corner the Palace of Ci-devant, the

Marquis of Aycinena, and completing the square in all majesty, the cathedral built in 1790.

Where an octagonal fountain, heavy in style and bad in taste, now shot up a stream of cold water piped down from two leagues' distance, had once stood the equestrian statue of Charles IV. It had been torn down in the first ebullitions of independence, but although the rider was gone, the horse remained.

Conquest had come early in Guatemala. No sooner had Mexico been reduced by Cortés than he sent Pedro de Alvarado southward, guided thence by Montezuma's tribute charts, to Guatemala. In 1524 Alvarado found three principal tribes inhabiting the villages about Lake Atitlán.

Living in fierce opposition to each other, the tribes sought to use Alvarado to liquidate one another. They were scarcely aware that the principle of *divide et impera* was an old Spanish custom.

Alvarado played tribe against tribe until he had completed his conquest. 'Seeing,' wrote Don Pedro to his liege, 'that by fire and sword I might bring these people to the service of his Majesty, I determined to burn the chiefs.'

After this he branded all the leaderless captives as slaves and exacted such gold as they had, turning over the royal fifth to the king's treasurer. It was all very legal. Pedro de Alvarado, followed the manner prescribed by established towns. In a lovely valley beneath the volcanoes Fuego and Agua, he built his capital, 'The City of St James, of the Gentlemen of Guatemala.'

The earth-land here was rich then; impecunious Spanish grandees came to America to take their ease in Guatemala's sun, to produce cochineal and cacao, enlarge Catholic Spain's orbit, and fill therewith their own empty coffers.

In time the city became a lake of sienna red roofs, and the City of St James grew in beauty and power until by the middle of the eighteenth century it contained, if the statistics can be trusted, 100,000 inhabitants. The City progressed until, in 1770, the restless inner earth broke its thin crust and tumbled most of its six thousand houses, its twenty public foundations, its college of San Tomás, it churches, its nunneries, its convent of Merced, Franciscanos, and Domenicanos, into a shapeless mass.

Then the Spaniards, like the migratory Maya, moved en masse twenty-five miles to the south, and there in 1775, the very year in which a shot in Concord, Massachusetts, 'was heard around the world,' the Capitán-General laid the foundation of modern Guatemala City.

John Lloyd Stephens entered into his diplomatic duties (somewhat delayed by discovering other civilizations) by taking possession of the American Legation.

He was very much pleased with its single-storied house, entered through a large double door which led into a paved courtyard emblazoned with bougainvillaea.

He found the salon of the legation tastefully furnished and lined with book cases filled with books in yellow bindings, which gave him 'twinging recollection of his law office' in New York. There, too, he found the archives of the legation and following his instructions (it must be owned for the first time), he prepared to ship them back to the United States.

Now it became incumbent upon him 'to look around for the government to which he was accredited'. The prescribed protocol suggested that he slip into his blue diplomatic jacket with the golden buttons, the one that had so overawed Don José at Copán, and present himself formally to the Minister of Foreign Affairs. But where was this person? And where, for that matter, was the President of the Confederación de Centro América? The French Minister, Baron Malelin, shrugged shoulders. Frederick Chatfield, the British chargé d'affaires, stated flatly that no such government existed. And then, all speaking at once, they tried to initiate Stephens into the mysteries of this political limbo.

They did not exactly begin at the beginning, for they missed the deluge. But they followed the American conquest, entered the stormy times of Philip II, the revolt of the Maya Indians et El Petén in the late seventeenth century, and then, by riding over the reign of Carlos III, they came full gallop into the times of Napoleon. Well – Napoleon had deposed Carlos IV, and had then, in 1809, with the instruments proper in the case, dethroned King Ferdinand too. At this the American colonies rose in royal rebellion; that is, they declared themselves loyal vassals of Fernando VII and would obey no Code Napoleon. A governmental junta was formed in Central America, headed by Lieutenant General José Bustamante y Guerra (famed more in history as second-in-command of the ill-fated oceanic expeditions of Alessandro Malaspina than for his statecraft), who was actuated in the royal name to collect the king's revenues and to suppress revolts.

The revolutionary standard was raised for a brief moment in 1811 in San Salvador, when Manuel José Acre captured a few thousand new muskets and $200,000 from the royal treasury with the intention of seeking independence, but Bustamante was an old hand at suppressing mutiny and the revolt was strangled.

The Capitancia-General of Central America did not have to fight, as South Americans had, for its independence, for when Fernando VII was re-enthroned in 1821 a delegation actually journeyed to Spain where the Central American junta gave the unhappy king the conditions under which they would remain within the Empire. He refused, recanted, hesitated; then it was too late. Mexico was in revolt.

South America was independent. By the time the delegates had returned to Guatemala, all of Central America was part of the new Mexican Empire under 'Emperor' Iturbide. Fifteen months later, with the rise of the liberal Republic, the five Central American provinces adopted a constitution, formed a federation, abolished slavery, and elected Marinas Calvéz president. With revolutionary social aims, they prepared to launch the ship of state. The coat-of-arms of the federation consisted of five volcanoes, each representing one of the five Republic states. The liberty cap of the *sans culotte* occupied its center, and, like a messenger of hope, a rainbow formed a lunette over the symbols of federation.

The state of Guatemala, composed of Indians, aristocrats, and clerics, the largest member in population and territory of the federal system, and thus saddled with the expense of maintaining a central government, lost within a year its enthusiasm for it.

The years that followed, 1825 until 1835, were filled with revolutions and counter-revolutions. Out of these conflicts came two vividly contrasting personalities: Francisco Morazán, a liberal, son of a French Creole, born in Tegucigalpa in 1799; and his antithesis, Rafael Carrera, the half-caste bastard of a Guatemala *ci-devant*, the personification of frustrated resentment.

Francisco Morazán had twice been president, rising spectacularly from the post of Secretary General of Honduras, which he held at twenty-five years of age, through higher offices to that of senator. He became the leading liberal and was elected president in 1831, and again in 1837. But his liberal reforms were launched too quickly. The people had hardly time to consider their newly won liberties when Morazán established the Livingston code, trial by jury, and broke the power of the clergy by exiling to Havana the Archbishop with a regiment of friars.

Reform followed reform with such rapidity that the people absorbed none of them, so neither King Ferdinand nor the Pope recognized the Central American Federation. And even though North America, Great Britain, and France gave diplomatic recognition, the Federation was so torn by unceasing civil war that the Republic doomed itself to failure.

In 1837, while Francisco Morazán was fighting revolution everywhere, cholera broke out in Guatemala. Morazán was charged by the opposition, mostly the clergy, with having poisoned the wells so as to liquidate the Indians.

This date marked the rise of Rafael Carrera. The army of the Federation marched with Morazán. He had entered Guatemala just a few months before Stephens had made his unspectacular entry into that city.

In a series of sharp battles Morazán dispersed the half-Indian army of Carrera and solemnly announced the revolution's end. Yet no sooner had he left for Salvador than Carrera came out of hiding, assembled his army, and again terrorized Guatemala.

Stephens was now brought up to date; for he had entered the city just when the unpaid soldiers of Carrera were exacting 'loans' from the citizenry.

Guatemala was very tense, for Rafael Carrera was expected. Through the whole city ran a feeling of expectancy, as if the people waited for a hurricane which would come out of nowhere, to sweep the town, or for the rumbling volcano de Fuego to burst its serrated peak. The churches, offering solace, had an unprecedented attendance.

When Stephens in his gold-laced diplomatic coat, was ushered into the presence of the absolute master of Guatemala, Rafael Carrera was sitting at a table, counting stacks of silver pesos.

His guards were fitted out with red bombazet jackets, tartan-plaid caps, which with their dark skins reminded Stephens of the organ grinders' monkeys he had seen as a boy about Bowling Green.

Rafael Carrera was surprisingly young – Stephens guessed him to be about twenty-five – with the straight black hair of the Indian and the copper-colored skin of a mestizo (his friends, in compliment, wrote Stephens, 'called him a mulatto; I, for the same reason, call him an Indian, considering *that* the better blood of the two'). He was beardless and short, bandy-legged, and barrel-chested. His military attire, when he rose to welcome Stephens, was seen to be a black bombazet jacket with matching trousers.

He told Stephens that two years ago he had 'begun' with

thirteen men, armed with muskets so old they had to be fired with lighted cigars, as one had fired an ancient harquebus.

Within a year he had a praetorian guard of Indians who carried banners, crying: '*Viva la religión y muerte a los extranjeros*' – which, since it was no idle threat, had sent the foreign population flying out of the country.

But when Carrera finally met and talked to some of the foreigners, his war cry was modified. Now he counted quite a number of Englishmen among his acquaintances, which exhibited, said Stephens, 'a happy illustration of the effect of personal intercourse in breaking down prejudices against individuals or classes.'

Carrera typified *personalismo*, the form of personal government which has plagued Hispanic America since its independence. After being drummer boy and pig herder he took up highway robbery and terrorized the country. Trade was disrupted, few traveled beyond the environs of the cities; the centralists, in their hatred of Morazán, clasped Carrera to their aristocratic bosoms, thinking that if each would declare war on the other, both factions would be eliminated; it is not the first time in history that a people have embraced the apocalypse for the purpose of ridding itself of a temporary problem.

Carrera, at the time of Stephens' audience, was riding the crest of a wave of triumph, yet feeling was still bitter; so when he found a broadside pasted on an adobe wall calling him a bandit and an *antropófage*, he demanded that the last word be defined; when, after several attempts, its meaning – 'man-cater' – seeped through his brain, his wrath was Jovian; it was only calmed by a flow of blood.

After two years of unprecedented power he could read, scrawl his name 'Carrera,' ending it in a flourish in the antique style. His dress improved, and he established himself as guardian of Guatemala.

The Presidential Agent relates:

Considering Carrera a promising young man, I told him that he had a long career before him, and might do much good to his country; and he laid his hand upon his heart, and with a burst of feeling that I did not expect, said he was determined to sacrifice his life for his country.

One can only applaud the political sagacity of Stephens, for although he liked neither the man nor his tactics he gauged, very accurately, the future of Rafael Carrera.

'I considered,' he wrote, 'that he was destined to exercise an important, if not a controlling influence on the affairs of Central America.'

Carrera in fact remained in power for twenty-five years, from 1840, when he was a mere *caudillo*, until 1865, when he died in office as president. In 1854 he was declared *presidente vitalicio*. His title: His most Excellent Señor Don Rafael Carrera, President for Life of the Republic, Capitán-general of the Forces, General Superintendent of the Treasury, Commander of the Royal Order of Leopold of Belgium, Honorary President of the Institute of Africa.

Unfortunately he had established the political formula for the coup d'état. It was given a quaint touch by a presidential aspirant in 1898, who walked into a cabinet meeting, laid his pistol on the table, and said: 'Gentlemen, I am Estrada and the new president of Guatemala.'

Stephens took a diplomatic tour of the country. He went to the ruins of Antigua, climbed the volcano de Fuego to obtain a panorama of the country, and later in a very gay company he rode to the city of Mixco, where the *simpático* 'Meester Estebans' won the hearts of the ladies and, we judge by the compliments given him, the respect of the men.

Everywhere he allowed his curiosity full license; he went to the Indian markets, he talked to the padres, and between his calls of courtesy wandered in the mountains. Arriving in Guatemala he summed up for the Secretary of State the whole distracted picture of Central America, ending his letter with:

The Federal Government was thus entirely broken up.
There was not the least prospect of its ever being restored,
nor for a long time to come of any other being organized
in its stead. Under these circumstances, I did not consider
myself justified in remaining any longer in the country.
I had no public business . . . Accordingly I secured the
Books and Archives of the Legation and forwarded them
to New York – having done this, I leave for Guatemala
and will travel at my own expense into the Mexican
provinces of Chiapas and Yucatán, for purposes of my
own, and at my own expense.

As a precautionary measure to insure his safety to Palenque,
Stephens called upon Rafael Carrera who, after the massacres
of Quetzaltenango, had taken up residence in Guatemala
City. He had obtained letters from the Archbishop of
Guatemala to all the padres along the route, but just in case
God was not on the side of those with the best artillery,
Stephens obtained a passport signed in the unalphabetic
scrawl of Carrera. He wrote:

It had taken him longer than it would have done to cut
off a head, and he seemed more proud of it. Indeed it
was the only occasion on which I saw in him the slightest
elevation of feeling.

By April 1840, Stephens' and Catherwood's plans were
complete, and they set off for Palenque. There was only one
way to reach the other of the 'Three Ancient Cities' mentioned in the literature and that was to ride from Guatemala
into Mexico, and thence by direction to the ruins of Palenque.
Their itinerary, in fact, had been published, whether by
design or accident, in the *Official Gazette* of Guatemala.
There, among the complicated rituals of government, one
could read that Señor Juan L. Stephens, Ministro de los
Estados Unidos, and his dauntless companion, the English-

man, Frederick Catherwood, were resuming their archaeological journeys, this time to the mysterious (the Editor said 'fabulosamente rico') ruined city of Palenque located in the Department of Tzendales, state of Chiapas, in Mexico.

During Stephens' absence, Frederick Catherwood had discovered the ruins of Quiriguá, thirty miles north of Copán, near to the Rio Motagua. Unquestionably a colony of Copán, Quiriguá is noted for its superb stelae carved out of red sandstone. Although Stephens, himself, did not visit the ruins, he was able to write correctly: 'The general character of these ruins is the same as at Copán.' Catherwood limned those monuments now known as Stelae 'E' and 'F'. Later, when Stephens found that they were near a river, he began negotiations with Señor Payes, their owner, for the purchase of the entire ruins. The negotiations were still in progress when they left Guatemala City, bound for Palenque.

In the meantime there was a search on for the missing two Englishmen who had preceded them to Palenque and were unheard of after 140 days. A letter was addressed from Belize to Frederick Chatfield H.M. Consul in Guatemala. Chatfield who thought that Central America was Britain's hunting grounds did not like Yankee intrusion at any level, and on 26 March he answered:

> I have no intelligence of the [British] Travellers. Stephens is flying about the Country to get materials for his Book, and if he escapes fevers and other mischiefs he may perhaps be here soon . . .

In responding to a second inquiry, Chatfield offered little encouragement to those seeking the ruins of Palenque. He wrote on 8 April:

> . . . I never heard that there existed a road from Peten to Palenque, it might be through the Monte or bushwood, and hardly practicable. Mr. Stephens and the Yankified

IV. *Catherwood's lithograph of the Temple of Kulkulkan, Chichén Itza.*

V. *Catherwood's lithograph of the Temple of the Dwarf, Uxmal.*

VI.   *Catherwood's lithograph of one of the Idols at Copán.*

English artist [Catherwood] who accompanies him, are gone to Quezaltenango, intending to get to Palenque across the Mexican frontiers. . . . To go by land is in my opinion foolhardy, especially as there is little or nothing to see when on the spot . . .*

On 7 April, 1840, Stephens and Catherwood had set off to Palenque. They followed on muleback the ribbon trail that wound through the high, pine-studded mountains of Guatemala, the whole breadth of the state. Within a week, they reached the environs of Lake Atitlán.

Atitlán lay shimmering between towering volcanoes, sparkling like a colored mirror of lapis lazuli. It was one of the great population centers of the pre-conquest Guatemala. The centuries had not changed Atitlán, except, perhaps, for its Indian masters.

A right angle turn on the main road brought the travelers, guided by a huipil-clad Indian, to the ruin of Utatlán, two miles south-west from the village of Santa Cruz de Quiché. The ruin of Utatlán was the center of the Quiché tribes which Pedro de Alvarado had assaulted in 1524.

The explorers reached it by climbing the precipitous hill on which it was perched. Although Catherwood found little to sketch among the ruins, he did make drawings, for here was another record.†

*The British also tried to undercut Stephens' negotiations at Copán. Lord Palmerston who was then Foreign Minister wrote to Frederick Chatfield. 'It appears . . . that these ruins [of Copán] are held in little or no estimation by the natives of the country, and it seems possible, therefore, that the chief difficulty to be encountered in removing specimens of the sculpture would consist in providing means of transporting them to some place of embarcation. You will be careful, therefore, that in making any inquiries in pursuance of this instruction, you do not lead the people of the country to attach any imaginary value to things which they consider at present as having no value at all.'

A German, Karl Scherzer, was commissioned to carry out the mission, but never reached Copán.

†In 1841 the ruins were thoroughly explored by the government of Guatemala, at the insistence of Francisco Morazán. Señor Don Miguel Rivera y Mistre, a man of some scientific attainments, gave Stephens a full copy of his report, which he used in his book.

At the end of their second day they saw a rotund figure panting up the steep sides of the ruins of Utatlán under the cover of a huge red silk umbrella. An old black coat which fell to his heels, rubbed bare by constant use, a broad-brimmed, glazed black hat, and a pair of plaid trousers covered the body of this extraordinary person who laughed outrageously as he came toward them. The natives quickly uncovered, and the explorers were aware that they were in the presence – despite his extraordinarily unclerical dress – of the *cura* of Santa Cruz de Quiché. In high spirits he introduced himself and passed around cigars.

He asked the news from Spain and then in the cultured tones of an Andalusian (using the *seseo* and *yeísmo* of Castilian Spanish) he told them his personal history.

He was a Dominicano. In his youth he had seen the Battle of Trafalgar, and he laughed every time he thought of it; the French were blown sky high and so were the Spanish. He had had enough of war and revolutions, and he had asked the Father Superior to send him to America.

On the high seas they were chased by a French corsair; in the waters of America they were shot at by an English ship; and then landing at Omoa, in Honduras, they were assailed by the revolutions which he thought he had escaped. He laughed at the irony of his position, and with tears of merriment, making the world the butt of his joke, he passed around more of those dark, richleafed cigars. His laughter was irresistible, and he directed his biting humour at everything. Stephens and Catherwood finished their measuring and followed the laughing padre with his red silk umbrella to the convent.

In the padre's room, a chaos of books, clothes, and religious effigies, they continued their conversation on politics, on history, and especially on the mysteries of the Maya. It was unexpected to find a priest in this out-of-the-way place so well-versed, so learned in half a lifetime spent in Los Altos.

There were, he said, some ruins peopled by a mysterious race of Indians beyond Santa Cruz de Quiché. Somewhere between the *cordilleras* of Guatemala and the flat jungle-bound lands of El Petén was a living city, occupied by Indians who still lived in the same palaces as they had before the coming of the Spaniard.

The padre had heard of it at the village of Chajul in Vera Paz, and when he was young he had climbed the highest peak of the Cordillera, some 12,000 feet, and there as the clouds parted he could see the flat plains of Yucatán and the undulating blue of the Caribbean.

Below him the padre avowed he had seen the white towers* of a great city rising from the vivid green jungle, glittering white in the sun. These Indians, he said, allowed no white man to come into their country. Money was unknown to them. They kept their roosters underground so that their crowing could not be heard and guide the hated white man to their jungle city.

The narrative had a considerable effect on Stephens. Four days from there – a great city – Indians living precisely in the same state as before the discovery of America!

This was no ordinary man who told them this tale, but a well-educated padre, skeptical and balanced. They who had seen the marvels of Copán, Quiriguá, and the cloud-perched ruins of Utatlán, now they were told of a living city of Indians.

When the padre took down a map and pointed out the location of the site, Stephens could no longer contain himself:

> One look at that city was worth ten years of an every-day life . . . there are living men who can solve the mystery that hangs over the ruined cities of America; perhaps who can go to Copán and read the inscriptions on its monuments. . . . Can it be true? Being now in my sober senses, I do verily believe there is much ground to suppose that what the padre told us is authentic.

*He probably had seen the ruined tall towering temples of Tikal.

175

Stephens was not a man to be stampeded by another's imaginings. Yet he thought that 'two young men of good constitution' who learned the language of the Indians, who were willing to give five years of their lives, might find the place. He thought himself of climbing the *cordilleras* to get a glimpse of this mysterious white city, but they were not to be diverted:

'Palenque was our great point.'

They left the laughing padre and his heavenly discourse to take the highroad across Los Altos. It was quite a procession; Bobon, an Indian, part buffoon, part guide, carried on a long stick, like a standard, a stuffed quetzal bird given to Stephens as a parting gift by the padre of Quiché. Another called Juan, half Indian, was the factotum of the expedition who kept the peace with the muleteers. He had a gargantuan appetite, and nothing edible was safe in his presence. One time he wolfed down a hamper of fresh bread that brought on a terrible indigestion, and Stephens found him rolling on the ground wailing: 'Mother of God I am going to die.' After that he settled down to a routine appetite which was terrible enough.

As for Stephens and 'Mr Catherwood,' they were gradually losing all appearance of foreigners. They had added to their native attire a piece called *aguas de arma*, undressed goatskins, embroidered with red leather, which covered their persons when it rained, and they wore the large hats of the country.

After riding over wild abyss-filled country where the odors of spiked agave plants in bloom and begonias intermingled, they came, during Holy Week, to heaven-high Quetzaltenango, which in ancient times was subject to the Aztecs.

A picturesque city, the largest between Guatemala City and Mexico, it was of red-tiled houses facing smooth, well-paved streets, and delightfully located; huge mountains rose at the end of the streets acting as a dramatic backdrop. It had an imposing cathedral, a tastefully arranged *cabildo* facing a wide plaza, and a fountain where man and beast slaked their thirst.

Catherwood was so impressed by its picturesque qualities that he made a fine panoramic watercolor of it.

There was a grandeur, a magnificence about the raw earth, mountains burst out of the high plains, abysses cut away the soil, leaving yawning chasms around the very edges of which mule paths followed. And the pungent smells of pine and cypress, begonia and trumpet flower, filled the raw, thin air. At Huehuetenango, not far from the Mexican border, where the expedition stopped to rest the galled mules, they were taken by a gentleman of the city to a river bank where not many months past he had excavated the bones of a mastodon elephant. He then accompanied them to ruins called 'Las Cuevas' – the Caves. The practised eye of Catherwood made out at once amorphous mounds, once pyramidal in shape. The travelers were quick to note that the ancient structures were not, as at Copán, made of cut stone, but of stone cemented with stucco.

The owner of the ruins was delighted to give them permission to excavate, if he be allowed all the treasure which he felt they would discover.

They were to find not pottery and funeral urns of Chorotegan pattern, but strangely enough an American, a living North American. He burst in on them and greeted them in English, calling them by name.

It took a moment for Stephens to recognize him. He was dressed in Guatemalan costume, a sort of jodphur with well-spurred jackboots, a woolen poncho, a large brimmed hat. A young man under thirty, his face was covered with a full black beard.

It was his blue eyes that jogged Stephens' memory; he remembered now – this was the American who was major-domo of a cochineal concern near Amatitlán; whereupon he introduced Henry Pawling to Catherwood.

Henry Pawling had seen Stephens' journey announced in the *Official Gazette*, and was suddenly overwhelmed with nostalgic memories of home and his own people.

He was born in Rhinebeck Landing on the Hudson, clerked in his father's store in New York City, and finally drifted to Mexico City where he met the owner of a circus. Impressed with Pawling's excellent Spanish and knowledge of the country the circus proprietor made him a proposal.

Anxious to see something of the world, Pawling traveled ahead of the circus distributing handbills to the astounded Mexican audiences and arranged accommodation.

He had deserted his circus profession in Guatemala and had taken over the cochineal concern near the environs of Amatitlán.

Pawling spoke of North America and home with great feeling.

Disgusted by the chaos of Guatemala, he had put all that he owned in his saddlebags, bought a fresh mule, and ridden night and day to catch up with Stephens.

Pawling's excellent command of Spanish, his knowledge of handling natives (not to mention his pair of pistols and short-muzzled, double-barrelled blunderbuss) were very welcome.

'Fortunately,' wrote Stephens, 'my passport was broad enough to cover him, and I immediately constituted him the general manager of the expedition.'

The last of April, after climbing over the mountain trails of Guatemala, they crossed the Rio Lagertero that marked the frontier, passed, without stopping, the first Mexican village of Zapoluta, then rode in, dust covered and famished, to the town of Comitán.

A frontier town of Chiapas, in Mexico, Comitán was a city of some substance, with a huge church, a well-fitted convent of Domenicanos, and a population of 10,000.

When they touched upon their proposed visit to the ruins of Palenque, the travelers were told that only recently three Belgian antiquarians had been turned back from Comitán while attempting to get to Palenque.

The commandant had an order from the Mexican dictator General Santa Ana that no one – whatever his credentials – was permitted to visit the mysterious city of Palenque.

It was suggested that Stephens visit Mexico City for permission, and so the expedition held a council of war. To ride a thousand miles to Mexico City and then, if granted permission – which was doubtful – to double back again was not an inviting prospect.

The ruins of Palenque, buried in the jungle would certainly not be garrisoned.

To Palenque, then – in defiance of General Santa Ana.

The road was over a landscape scarred with barrancas, cut by rivers, and, as they dropped to fifteen hundred feet altitude, enveloped by jungle.

There were no bridges, suspended or otherwise, and every abyss had to be crossed by descending and ascending.

Nor was the thin ribbon of trail, used mostly by natives taking contraband from Campeche, improved at all by the rain. Storms, sweeping in from the Caribbean – for it was the beginning of the rainy season – deluged the party night and day, upsetting Henry Pawling so much that he wanted to desert the expedition, only continuing when Stephens had made an attractive offer.

They were already among the archaeological preludes of Palenque, for at Ocosingo, three days from Comitán, they discovered the vestiges of what had once been a stucco-embellished city, still bearing traces of the ornaments that had enlivened it. Had they stopped longer (although Catherwood made several drawings of the ruins), they would have found near by a constellation of archaeological sites.*

They were irresistibly drawn to Palenque, so with Indians going ahead as carriers, and following the mountain ridges, they moved over the same trail taken by Capitán Dupaix on his expedition in 1807. The poor Capitán, doubly bedeviled by rain and fatigue, said:

*About Ocosingo, within a ten-mile radius, there are many major ruins, probably colonies from Palenque, at Ubala, Chacal Chib, Campomtic, Pamtela, Tonina, Laltic, Cololte, Quechil, etc.

The roads, if they can be called thus, are only narrow and difficult paths, which wind across mountains and precipices, and which it is necessary to follow sometimes on mules, sometimes on foot, sometimes on the shoulders of the Indians, and sometimes in Hammocks. In some places it is necessary to pass on bridges, or rather trunks of trees badly secured and over lands covered with jungle . . . and entirely dispeopled. . . . . After having experienced in this long and painful journey every kind of fatigue and discomfort, we arrived, thank God, at the village of Palenque.

Thirty years of rain and revolution had made the trails to Palenque even worse than those pictured by Capitán Dupaix. Indian carriers had to be changed at every village – for none wished to go beyond the limits of their tribe – food was almost non-existent. Like the labors of Sisyphus; they went up, they went down. On the eighth day, they reached the heights of Tumbalá. Below them a ravine dropped a thousand feet. In the distance, some hundred miles away, they could see the Laguna de Terminos and the Caribbean Sea. Below them, buried somewhere in that immensity of jungle, were the ruins of Palenque.

On the tenth day, they echoed Capitán Dupaix:

'Thank God, we arrived at the village of Palenque.'

CHAPTER XII

Palenque: The Second City

After the horrible journey, even the little village of Palenque seemed a paradise. It consisted merely of rows of wattle and daub houses, magnificently shadowed by huge *ceiba* trees invading the village and was as peaceful as fabled Arcadia.

Crossing the Rio Michol, they observed women bathing in the limpid stream or braiding their long black hair under vine-festooned trees, garbed only in a blue skirt that clung to their wet loins.

In Palenque there was, as expected, a church thatched with palm-leaves, a belfry and wooden cross before it. The whole aspect was curiously halcyon, 'the most dead-and-alive place I ever saw,' said Stephens.

Directed to a house no different from the rest, Stephens aroused the alcalde and presented his passport.

The irritable nature of the alcalde was known far and wide. What had he to do with Stephens' passport? Since the question was rhetorical, he answered it himself: 'Nothing.'

The travelers asked for food, he said there was none; they specifically detailed corn, coffee, chocolate – to which he answered 'None.'

Conscious of what must be passing in their minds, he told them complaints had been made against him before, but it simply was of no use; they could not remove him from office, and if they did, he did not care.

He recommended them to the prefect of the village, who was courteous, helpful, and solicitous. He offered Stephens a chair and a cigar. He was not in the least surprised to see the American; in fact, he said he had expected him for some time. This was very puzzling to Stephens; how, in this corner of American earth, as isolated as Saturn, could this official have known that he was coming to Palenque?

Very simply, he was told. The prefect was informed thus by Don Patricio. Gradually it dawned on Stephens that by Don Patricio was meant Patrick Walker of the Belize colony.

He was aware that the information that Captain Caddy had been killed by Indians was not true.* They had spent two weeks at the ruins where Captain Caddy had made some drawings, before leaving for Belize.†

Santo Domingo del Palenque, from which the ruins near-by got their name, had been founded on the savannahs of Tumbalá in 1564 by Pedro Laurencio, A Dominicano missionary. Nothing, even in that early time, was known of the great stone city that lay eight miles distant. The memory of it had disappeared long before the arrival of the white man.

Even the original name of the site was unknown; no one knew what the Maya called it. 'Palenque' ('*palisade*' in Spanish) was given it by early explorers only because it approximated the village of Santo Domingo del Palenque.

The memory of the city had been blotted out so completely that when Hernán Cortés made his famous march from Mexico, through Yucatán to Honduras, it was unknown even to his Indian guides; even though they passed within thirty miles of it, for 'if it had been a living city,' thought

*Patrick Walker's original report was found in the Colonial Foreign Office in England. The Museum of the American Indian photographs were found among Caddy's illustrations made by aforementioned Dr Marshall Saville: all these with narrative were put together as a book by David M. Pendergast, *Palenque: The Walker-Caddy Expedition to the Ancient Maya City 1839–1840*. Univ. of Oklahoma Press, Norman, 1967.

†John Herbert Caddy made a report on his explorations, *The City of Palenque*, 36 pp., with portfolio 15 x 21 inches containing a plan of the palace, twenty-four sepia paintings of buildings and sculptures, a folding map of the peninsula of Yucatán, and a sketch map of the ruins.

The paper was read before the Society of Antiquarians in London on 13 January, 1842, but the prompt appearance of the Stephens-Catherwood work forestalled publication. In 1932, Dr Marshall Saville, the late American archaeologist, had the good fortune of meeting in New York Miss Alice Caddy, the explorer's granddaughter, who placed the portfolio in Saville's hands for publication. 'The Caddy drawings contain some sketches not found in Stephens' work,' said Dr Saville 'a number more accurate than Catherwood's. Saville died before he could arrange their publication.' *Bibliographic Notes on Palenque, Chiapas, Indian Notes and Monographs*, Vol. VI, No. 5, 1928, 137–138.

Stephens, 'its fame would have reached his ears, and he would have turned aside from this road to subdue it and plunder it.'

Sometime in the eighteenth century, the Indians who lived in scattered communities in the geographical violence of the Tumbalá hills, where they planted corn twice yearly, discovered the ruined stone buildings, and for years, thereafter, the favorite tale of those who traveled through Chiapas, was of the fabulous ruins of Palenque.

Then it was not the fashion of the time to expend energy on things past, people were overtly employed in cutting out a place for themselves in unsettled America.

Count Constantin de Volney had still to write his romantic rhapsody on *Ruins* that was to send antiquarian-minded men scurrying to forgotten lands to discover moldering ruins on which to meditate the transience of empires.

Besides, all sensible men of the eighteenth century disliked 'wild nature.' There is good reason why the discovery of the ruins, wafted from tongue to tongue, did not move the Capitán-General of Guatemala. In the past, too many, far too many, expeditions had been sent out in search of golden El Dorado: yet rumors persisted.

The Canon of the Cathedral of Ciudad Real de Chiapas could no longer resist them; he gathered together a retinue of Indians and had them fashion a rude palanquin, and on this he was carried from Ciudad Real to Palenque.

Arriving there, he tucked up his religious habit and assisted by machete-wielding Indians, cut the way through to the stone 'palaces' of Palenque.

So impressed was Fray Ramón de Ordoñez y Aguiar by what he saw in 1773 that he wrote a *Memoria** which he addressed to Don José de Estachería, president of the Royal Audience of Guatemala. This report reached his periwigged Excellency about the time that his own city was being over-

---

*A quaint document of twenty-three pages deposited in the Real Academia de Madrid, entitled *Memoria relativa a las ruinas de la ciudad descubierta en las imediaciones del pueblo de Palenque de la provincia de los Tzendales del obispado de Chiapa, dirigida al Ilmo y Rmo. Snr. Obispo désta diosceses*, 1784.

whelmed by earthquake; he had little time for ancient ruins when Guatemala was being overwhelmed with destruction. However, in 1776, when he had established the new capital, he wrote an official directive to José Antonio Calderón, mayor of Santo Domingo del Palenque, directing him to survey the Palenque ruins.

In the meantime the original discoverer of Palenque sat in his cell in the Chiapas convent and wrote: 'A History of the Creation of Heaven and Earth,' now unimportant to us save that the padre, in order to explain Palenque, had a race of people appear out of the Atlantic, guided by a distinguished leader called – he alone knew why – 'Votán.' It was he, according to this chronology, who penetrated Central America and – without opposition from the original natives – halted his expedition at the base of the Tumbalá Mountains and there built a stone city, called 'Nachán' – 'the city of serpents,' now called Palenque.

José Antonio Calderón knew nothing of this 'Votán', when, following the directive from Guatemala, he visited Palenque in December 1784. He was accompanied by Antonio Bernasconi, an Italian-born architect and a resident of Guatemala. Their report, an intelligent one, was forwarded to Spain, where in time the royal historiographer, the most able Juan Bautista Muñoz (whose bibliographical labors were to assist William Prescott), used the manuscripts to fashion a report on American antiquities.

The next royal decree of 1786 sent out Captain Don Antonio del Río to the ruins. He came in his three-cornered hat and powdered periwig, and made up for his lack of antiquarian training by his zeal; he assembled two hundred Tzotzil Indians, armed them with adzes, hook-bills, and mattocks; with these he assaulted tree-engulfed Palenque.

With an energy matched only by the flamboyance of his language, Del Río tumbled the trees, cut the vines that bound the ruins, and for the first time since they had been abandoned in the ninth century, the pallid, embellished stuccos of

Palenque were exposed to the sun. 'And so,' said Del Río, 'in pursuance of my desires to explore the place, I effected all that was necessary to be done, so that ultimately there remained neither a window nor a doorway, nor a room, corridor, court towner, nor subterranean passage in which excavations were not effected from two to three yards in depth; for such was the object of my mission.'

This report of Del Río, illustrated by pencil drawings, was sent to Madrid, where it promptly disappeared into the mountains of unpublished reports; but in Guatemala, where it was copied before being sent to Spain, the manuscript report of 'Palenque' was seized upon by one Dr Felix Cabrera, a gentleman of fatuous erudition. He carefully edited it, expunging Captain del Río's barracks language, filled it with learned asides, and wrote a preface which he called 'Teatro Critico Americano' wherein, following the prevailing cosmogony of the time, he ascribed the ruins of Palenque to people of Egyptian culture.

This was to remain in manuscript until Dr Thomas McQay, a British resident of Guatemala City, obtained the Del Río manuscript and sent it to London, where in 1822 it was published with crude line engravings by Waldeck.

This was the first published book on the ruins in Central America even though Humboldt had noticed Palenque in his book in 1810. It was destined to inspire the expeditions of John Lloyd Stephens.

Yet between the long interval of Del Río's expedition and the publication of the account of it in London, the Spanish government, finally alive to the importance of the civilizations that their *conquistadores* had leveled, sent Guillelmo Dupaix, a retired officer of the Mexican Dragoons, to Palenque. Dupaix, however, fell under the suspicion of Viceroy Iturrigaray, who thought his expedition was mere cover for a revolution, and he was subsequently jailed.

Luciano Castañeda accompanied Dupaix as engineer-draughtsman; and in 1807 they reached Palenque, where they felled the trees that had, once more, enveloped the ruins. Castañeda then made drawings of the ruins somewhat in the technique of Piranesi. These illustrations went the way of much of Spanish science, for Castañeda, before he was run through with a lance, put them in the Cabinet of Natural History in Mexico, and there they lay until they were rescued by Monsieur l'Abbé Baradre from an unearned oblivion and published in France.

Palenque had, curiously enough, little attraction in Europe, even though reports appeared in various journals. But it excited the imagination of Jean-Frédérik Maximillien, Count de Waldeck. At the end of his long life (he lived to be one hundred and nine years old) he styled himself 'dean of travellers and artists'; and 'the first Americanist.'

However, the technical deficiencies of his work, the over extension of his imagination – he saw elephants everywhere in the Maya glyphs – and his actual falsifications of Maya carvings in the attempt to prove that the Maya originated out of Phoenicians, Chaldeans, and Hindus; has left his contributions to Maya culture of relative minor value. His own life-adventures were blown up into a wonderful fantasy which he recounted again and again with Munchausen-like virtuosity.

Waldeck's life story, like his drawings of the Maya ruins, was a strange mixture of inaccuracy, unjustified restoration, overdrawing and exaggeration. There is no agreement on the simplest facts of his life. He was born in April 1766, but whether in Vienna, Prague or Paris, no one precisely knows. Waldeck once said he was an Austrian subject, and became a French citizen. Yet, in Mexico a German journalist, in 1830, referred to him as '. . . . *unser sehr getreicher deutscher Landsmann.*'

Waldeck said that he was a descendant of the Dukes of Waldeck-Pyrmo, but the Graf Waldeck who appears in the pages of the *Almanach de Gotha* is not our Waldeck.

At the age of nineteen, according to his own account, he accompanied the French explorer François Le Vaillant, in the year 1785, into the interior of Africa, yet Waldeck was never mentioned by Le Vaillant; all he had with him was a faithful Hottentot named Klass and a trained ape named Kees, 'free from the faults of his species. . . .' Still, Waldeck persisted in this fiction:

'. . . for me, voyages are merely promenades. I have been accustomed to them since 1785, with François Le Vaillant.'

After five adventurous years Waldeck returned to Paris, where, according to his own account, he studied art at the atelier of Jacques Louis David. This could be possible; for Waldeck was a superb artist and had the facile brushwork of David. However, his name is not mentioned in the *Liste des élèves de Louis David*.

How Waldeck was involved in the French Revolution is unclear. He himself said he fought under Napoleon at the siege of Toulon. He also said that he was friendly enough with the doomed Marie Antoinette to have painted her portrait: yet his name is not included in the lists of those who visited her. According to his own account, he then went to Egypt with Napoleon; yet his name is not on the army lists.

It was while in London, in 1823, when he made the illustrations for the book on the ruins of Palenque, that facts are borne out by what he did:

'. . . from the moment I saw the pen-and-ink sketches,' Waldeck said, 'of that work I doubted that they were faithful and I nourished the secret desire to see the ruins of Palenque for myself and draw the originals. . . .'

Permission to get to Palenque at that time was hard to seek. It seems that Waldeck lived in Mexico City for quite a time, for he was interviewed there in 1830, by German journalists. He worked for a mining company in Mexico, and later designed and acted scenes for the stage and an *opéra bouffe;* there is a contract still extant* which

---

*The Waldeck papers; journals; letters and contracts are still in the Edward E. Ayer collection, in the Newberry Library, Chicago, along with a sizeable number of his original drawings.

... obliges him to sing and to clothe himself all the operas, serious, semi-serious, farcical, comic, cantatas and concerts, classed as a singing bass, serious and characteristic ... all of which shall be of appropriate delicacy and conform to the roles he is portraying.

In 1831 he was given permission by General Bustamante to visit the ruins of Palenque, to which official rubric was added to a stipend from the Mexican treasury.

Inside a year he took up residence at Palenque, building himself a small, palm-thatched lean-to at the foot of the pyramid of the Temple of the Cross. There, between exploring the ruins of Palenque, as well as the bed of a dark-breasted *mestiza*, Comte de Waldeck, at an age when most men would seek comfort, weathered the climate of Palenque for two years.

While drawing the ruins he kept an elaborate notebook, trying to ravel out the complicated Mayan glyphs. He made sketches of the flattened heads of the Indians, the naked bodies of women, animals, and birds; in short, everything that his cosmopolitan enthusiasm could embrace. His drawings of Maya sculptures, typical period pieces, were beautifully done in the facile manner of Jacques Louis David.

A broken Maya stone head became, under the alchemy of Waldeck's brush, a vibrantly alive modern sculpture; a tumbled ruin metamorphosed into a building of classical finish. As archaeological drawings, they were relatively useless, as works of art, superb. 'I had a *soupçon*,' said William Prescott, 'that Waldeck was a good deal of a charlatan ... his coloring does not bear the true weather-tints of antiquity.'

This 'soupçon' was shared for other reasons by General Santa Ana, for in Waldeck's two-year absence from Mexico City, Bustamante, his patrón, had been 'replaced' – which is to say assassinated – by Antonio Lopez de Santa Ana.

All Bustamante's 'works' – including Waldeck's – came under suspicion. Santa Ana set his police upon him and sequestered most of his drawings (although Waldeck managed somehow to keep his original sketches).

Fleeing to the Yucatán, where he continued his archaeological wandering, Waldeck vociferously complained of the Mexicans' treatment of him, calling them 'barbarians who want to be considered an enlightened people'. With bitter hatred he sailed for Paris, where in 1838, at the age of seventy-two, he published his first book, *Voyage Pittoresque et Archéologique.*

There was little on Palenque in this book; this was reserved for his dotage, for Jean-Frédéric de Waldeck lived to be a veritable Methuselah, publishing his second book on Maya archaeology in the year of his centennial. He died in 1875, from a stroke, while looking at a girl in a swishing petticoat on the Champs Élysées. He was then 109 years old.

At dawn, while the jungles were still opaque with vapors, Stephens and Catherwood advanced on Palenque in proper military fashion.

First came Stephens with the Indian guides, his pants rolled up above his boots and trailing a blue line of smoke from his morning cigar, then Catherwood, trying to keep his spectacles dry despite the deluge from the water-laden branches. Next came Henry Pawling, who in his capacity of manager kept his eyes on the many Tzotzil Indians, who carried on their backs the impedimenta of the expedition. All were nervously expectant – all, that is, except Juan, for upon him of the Gargantuan appetite was to fall the problem of provender. He had to see to the entire market of fowls, beans, rice and corn; chocolate and sugar. The alcalde had unbent sufficiently to allow them the use of a water jug; but what they really wanted they could not get – a woman cook. 'No woman would trust herself alone with us,' Stephens complained: 'This was a great privation; a woman desirable, not for what she may suppose, but to make tortillas.'

In the luxuriant forest, rills cascaded down between rock

and root. Birdcalls echoed in the stillness. The delicate trill of the modestly plumed hilguero broke out, ran the length of its avian scale, and broke midway in its song as a flock of scolding toucans, huge-beaked and black of wing, clattered noisily down to see who broke the jungle peace.

Stephens seemed hardly aware of the tumbling Rio Michol which brawled noisily on his left or of the throbbing moans of the howling monkeys, for his mind was 'set on Palenque.'

Within three hours they had reached a steep ascent. Dismounted, they left their mules behind, and turned left at the smaller Rio Otolum, which was filling the jungle with its tinkling music.

Sculptured stones began to appear in the shaded aisle of the forest, a certain index of Maya occupancy.

This stirred Stephens' imagination on the wrecks of empires and the world's mutations, for here he found a gleaming white stone road over which feathered-bedecked people had once come in the pageantry of empire.

Above the stream pouring from a vaulted culvert sixty feet overhead was the vague, shadowy outline of a huge white building.

Stephens, in his eagerness to lead the rest, clambered over a stone terrace, reached the top first, and gained the edge of the Palace.

Palenque was barely visible in the verdant sea of the jungle. It seemed to hang on the brink of the mountains, set at the very edge of an outlying finger of a jungle range projecting from the Tumbalá escarpment.

It looked down over a gently undulating plain, where once, a thousand years ago, checkered cornfields had fed the builders and later the occupants of Palenque. Eighty miles in the distance lay the Laguna de Terminos.

The Maya craftsmen had shown great architectural daring in setting their buildings at the very edge of a steep gorge six hundred feet above the coastal plain where Palenque hung like an unshed tear. Above it, back of it, the forest-clad mountains rose abruptly, huge and dominant, projecting verdure-covered peaks three thousand feet into the sky.

The Palace, which Stephens immediately commandeered as a residence, consisted of thick walls, many chambered rooms grouped about the four main courtyards which formed the Palace complex. From its center rose a three-storied square – unique in Maya architecture and like all the rest engulfed by roots of strangler-fig trees.

On the main stairway were gigantic figures in bas-relief. On the frieze and roof combs, crumbled by time, were fragments of stucco serpents still tinted in violent polychromy. From within the darkened ruins there poured out the moldy damp smell of a potato cellar.

Three huge fruit bats, disturbed by the noise, detached themselves and circled the ruins, sending the Indian guides scrambling with startled shouts down the side of the pyramid.

On the walls of the Palace Stephens found the names of those who had visited the ruins before them: Count Waldeck's led the list with a faded drawing of a woman, under which he had scribbled the date, '1832'; there was Captain John Herbert Caddy and Patrick Walker, who had arrived a few months earlier, and Noah O. Platt, a New York merchant looking for logwood, who had come miles out of his way to the living enchantment of the ruins.

In a corridor Stephens found a piece of doggerel which 'breathed deep sense of the moral sublimity pervading these unknown ruins' written by a young Irish merchant of Tabasco, William Beanham, later found murdered in his hammock.

Darkness descended suddenly. The indigo black night loosened a storm, and the place rocked with claps of thunder. The winds roaring in from the Caribbean blew out the candles and as the men lay in their hammocks besieged by the darkness, wondering what next would descend upon them, large luminous fireflies, called *cucuyos*, began to flick on their lamps.

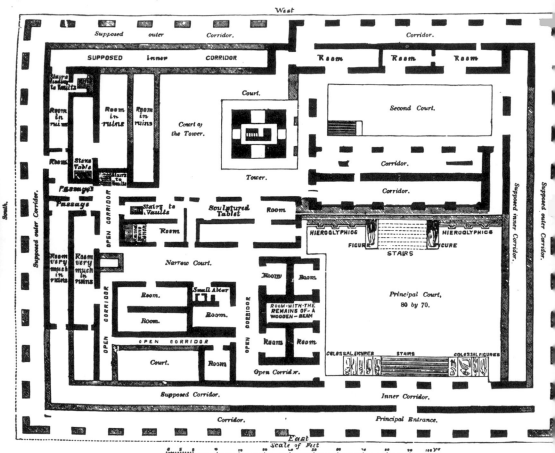

43. *Panorama of Palenque drawn by W. H. Holmes in 1895.*

44. *Palenque. Catherwood's survey of the Palace.*

In the cold light of the *cucuyos*, the ruins appeared to be enchanted, the stucco bas-relief invested with life.

Headless warriors stepped out of their walls and stalked through the sombre, lighted galleries, as Stephens and Catherwood lay awake in the darkness, their ears strained to pick up the strange night sounds. Outside, there was the bleat of tiny tree frogs, like the tinkling of silver bells, and something like a plaintive human voice called in the distance. Then silence.

Now with the distant roar of thunder on fierce gusts of wind, the rains came, pouring in through all the interstices, drenching the travelers in the chill of the falling barometer. They could not hope for sleep that night, and Stephens composed himself with a cigar.

'Blessed be the man,' said the irrepressible Mr Stephens, 'who invented smoking, the soother and composer of a troubled spirit, allayer of angry passions, a comfort under the loss of breakfast, and to the roamer in desolate places; the solitary wayfarer through life, serving for "wife, children, and friends".'

The architectural complex of the Palace, with its thick walled rooms grouped about courtyards (the outside measurement of which Stephens correctly estimated at 228 feet by 180 feet), was the first to be investigated.

Stephens, with the aid of Henry Pawling, used the measuring rods to lay the mathematical basis for Catherwood's floor plan which was amazingly accurate even when compared with those taken by better-equipped twentieth-century explorers.

They erected the scaffolding to hold Catherwood's camera lucida, and he then began to draw the stucco portraits of the priests that ornamented the walls.

Catherwood found that the Maya art at Palenque was restrained; the luxuriant complexity of detail that so befuddled him at Copán did not exist. Architecturally this site seemed of later date and more advanced than the others he had seen.

193

He had no difficulty in drawing the huge stone bas-reliefs in the main court, colossal figures with sloping foreheads and protruding lips. Although assailed by small black flies that hovered before his eyes, and larger ones that bit his ears, and mosquitoes that plunged their stings into his pallid skin, these annoyances were not enough to quench his interest. Catherwood stuck to the Palace.

In the first ten days the crumbling mass that the chaos of a thousand years had tumbled was being measured, drawn, and explored despite wind and rain, insects, and bats. But lack of sleep was having a telling effect on everyone. Catherwood would suddenly slump at his easel, and only the persistent whirling buzz of insects could awaken him.

They soon found that they could no more exist without sleep than the nitwit of Aesop's fable could live without eating, who, at the moment he learned to do so, died.

Niguas were another enemy. The explorers were well-armed against what they believed to be their real dangers, prowling jaguars, and Indians for whom they had laid traps should they try to ambush them in the blackness of a thundery night. Yet who would believe that they could be felled by niguas?

Early in their conquest, the Spaniards had made acquaintance with niguas, horrible insects which

> ate their way into the Flesh under the Nails of the Toes, then laid their NITS there-within, and multiplied in such manner that there was no ridding them but by Cauteries.

Stephens thought he had the gout, his toes pulsated like those of an eighteenth-century debauchee, but Henry Pawling soon corrected this first impression, announced that he had niguas, and set about with a needle to remove them. Stephens' foot was inflamed and swollen to twice its size and he was soon hammock-ridden. Once he could walk with the aid of Juan it was decided that he was to return to the village.

All Santo Domingo it seemed had been expecting the arrival of the padres on their annual visit. People crowded the village street and when Stephens appeared, three men rode out to meet him, mistaking him for one of the illustrious visitors.

'If the mistake had continued,' he said recalling his empty stomach, 'I should have had dinner enough for six at least.'

Still, he was given a hammock and a poultice of hot salt water and in two days the swelling of his foot was reduced sufficiently to allow him to appear among the three hundred inhabitants waiting to welcome the padres to Santo Domingo.

A retinue of a hundred Tzotzil Indians, clad in pinstripe knee-length ponchos, accompanied the padres who had come over the mountains with the express purpose of visiting the ruins of Palenque.

The black-bearded padre from Tumbalá was a young man of twenty-eight; weighing one-eighth of a ton, he had been carried in a palanquin over the mountains to Palenque, requiring the services of fifty Indians.

The Dominicano from the Indian village of Ayalon was somewhat older, with a majestic manner which befitted him, for he was not only a priest but a member of the Mexican Congress. He had taken part in the revolutions that had unhinged New Spain from the mother country and had been twice wounded on the field of battle, where he varied his conduct in the struggle between killing and then confessing the dying.

The third was a black-cowled padre from Ciudad Real.

'It is a glorious thing in this country to be a padre,' said Stephens, 'and next to being a padre oneself is the position of being a padre's friend.' For now Stephens, as resident-explorer of the ruins of Palenque, was invited to take chocolate with them inside the white calcimined houses.

The *cura* of the village soon appeared. A tall dark-visaged man, an Indian of uncertain appearance with his checkered shirt and yellow buck-skin shoes, his black waistcoat and pants held two inches apart by a protruding stomach, he was as charmingly affable as he was singular in appearance, and tossing his old straw hat into a corner he pulled out a pack of much used cards and suggested a game of *monte*.

The whole scene was like a tableau out of the life of Jèrôme Coignard, the lovable abbé of *La Rotisserie de la Reine Pédauque*, who played *ombre en philosophe*, reflecting 'that at play men are much more sensitive than in serious business and that they employ the whole of their probity at the backgammon board.'

The padres' game of *monte* began easily, with witty, earthy, discourse; then it 'settled down seriously,' said Stephens, who watched on the sidelines, and 'I left them playing as if the souls of the unconverted Indians were at stake.'

The next day, the padres put away their cards and donned their surplices for a Mass in the tumbled village church, appearing afterwards with the 'padres' friend' (Mr Stephens) for dinner at the home of Santiago Froncoso. Although the inventory of Don Santiago's entire stock – macaroni, flour, and nails – could not have totaled thirty dollars, he was well dressed in red slippers, white coarse-cloth trousers, and a white shirt, the bosom embroidered with little animal figures in the Maya fashion. He was a man of immense courtesy, with an erudition entirely out of place in this tiny termite-eaten village. His most intimate 'foreign relations' were in New York City.

The padres, in anticipation of Don Santiago's dinner, arrived rather noisily, the obese *cura* of Tumbalá carrying a violin which he at once offered politely to Stephens, asking him to play some musical airs of his country. Since Stephens could not perform, the padre put the warped fiddle under one of his six chins and played while the other padres continued their game of *monte*.

Considering himself on a social footing, Stephens said: 'Señores, in my country, were you seen playing cards on Sunday you would be thrown out of the church.'

'An Englishman', replied the priest politician, hardly looking up from his cards, 'once told me the same thing. He also went into detail of the manner of observing the Sunday in England. You will pardon me Señor Esteebans but we think it very stupid'.

And they fell to playing again with grains of maize as counters until the other guests arrived. Stephens, reflecting on this scene, said: '. . . the whole Spanish American priesthood has at times been denounced as a set of unprincipled gamblers, but I had too warm a recollection of their many kindnesses to hold them up in this light. They were all intelligent and good men, who would rather do benefits than an injury; in matters connected with religion they were most reverential. . . . I would fain save them from denunciations of utter unworthiness which might be cast upon them. Nevertheless, it is true that dinner was delayed, and all the company kept waiting until they had finished their game of cards.'

In the morning Stephens led the padres and their Indians over the escarpments of the Tumbalá mountains, whence, after much vexatious bickering, they moved to the pyramids and to the Palace.

Catherwood, drawn out of his solitude by all the clatter, came out on the projecting steps. In his emaciated state he was hardly recognizable. He was as gaunt as a skeleton. The insects had played havoc with his face; it was swollen about the eyes, with red blotches where furious Diptera had sucked his blood. His left arm hung paralysed from rheumatism. In no mood for pleasantries, he gave the priests a frigid welcome.

Despite the horrible conditions, Catherwood had kept on working; the food Stephens brought was welcome, and he and Pawling fell upon it like famished wolves. Fortunately the divine visitors did not long remain, but departed lavishing praises on the ruins in the melliferous Spanish hyperbole.

While Stephens had been nursing his niguas, Catherwood had 'finished' the Palace. Now they were ready for the other structures of the site, none of which were wholly visible for everything was obscured by the forest, entangled, engulfed, blotted out by a profusion of trees, strangling yet protecting the architectural work of the builders of Palenque.

It was only when Stephens climbed the triple-storied crumbling tower that he descried another building to the south-west, through its disorder of fallen rubble. Well over one hundred feet high, it lay obscured by a chaos of vegetation on top of a pyramid. This structure was the next to be uncovered.

To the accompaniment of the soft patter of rain, they cut their way through the encumbering brush, slowly mounting the stones of the pyramid until they burst upon the Temple. Plants grew out of the roof, trees with naked roots tried to dislodge the stones, but even though it had suffered greatly from the sapping of roots and creepers, this, The Temple of Inscriptions (Stephens called it 'No. 1 Casa de Piedra') was the best preserved of the isolated temples of Palenque.

The front of the Temple, facing north, was entered by five doorways decorated by four stuccoed reliefs. All had lost their faces, but the elaborate garments of the figures could be made out even though exposed to a thousand years of alternate fierce rain and fierce sun, enough of form and figure for Frederick Catherwood to draw.

The stucco mosaic had been violently colored and still exhibited something of its yellows, obtained from the ocherous earths, its scarlets taken from the cochineal insect, and its purples extracted from the immemorial Purpura, the thick-shelled snail of the Yucatán coast.

But imagination alone could recreate the barbaric beauty that was this temple, with its stuccoed sculptures, with colors still alive and sentient; a towering mountain as a backdrop.

Catherwood faithfully copied the figures, making little attempt at restoration. He drew what time had spared in outline and shaded in the parts irretrievably lost.

Then they entered the darkened vault pausing for a brief moment before the great doorway and peering into the inky blackness of the interior.

A lizard came out of the fetid fault, blinked its eyes, and ran into the open. The only sound within was the baleful screech of the fruit bats hanging from the ceiling.

Juan went slowly forward, a pine torch in his hand, causing the shadows of their figures to dance on the ancient, eroded walls. They examined the seventy-foot-long vault; it was empty as a tomb. Then Juan gave out a startled cry and they followed his pointing finger to the side wall, where under green-grey moss were two huge limestone slabs, covered with glyphs.

The expeditious Juan, silenced by the solemnity of the moment quickly brought up a pair of brushes, dipped them into a pool of water and began to rub off the verdure of centuries. Catherwood leaned against the eroding stucco walls, waiting expectantly, while Stephens, holding the pine torch, had forgotten for the last minutes to puff upon his cheroot.

'The impression made upon our minds by these speaking but unintelligible tablets I shall not attempt to describe,' he remembered later.

Slowly the carvings were revealed. They were written, or better, sculptured in characteristic pebble-shaped glyphs, each completely filling its appointed square, wildly grotesque face symbols coupled with bars and dots as if trying to ape Roman numerals.

There was no mistaking these; Stephens knew them to be the same as they had found in Copán and Quiriguá. It was perfectly maddening to Stephens that they could not read them. He was certain that 'hieroglyphics . . . tell Palenque history.'

Standing before these newly-found Maya glyphs, he was beside himself, for they had no key to the unraveling of these strange face symbols, which he fervently believed would tell something of the people who had built this stone city.

Hoping that they would find an answer, he had Catherwood copy them accurately. Until recently all that had been deciphered were glyphs which told of time. Today the study has broadened. Maya codices and glyphs from all the monuments are being classified by electric computer and Maya scholars are beginning to find something more than impersonal records of dates and rituals; from the carved texts actual named rulers are appearing, personal names and specific references to women, who were held in high esteem. This Palenque had held a high place, as Stephens and Catherwood then surmised from the length of the texts: they believed it to be adjutant to Maya history.

At Palenque only two dated stelae had been found, the earliest A.D. 685, the latest A.D. 783, which gave it a suggested one hundred years of life. But this is illusory, for Palenque is unique among all Maya cities in having recorded many hieroglyphic texts not only on stelae but on the outside and inside of buildings such as Catherwood was now copying in the Temple of the Inscriptions.

Even when Catherwood had finished copying the tablets – and so accurately that archaeologists a century later could read what he had copied – the travelers did not know that they had walked over and continually stepped upon one of the great Maya secrets.

In June 1952 the Mexican archaeologist Albert Ruz Lhullier was assigned to restore the structures at Palenque.

This brought him to the Temple of the Inscriptions where Catherwood had worked one hundred and eleven years before. He noticed in the inner room a large slab set neatly into the floor, with finger holes in it so it could be raised.

Raising it, he followed a narrow cobbled stairway downward, first in one direction and then another, until he and his workmen reached another large slab poised horizontally, sixty feet below the surface.

In front of the door were the skeletons of six Maya who had 'elected' to remain as guardians of the tomb. Inside was

45.   Cross section of the Temple of the Inscriptions.

a veritable fairy palace, through centuries of dripping
lime-saturated water, it had formed long tenuous stalactites.
Over the tomb was a beautifully carved slab in relief.
A portrait with hieroglyphics, it weighed five tons. Within
the tomb was a skeleton of the *halach uinic* of the Palenque
'true man', bedecked with enormous jade earrings, a jade
necklace, and a pear-shaped baroque pearl. It had long been
thought that the Maya pyramids were built solely to support
temples and did not contain the tombs of important person-
ages, as did pyramids in other lands.

Unaware of what they had missed, when Frederick

Catherwood had finished copying the tablets within the Temple of the Inscriptions, they stumbled down the pyramid into a *quebrada*, where the river stream had been artificially sewered by the Maya.

They had suspected, in reading the works of Dupaix and Del Rio, that there were more buildings to be found in Palenque, but there was nothing to follow in the jungle save a solid wall or instinct.

Juan stumbled across a profusion of cut stones and his shouts drew Stephens, who was inspecting a ten-foot monolith. He passed the call along and the four drew together, moving toward the purple shadows of an artificial rise of ground. Slinking between the trees and ducking under the lianas that crossed their path like bell ropes, and on climbing the sides of another pyramid they found a crumbling building, an edifice with three doorways.

The Temple of the Cross was a magnificent erection with a roof crest forty-two feet high, a roof comb boldly conceived. It became 'Cassa No. 2' in Stephens' identification. The Temple was once decorated with stucco design of bewildering complexity, the carved wooden lintels of sapote wood had decayed, causing the whole of the façade to tumble down in a mass of rubble. Catherwood thought that he had been forestalled by time, until, looking within the vaulted interior, he found a stone triptych on the wall. This was the carved tablet with a cross that was to cause so much weary logomachy, more learned controversy than any other piece of art in America.

The principle decoration of this triptych was a cross, resting on a symbol of a death's head (suggested by two jawbones). On top of the cross was a grotesquely sculptured *quetzal*, the famous golden-green trogon, sacred bird. Two life-sized Indians, carved in exquisite low-relief, flanked the cross; figures fashioned without distortion of features which are among the prime and faultless masterpieces of Mayan art. The grotesqueries were reserved for the 'cross' at Palenque proved to those who held such a view that Christians before Columbus had lived in America. Yet the Maya 'cross' is not a cross at all but a conventionalized tree combined with the sun and death symbols which point towards the four principal earth directions. Frederick Catherwood, now assured of his mastery of Maya style, set about in his own way to draw the ten-foot-long tablet.*

In Stephens' mind, benefited greatly by Catherwood's analysis, there was no longer any doubt of what he saw. As art, it ranked with all other old world cultures.

What we had before our eyes was grand, curious and remarkable enough. Here were the remains of a cultivated polished and peculiar people, who had passed through all the stages incident of the rise and fall of nations; reached their golden age, and perished. . . . We lived in the ruined palaces . . . we went to their desolated temples and fallen stars; and wherever we moved we saw the evidences of their taste, their skill in arts. . . . In the midst of desolation and ruin we looked back to the past, cleared away the gloomy forest, and fancied every building perfect, with its terraces and pyramids, its sculptured and painted ornaments, grand, lofty, and imposing, and overlooking an immense inhabited plain; we called back into life the strange people who gazed at us in sadness from the walls; pictured them, in fanciful costumes and adorned with plumes of feathers, ascending the terraces of the palace and the steps leading to the temples. . . . In the romance of the world's history nothing ever impressed me more forcibly than the spectacle of this once great and lovely city, over-turned, desolate, and lost . . . overgrown with trees for miles around and without even a name to distinguish it.

*Another tablet, somewhat similar, was discovered at Palenque fifty years later, which its discoverer, Alfred P. Maudslay, called The Tablet of the Foliated Cross.

Thus mused John Lloyd Stephens while sitting on the steps of the crumbling ruin of The Temple of the Cross.*

In the distance, veiled by a thin, persistent rain, the howling monkeys gave out a pulsating moan; cicadas beat upon their membraned drums, and hawks on extended wings circled the ruins. All the while Stephens, lost in a trance, spun out his archaeological dream.

Stephens was unaware that close to Palenque lay a galaxy of ruins, and that thirty miles distant on the Rio Usumacinta there were other ruins of the same period as Palenque. On that river which drained most of Los Altos of Guatemala (which another author a century later would call the 'River of Ruins') there were other Maya cities buried by the jungle – Yaxchilán, Piedras Negras, El Desempeño – which, as a result of the stimulus given by Stephens's books, others were to discover in a later century. Within the Maya area marked by extremes of Copán and Palenque, spread a vast sixty thousand square miles which hid the remains of hundreds upon hundreds of these ancient structures.†

Although Palenque was a distant three hundred air miles from Copán, separated by a bewildering clefted space of mountains, jungles, rivers, and savannahs; although Palenque's medium was stucco while that of Copán was stone, they who built them wrote the same language. Stephens had explored the two extremes – north and south – of the Maya cultural

*Plans of The Temple of the Cross as well as an entire schematic drawing of the Ruins of Palenque were executed fifty years later by William H. Holmes (*Archaeological Studies Among the Ancient Cities of Mexico*) (Chicago, 1895–7) and have been reproduced in almost every book published on the Maya since then. Holmes was one of the great topographer draughtsmen of the American West in the 1870s. Born in Ohio in 1846, he studied art and was attached at the age of twenty-six to the Far Western Surveys. He contributed pioneer reports on Yellowstone Park, made the classic illustrative material on the Grand Canyon and while exploring became interested in early American cultures. Before he died in 1933 he reached international eminence in depicting antiquities and organizing ethnological collections within Museums.

†American archaeologists have honored the memory of these two archaeological pioneers by naming a newly discovered Maya site near the celebrated ruins of Bonampak *Stephens* (Lacanah) and in the same general area a small Maya site called *Catherwood*.

empire. He had, in the language of a modern archaeologist 'proved the homogenity of Maya art despite differences of space and geography.'

Above the jungle's sound Stephens heard the muted calls of helpers who had disappeared in the jungle.

They had found another ruin. Stephens waited until Catherwood had done; then, gathering up the easels, they made their way down the pyramid.

So dense was the jungle that they had not seen the outlines of yet another pyramid. Now, following the sound of Juan's voice, they arrived at a truncated pyramid surmounted by another temple.

Reaching the top, Stephens quickly took its measurements, noted the slanting stucco roof, the high lattice-work roof comb, the two vacant niches where huge carvings had once been placed. These carvings, which he had first seen in the village, were to be the cause of a humorous sequel. At either end were two vast glyphs – somewhat battered by centurial erosion – proclaiming to those who could read them: the building was erected in A.D. 692.

Within a darkened room giving out the fetid staleness of centuries, they found the apothoesis of Maya art. Contained in a vault was a huge altar, a sort of altar within an altar. A stone mural dominated by two life-sized figures flanking the Sun Face symbol, with its protruding Gorgonlike tongue. It was backed by two spears and a double row of glyphs.

The carved human figures offered in homage to the sun cross-legged *mannequins*. Glyphs coursed the sides. There were other typical Maya intrusions and distractions, yet on the whole it was a magnificent piece.

Catherwood, who had seen much of the ancient art in the East, said it was as fine as anything he had seen in Egypt.

One can find little else in Maya art so perfect in its essential simplicity, so fluent, so completely achieved. It had a delicacy, an almost epicene quality. The Maya artist knew here the value of empty space.

Stephens too was deeply impressed and if they did not go through their usual exchange of mutual enthusiasms, it was only because after twenty-eight mostly sleepless nights and often foodless days, their minds would no longer respond.

The copying of the relief at The Temple of the Sun was almost the last thing that Catherwood accomplished at Palenque. It was to be his Maya masterpriece. So impressed was he by the design of the Sun that he had it stamped on the cover of Stephens's book on Central America.

The rains were now the Furies unbound. The wind whipped gusts of water into the ruins; there seemed not a single dry place of refuge.

Catherwood worked as in a trance. He allowed himself to be dragged a few hundred feet more through the jungle to yet another ruin – an architectural fragment now called The Temple of the Beau Relief. There he was able only to make a feeble sketch of an allegorical piece of a stucco – which unknown to them Count Waldeck had done five years before (ending his work by chopping off the face of the piece).

After that, Catherwood, like a massive oak deprived of its roots, slipped slowly to the ground. The hurricane lashed across the exposed hills, toppling trees, pulling down whole sections of forest. Above the din of the storm the howling monkeys sounded like wailing banshees. And Juan, to top the disasters; tipped over the pot of cooking fat – that was the end.

On 1 June, 1840, they quit the ruins.

There was no satisfying Stephens' lordly ambitions. Since he had possessed himself of the ruins of Copán for fifty dollars and was in negotiation for the purchase of the ruins of Quiriguá, he thought he might as well add Palenque to his archaeological real estate. Thus far, he had been frustrated in his attempt to remove some of the monuments to take back and set up in America as an archaeological museum. So while Catherwood recovered from an illness brought on by exposure, Stephens negotiated for Palenque.

He informed the village prefect of his plan and ascertained from him its value:

> The tract, containing the ruins consisted of about six thousand acres of good land, which according to the usual appraisement, would cost about fifteen hundred dollars and the prefect said it would not be valued a cent higher on account of the ruins. *I resolved immediately to buy it.*

This was not so simple as it had been in Honduras. In Mexico, the land laws required that a foreigner must be married to a Mexican woman before he could purchase property. Although Stephens was a young man of thirty-four, attractive to women and very much attracted to them, he retained a firm grip on his single state. 'On principle I always resisted . . . I never before found it to my interest to give way [but], the ruined city of Palenque was a most desirable piece of property.'

Archaeology must have taken a deep hold on Stephens if he was willing to allow his principles to be usurped by the purchase of Palenque. Apparently in serious mood he began to look over the prospects. Santo Domingo was a small village with few women and the prettiest girl on whom his eye had long rested and who had contributed most to his happiness ('she made our cigars') was only fourteen – hardly a deterrent, except that she was already married. The only remaining possibilities were the two neatly dressed ladies occupying a pink calcimined wattle and daub house which had embedded in its stucco front the two carvings from the Temple of the Sun.

Stephens liked the house. He liked the ladies. He especially liked those Maya tablets. He might have had either of them. Apparently Stephens plumbed the possibilities, in more ways than one, for reporting to Catherwood on the progress of this nebulous archaeological romance with the sisters

Bravo, he said: 'Both were equally interesting and equally interested.' Yet nothing came of it, and Stephens, as a last resort, instructed the prefect that he would try to arrange the purchase after his departure, through the American consul at Laguna. He allowed his firm offer of $1,500 to stand. There was correspondence over it in Spanish, which Stephens preserved in his personal papers, but nothing finally came of it. The removal of the Copán monuments was then quite impossible and getting those from Palenque equally impossible for political reasons as well as lack of proper transport.

North of the little village of Santo Domingo del Palenque, the pinnacled Tumbalá Mountains melt into the ground and become palmetto-studded savannahs. Here and beyond is a tangled skein of rivers pouring down from the Guatemala highlands onto the Tabasco-Campeche plain. In a confusing pattern of water these lands are transformed by the caprice of weather into either desert, hot savannah or hyacinth-covered lakes.

A historic land, this section. Here tribes of Mayance speech in historyless times moved down from Vera Cruz to lay tribal claim to all of Yucatán.

Here in 1519 on the shores of Tabasco, at Cintla, Hernán Cortés made his first landfall that was to eventuate in his conquest of the Aztec. Here, too, not many years afterward, he struggled through the quagmires of Tabasco on his way to Honduras to punish Crisóbal de Olíd, who had revolted against his rule. And here, in June 1840, following an immemorial route of Indian, conquistador, and colonist John Lloyd Stephens led his three fatigued expeditionists across the savannahs.

After traveling most of the day through quagmires of stump grass and palmettos they came at night, with the rain, to the village of Las Playas. Not so much a village as a single street with huts of leaf-thatch, its puddles filled with ill-fed dogs and scavenger pigs.

Unable to find a *posada*, and with the blessings of the padre, the travelers took refuge in a church which stood, or rather tumbled, at the end of the street.

They quit Las Playas next morning, and began the descent to the sea in a thirty-foot canoe loaned to them by the alcalde, and poled by three men.

Beyond Las Playas is the Catazaja Lagoon, a broad sheet of hyacinth-covered water surrounded by forest. In the distance the mountains of Palenque were visible, forming a perfect trapezium against the horizon.

Catazaja was an Elysium for birds. There were web-footed and long-legged wading birds, swimming, plunging. There in small flocks, was the *tantale* with its crooked beak. There were infinite varieties of ducks, cranes walked slowly and stately by, stopping to stare quite unafraid of the canoe gliding through the maze of lily pads. The graceful *jacaná* with its yellow tipped wings and irridescent green neck, tripped dexterously over the floating leaves, fluttering down like a butterfly from one pad to the next. The shy spoonbills kept to the shore. There were the flamingoes with their flaming wings, and ghostly herons rose in effortless flight. Even in their discomfort, Stephens and company felt the beauty of the moment. There was little of the naturalist in John Lloyd Stephens; his preoccupation was man – the measurer of all things. He could pass through the entire length of the jungle without once conveying that life, in bewildering forms, swarmed about him. But now, with hundreds of varieties of birds about him, nameless and unknown, he felt the lack of this knowledge, and at the Catazaja Lagoon he decided, should he ever return to Central America, to bring a naturalist with him.

Following the channel, they glided past alligators floating on the surface like partially submerged mahogany logs. Then they entered the Rio Chico, a sluggish, stagnant channel. Monkeys peered down at them through the leaves; and a huge green iguana, with three feet of whiplash tail, looked at them briefly – and continued to climb the sides of a smooth-trunked tree.

Toward evening the Rio Chico grew wider and became, no one knew why, the Rio Chiquito; with a roar it joined the turbulent Rio Usumacinta, one of the noblest rivers in Central America. The Usumacinta, drains three-quarters of the Guatemalan highlands, and flows through the provinces of Yucatán, Campeche, and Tabasco to empty into the Gulf of Mexico.

It was a wild country uninhabited and desolate. The howling monkeys screeched the whole night long, a gigantic screaming wail that quivered and rose, fell and rose again, trailing its banshee echoes across the brawling river.

Moving through the heart of the logwood country, they came to the village of Palizada, which lay on an open plain. Willows hung over the banks, a herd of cattle all but hidden grazed on the tall luxuriant grass. The tall straight *bojon* trees stood on the banks with their spreading umbrella-shaped tops reminded Catherwood of Italian pines and the ghostly-stemmed Cecropias looked like gigantic candelabra.

Palizada, then a small hamlet of straggling palm-leafed huts, was to become a boom town in a few years, when a forest of logwood was discovered there. Logwood had been a source of Spain's wealth and misery for centuries. The red dyes obtained from it were much in demand by the rest of Europe. Pirates – British, French, and Dutch – when not sacking Spanish galleons, would come into the dyewood country to log; their continued presence throughout the peninsula caused endless diplomatic disputes between England and Spain and resulted eventually in the British getting the Crown Colony of Belize.

Stephens and Catherwood went down to the sea, with a cargo of dyewoods, bananas, mangoes, and papayas, and with a crew whom Stephens called 'breechless marineros', miserable half-clothed *lazzaroni* who scarcely knew a jib from a halyard.

Down to the Laguna they went, through an inferno of mosquitoes and alligators, along the furiously rushing river where bamboos and aquatic *jahuacte* palms rose above the grasses. Rain, biting like hail, came with the wind, increasing in violence as they reached the Boca Chica of the lagoon.

The blasts of the Carib wind god Huracán were agitating the whole lagoon when the bungo plunged into it. Waves broke over the vessel, and Stephens did not expect they would reach the port of Carmen alive. He put the balsa-wood life preserver on Catherwood, and they took off their boots and coats and waited.

Into Laguna de Terminos, fifty miles long, hundreds of jungle-spawned rivers debouch their sediment-filled water. It had been discovered in 1518 and named by Bernal Díaz del Castillo, the famous soldier historian of the *True History* who had at first fancied it an arm of the ocean encircling Yucatán,* then believed to be an island.

Terminos was partially enclosed by the island of Carmen, a low, flat, sandy stretch seven miles long, lying like a shriveled appendix facing the Caribbean. The port of Carmen lay at the eastern end, an outsize village of two thousand persons, nurtured by the commerce of logwood.

After tacking under a close-reefed sail, the bungo was brought into the open roadstead of Carmen and the travelers were happy to be quit of her. In their saturated clothes they walked the entire length of the town, past hotels, cafés, even barber shops.

The houses, mostly frame, were huddled together, banana trees spread their luxurious shade, and red and white flowers like periwinkles were tastefully planted in and about

---

*Yucatán was not the name of the region. In reply to a Spanish question about the name of the land the Maya replied: *Ci uthan* (you say so). The name mostly used for the peninsula of Yucatán seemed to have been *uluumil cutz yetel ceh* (the land of the turkey and the deer). There was in all probability no general name for the Maya area. 'Maya' first appears in 1502 as the city-state of Mayapan. Lothrop, Samuel, L., *The Word Maya and the Fourth Voyage of Columbus*, Museum of American Indian Notes, 4: pp. 350–356, 1927.

the piazzas. The streets ended in the jungle, and on its outskirts, in a neat, freshly painted house, was the United States consulate. In attendance to its problems was 'Don Carlos.'

Charles Russell, Esq., called familiarly Don Carlos, was a Philadelphia-born American, long resident in the tropics. He had been an importer of logwood, and had married, says Stephens, 'a Lady belonging to one of the first families of the country.'

A merry blue-eyed man, with grey-streaked hair and grizzled eyebrows, he was intrigued by Stephens's description of Palenque. He had always wanted to go there but now the cold of many winters had diminished the enthusiasm of his younger years and Palenque remained unvisited. He agreed to the scheme to buy the site of Palenque for $1,500 in Stephens's name, for being married to an '*hija del pais*,' he could conform to Mexican law.

It was Stephens's intention to continue his explorations – the search for ruined cities – into Yucatán, for he had read of a great walled city called Uxmal, but it depended wholly on Frederick Catherwood, who was racked with malaria.

Rather than break up the expedition, Catherwood insisted that he was well enough to take the journey. Fortunately there was a vessel rocking in the open harbor at Carmen, and the shipmaster took Stephens and Catherwood one hundred and twenty miles north-west to land at the port of Sisal, entrepôt to Mérida, the capital of Yucatán.

They reached Mérida on the eve of the fête of Corpus Christi, having bounced in from the coast in a springless buckboard affair, a *valon-coché*, and at dusk, the twilight scarcely intervening, they passed under the ruins of three lofty stone gateways, miniature arches of triumph for the explorers who had, thus far, braved two thousand miles of Central American geography.

The whole flat, drab countryside was pleasantly animated by the approaching fiesta.

The white clad Indians whom they passed in the streets doffed their straw hats, uttering *Dios botik*; the women, neatly dressed in white huipils, waved to them. On the horizon, above the stern-piked pads of the maguey, they could see the church spires of the city.

Houses lined the streets, neatly calcimined in pastel shades of pink, cream, green, and yellow, 'very pleasing to the eye,' Stephens admitted. The well-paved streets were decorated with pine branches. On the roofs of the corner buildings stood models of animals – elephants, deer, flamingoes – which served as street guides since the natives were unable to read Spanish: 'Meet me at the street of the flamingo.' Simple monolithic houses turned their posterns to the street – in the Spanish – Moorish fashion – the iron-studded doors and grilled windows gave them a forbidding, mysterious appearance, yet once within the gates lovely patios were aflame with riotous tropical flowers.

Stephens wrote:

The streets were clean, and many people in them well dressed, animated, and cheerful in appearance; *calèches* fancifully painted and curtained, having ladies in them handsomely dressed, without hats, and their hair ornamented with flowers, gave it an air of gaiety and beauty . . . we felt as if by some accident we had fallen upon a European city.

Catherwood, too ill from malaria to travel, was unable to follow Stephens who rode with a guide through the scrub jungle to visit 'the fabled ruins of Uxmal' which lay fifty miles from Mérida.

When Stephens saw through the interstices of the scrub forest the outlines of pyramids, standing stark and bare in the fierce sun, the nerve tingling sensation he had experienced at Copán and at Palenque again possessed him. '. . . To my astonishment I came at once upon a large open field strewn with mounds of ruins, and vast buildings on terraces, and pyramidal structures; grand and in good preservation, richly ornamented, without a bush to obstruct the view, and in picturesque effect almost equal to the ruins at Thebes.'

Stephens could hardly contain himself. He rode back to the hacienda and burst in upon Catherwood, who lay with a wet cloth over his head. Catherwood sat up unsteadily in the hammock, looked at him with bloodshot eyes and said: 'Stephens you are romancing.'

Catherwood, weakened but unyielding, went out the next day to Uxmal, inspected the vast ruins lying under an oven-hot sun. He agreed that the 'reality exceeded Stephens' description,' and promptly put up his easel and began with practised hand to draw a panorama of the pyramid of the House of the Dwarf.

His fever mounted and at three in the afternoon Stephens found him collapsed beside his unfinished drawing and so the first expedition to Central America came to an end.

Stephens was satisfied, though only partially. They had set off to find three cities: Copán, Palenque and Uxmal, and they had found them all.

Catherwood had made the first accurate drawings of these cities as well as others along the way which had not been mentioned. The exploration of Uxmal had been abandoned because of Catherwood's illness, and Stephens, as is evident in his letters, resolved to return and this time to broaden their search.

On 24 June, 1840, Catherwood was put aboard the Spanish brig *Alexandre* bound for Havana, with Stephens in 'great apprehensions for his health,' taking over his care as well as the guardianship of his drawings and notebooks.

As if the gods willed their perishing, the *Alexandre* ran into the equatorial doldrums. It sat for days like a Muscovy duck on a sea of glass. By 13 July, the drinking water ran out. Sharks, as if summoned by some telepathic instinct, began to course the ship. In the afternoon a wind came up in gusts, but not strong enough to move the vessel. Then, just as Stephens had given up, thinking that their discovery of the Central American ruins would be lost on the *Alexandre*, the wind strengthened and another vessel hove into sight.

Stephens hailed it in English, and it turned out to be the *Helen Maria*. It came about, the sailors pulled Catherwood and Stephens aboard, then it sped north, reaching New York harbor on the last day of July.

CHAPTER XIII

Incidents of Travel in Central America

Interests in the Maya discoveries was as intense then as the public curiosity in Egypt which prevailed after the twentieth-century discovery of the tomb of Tutankhamun. Stephens had promised the public a book on his adventures, and a reading public seemed impatiently waiting for it.

The Harper Brothers – all four of them – called upon Stephens and insisted that he lose not a moment before beginning on his book, for the publicity attending his return had been such that it would send others flying off to Central America in search of ruins: so that he might be forestalled.

As Harper and Brothers' best selling author, Stephens was now in a position to insist on certain conditions. The work must be in two volumes, larger in size, 'suitably octavo,' he said; it must be well printed, and yet priced within the range of the common man, for Stephens's other significant contribution to archaeology was to tumble it from its fabulous price heights. Lord Kingsborough's massive nine-volume work sold at £150 the volume and Waldeck's folio at 3,200 francs which were beyond the means of the audience Stephens wished to reach.

Catherwood was to have charge of the illustrations and was to personally choose the engravers, inspect the final work, and also design the binding.

Frederick Catherwood was at that moment still confined to his house at 89 Prince Street suffering from the after effects of malaria. His wife took charge of his wasted body and whether it was the tumultuous political parades that drove him from his bed, or his rugged constitution, or his wife's loving care, we know not. He recovered, in time to meet with Stephens and arrange the illustrations for the book.

Catherwood's panorama had also prospered during his absence. New York was now a cosmopolis of 300,000 inhabitants, and growing daily with an influx of immigrants. Being thus allowed the financial leisure to direct the illustrations of Stephens's book, he selected five well-known engravers to work from his sepia and pencil drawings, and so with eighty or more plates to prepare for the book, Catherwood left his panorama for some months and disappeared into an engraver's world filled with its scrapers, burins, roulettes, and copper plates. In the meanwhile, with his sister Elizabeth in quiet attendance sharpening his quill pens, Stephens kept to his manuscript.

America's literary air was becoming vibrant with Hispanic-American themes. James Fenimore Cooper had left his Leatherstocking world to write a lurid, heavy tale called *Mercedes of Castille*. Herman Melville had sailed that year on the *Acushnet* around South America into the Pacific out of which would come *Omoa*. And in a different milieu, fashioned by the same Hispanic interest, Walt Whitman was turning out such literary potpourri as *The Inca's Daughter* and *The Spanish Lady*.

But it was in Boston, on Beacon Street, that literary themes of Spanish-America were the most insistent. There, in a darkened room of a fashionable house, William Prescott was dictating the first pages of *The Conquest of Mexico*. On completing *Ferdinand and Isabella*, he had decided to write on Cortés and his conquest of Mexico. Since his connections were boundless and his purse ample, he began by writing to a London bookseller and placing fifteen hundred dollars at his disposal for the purchase of books on the subject of Mexico. He soon learned (as did Stephens) that little was purchasable in book form, but he had the aid of Pascual de Gayangos; a learned Spanish scholar living in London who ransacked the libraries with persistency and devotion. Meanwhile Frederich Wilhelm Lembke, who knew the Spanish archives thoroughly as a result of his researches on his own *Geschichte von Spanien*, responded to Prescott's request and put a corps of copyists to work.

In time they amassed a huge box of unpublished material for shipment to America. 'This learned Theban,' wrote Prescott, 'who happens to be in Madrid, has taken charge of my own affairs and, like a true German, inspecting everything and selecting just what has reference to my subject.'

William Hickling Prescott was born on 4 May, 1796. A proper Bostonian 'in its most attractive form,' as Van Wyck Brooks said: 'a positivist, clear, full of romantic feeling, with scarcely a shred of intuition. One might well ask for different things, but one could scarcely ask for anything better. . . .'

Since Prescott did not write for bread, he had to keep to a schedule if work was to be delivered on time, and every morning, wet or fine, he would mount his horse 'and gallop to Jamaica Plain, to see the sunrise on the hill.'

On his way he would rehearse in his mind the words he would that day commit to paper.

On one of these mornings, 5 December, 1840, he wrote: 'I am now setting about the conquest of Mexico.'

While John Lloyd Stephens was composing his personal narrative of exploration in the legendary field of Mexican archaeology, Prescott was feeling his way through the antiquities of Mexico: 'a fathomless gulf,' as he called them.

Prescott's personal drama began in 1811.

As every boy of substantial background in Boston then did, Prescott entered Harvard College, and at fifteen years of age was preparing to read law and to echo the profession of his father, Judge Prescott.

In a bout of student horseplay in his first year, he lost the sight of his left eye, and had subsequently to abandon his career and travel to Europe in search of some alleviation from the ophthalmic surgeons there.

At the age of twenty-five he set out to mould himself into a historian. He first taught himself the use of the noctograph,

46.   William Prescott in 1856.

by means of which, with the aid of an ivory stylus guided by silver wires and pressing on a sheet of carbon paper, he wrote his notes. He learned to use it in semi-darkness.

A secretary was hired to read the books which he selected. He gave himself a year to learn French, another year for Spanish; he studied the great historical theories. Like Taine, he felt that literary criticism was one of the branches of history.

Though it was one of the last of literary forms and perhaps would end in absorbing them all, Prescott thought it must be the guiding point in selecting and judging authors.

In 1827, after long preparation Prescott began to lay down the broad outline for a history of Ferdinand and Isabella of Spain; ten years later the work appeared.

Van Wyck Brooks wrote:

> Suddenly, in 1837, a great work appeared, like a wonder of nature as it seemed to American readers. It was a brilliant performance, as any child could see, and no scholar was ever to deny. . . . As a work of art, a great historical narrative, grounded at every point in historical fact, and within the glow and color of Livy and Froissart, it was a magnificent success.

It was natural that, having succeeded in finding theme and style in a new form of history, Prescott should go on – to the Spanish conquest.

By 1838 Prescott realized that his proposed history of the conquest of Mexico would require a prodigious amount of research, for many of the contemporary accounts had never been published, but were hidden away in the official archives of Spain.

If he could not travel to see the geographical milieu of his subject, he had the eyes of a friend to supply him with the scenic detail of the topography of the conquest. Prescott was a spectator, not a man of action, and so the news of the discoveries of John Lloyd Stephens, in the very earth in which he struggled, came as a most providential coincidence. The first letter Stephens wrote announcing his discoveries went to Prescott:

Feb. 2, 1841

. . . I have delayed publishing Central America for I am engaged in a scheme for bringing to this country some very interesting monuments, which might be defeated by newspapers reaching Guatemala and giving the owners exaggerated ideas of their value, but if I have any knowledge worth your perusing I shall be most happy to communicate it. . . .

I wish you could see these drawings [of Catherwood] and still more I could have a few hours conversation with you. . . . Some of the sculptured columns at Copán and Quiriguá are equal to the finest of the Egyptians and the buildings at Palenque and Uxmal are very large and really one can hardly help speaking of them extravagantly, but I am afraid they are not as old as I wish them to be. . . .

Please do not mention my schemes . . . for the monuments.

Prescott answered:

You have made a tour over a most interesting ground, the very forum of American ruins, none of which has been given to the public, even in description I believe, except Palenque, Uxmal, Mitla, and Copán – and there are no drawings of these latter. . . . It would help us much if all the conquistadores had condescended to give some particulars of the state of the buildings in Yucatán at the time of their arrival. But I have found nothing beyond a general allusion to remarkable buildings of stone and lime and curious architecture scattered over the country. . . .

Your opinion as to the comparitively modern date of these remains agrees entirely with the conclusions I had come to from much more inadequate sources of information, of course, than you possess. But I have met with no facts to warrant the antiquity assigned by Waldeck and other travelers of thousands of years, like the Egyptian. . . . (One can never read of such antiquarian speculations, however, without thinking of Membrino's basin helmet [the barber's basin asserted by Don Quixote to be King Membrino's helmet].)

I was not aware that the buildings were so well executed as to equal in this respect the Egyptian. Robertson* underestimated them, and distrust which had a knowing air, at least, was the safer side for the historian. The French and Spanish travelers, however, write with such swell of glorification and Waldeck's designs in particular are so little like the pictures of *Ruins*, that I had supposed there was some exaggeration in this respect. No one can be a better judge than yourself, however, who are familiar with the best models in the Old World to compare them with.

Encouraged by scholars, Stephens went on with his book, but, try as he would, he could not keep the secrecy that he wished for the publicity attending his discoveries had already inspired others to follow in his footsteps.

In 1840, an elegant young Viennese, Baron Emanuel von Friedrichsthal, had come to Boston where he was presented to Prescott.

Prescott informed Calderón de la Barca who was then in Mexico:

*William Robertson (1721–1793), Scottish historian, wrote: 'Neither the Mexicans nor the Peruvians were entitled to rank with those nations which merit the name of civilized.' Their houses were 'more fit to be the habitation of men iust emerging from barbarity . . . low straggling huts . . . scattered about irregularly.'

An Austrian gentleman is here just now, and proposes to visit Palenque which he has been studying in my Lord Kingsborough's publications. He may possibly visit Mexico in which case I shall take the liberty to give him a note to you. He is an accomplished man in whose society you and your wife will take pleasure.

Friedrichsthal was, in fact, the first Secretary of the Austrian Legation in Mexico. He was fairly well known to Europe's *literati* for his description of plant life in Greece and Serbia.

Upon hearing of Stephens' discoveries, having been aware of the publications of Waldeck, and after visiting Prescott, he purchased a complete daguerreotype apparatus to expose the first photographs of American ruins ever taken.

His observations, for the short time he wandered in Yucatán, were quite acute; he sensed that

> In comparing the many vast monumental sites of Yucatán and those of Palenque, Quiriguá and Copán, despite obvious architectural variations, one cannot fail to notice the general character of resemblance, *indicating identical origins.* . . .

His description of Chichén Itzá, so far as is known, is the first detailed one by a European.

> At Chichén Itzá, situated some 33 leagues from Valladolid and about 25 from Mérida, one finds cells and interior walls decorated with human figures and symbolic signs cut into the stone. There are pyramids with steps and terraces, generally crowned by a building that is composed of several chambers. Their height varies from 40 to 120 feet, rising at an angle of 54 to 58 degrees. The exterior is often covered with innumerable figurative sculptures, the subjects of which share the somewhat obscene character of certain religious Hindu monuments.

To the north and to the south of the city stretch two huge parallel walls of 262 feet length, which once supported a number of buildings that have now crumbled, with the exception of one temple, forming the western angle of one of the walls. In the center of each wall, the plain surface is adorned with two stone rings, representing two coiled snakes, on each side.

There are several huge religious buildings of long rectangular shape. One of them, the so-called '*Casa de las Monjas*,' has no entrance on the ground floor; the upper floor holds numerous rooms with carved lintels over its doors, covered with hieroglyphs.

The dwellings were constructed in a square, enclosing a courtyard. The wing containing the single entrance was somewhat smaller than the other three.

The wide paved streets have low ramparts composed of ashlars that are piled up without order; there are graves surrounded by sculptured and chiseled stones; numerous and fairly well-preserved cisterns; and the pillars that served for the torture of criminals.*

In exposing daguerreotype photographs of Maya structures Friedrichsthal anticipated by several years the work of another Austrian, Capitán Teobert Maler, who escaped the débâcle of the Mexican Empire when Maximilian was executed, in 1867, and wandered throughout Maya country, making a wonderful photographic record of the Maya.

On his return to Europe, Friedrichsthal was warmly received by Humboldt and, in appreciation of his accomplishments, was awarded recognition by the Académie Royale des Inscriptions et Belles Lettres at Paris. His Maya tour, however, left a bad taste in Stephens' mouth.

Writing to Prescott, he said:

*Friedrichsthal, Chevalier Emanuel de, *Les Monuments de l'Yucatán*, Eyries, *Nouvelles Annales de Voyages*, Vol. 92, Paris, 1841, pp: 291–314.

I gave Friedrichsthal a *carte du pays* for Yucatán and letters, and the result is a publication in the newspapers impeaching the correctness of Mr. Catherwood's drawings. I did not see him when he passed through this city and I cannot believe that he authorized so unfounded a publication.

In May 1841, Stephens' manuscript on Central America, equivalent in length to three standard novels, was finished. It had been written with Trollope-like speed. It was destined to be one of the notable books in American literature, not alone for the influence it would exert on American archaeology; it was to give Americans their first real glimpse of ancient America.

The opening gambit in Stephens's archaeological epic was simple and without literary artifice:

'On Wednesday the third of October 1839, I embarked on board the British brig *Mary Ann*, Hampton, master, for the Bay of Honduras.'

Once in the stream of narrative he wrote quickly, easily, spontaneously, for Stephens's writing was like his conversation: alive, full of anecdote and rich in detail.

One was held to the book by the personality of Stephens. Through all his difficulties, his imprisonment, his disagreements, he showed a natural playfulness and exuberance. The detached amusement was always at his own expense, and his perception of incongruities was deft and penetrating. In the depths of seriousness he was always able to achieve some form of solvent laughter. One was won over immediately to his enthusiasms; his curiosity was infectious. Before everything Stephens was a New Yorker, analogies were always made – be it banks, women, canals, or ruins – with New York City; the city became his measurer of all things.

Prescott – who was in the middle of dragging his hero, Hernán Cortés, over the blood-strewn Mexican earth – was enthusiastic about Stephens' book. He almost ruined the sight of his one good eye, he said, by reading it himself. On 2 August, 1841, he wrote Stephens from Boston:

> I cannot well express to you the great delight I have received from your volumes. I suppose few persons will enjoy them more, as very few have been led to pay attention to the subject. You have indeed much exceeded the expectations I had formed . . . You have shown how accessible many of these places are, and have furnished a sort of *carte du pays* for the future traveller. I have no doubt that your volumes will be the means of stimulating researchers in this interesting country, which has been looked on as a kind of enchanted ground guarded by dragons and giants . . . Too much praise cannot be given Mr. Catherwood's drawings in this connection. They carry with them a perfect assurance of his fidelity. *How different from his predecessors.*

The *Incidents of Travel in Central America* continued to go through edition after edition.*

It is the archaeological sections – by far the greater part of the work – that time, the great test of masterpieces, has made classic. In ten months Stephens had discovered, and then uncovered, several lost Maya cities. The unearthing of this ancient civilization remains one of the greatest achievements in American history, and Stephens' fame rests not on sterile discovery alone: he cut through the web of fabled history to prove the homogeneity of Maya culture. He showed that the people who built Copán in Honduras also built the stucco-embellished city of Palenque in Mexico, even though they were separated by hundreds of miles of jungles and mountains.

*As the result of this author's first biography of Stephens' *Maya Explorer*, published in 1947, the interest in Stephens swept all the second-hand copies of Stephens' book off the market. To meet the new interest Rutgers University Press re-issued *Central America* in 1949.

He was the first to speak of the Maya remains as 'works of art.'

He took issue with the world's authorities – Lord Kingsborough, Robertson, Grotius, Waldeck – when he insisted upon the American origin of the ruins.

They were neither Egyptian, Roman, Grecian, nor Cambodian – 'for unless I am wrong,' he wrote at the end of 300,000 words,

> We have a conclusion far more interesting and wonderful than that of connecting the builders of these cities with the Egyptians or any other people. It is the spectacle of a people skilled in architecture, sculpture, and drawing, and, beyond doubt, other more perishable arts, and possessing the cultivation and refinement attendant upon these, not derived from the Old World but, originating and growing up here without models or masters, having a distinct, separate, and independent existence; like the plants and fruits of the soil, indigenous.

With that Stephens laid the archaeological groundwork of American pre-history. What he saw, he described well and accurately; what he did not know, he hypothesized with great perspicacity; as Dr S. G. Morley said:

> . . . although he was unable to decipher the hieroglyphic inscriptions, that discovery being reserved for another generation, Stephens accurately gauged the importance of what he saw and left behind him a vivid, glowing description of its wonders, which will stimulate research in this field for all time.

In England the *Incidents* had great vogue. The British were delighted with this new contribution to American literature.*

*John Murray, the London publisher, wrote to Edward Everett, American Minister to England: 'Mr. Stephens sent over the American edition of his work on chance and I have already sold 2,500 copies.'

The London *Athenaeum*, whose criticisms were *dicta* in the literary world was elated to find another book from Stephens' quill:

'The readers of the *Athenaeum*,' wrote the reviewer, 'have not to be told in what high esteem we hold Mr. Stephens.'

They spoke of him as 'cheerful . . . manly . . . observant . . . graphic' and one who 'never indulges in the rhapsody of fine writing.'

But in a querulous review, George Jones, who was then writing a book to prove 'the identity of the aborigines with the people of Tyrus and Israel and the introduction of Christianity into pre-colonial America, by the Apostle Saint Thomas,' insisted in the pages of the *Edinburgh Review* that Stephens' book:

> Stimulates rather than gratifies curiosity . . . and even though in justice to him Central America was in violent disorder . . . it seems questionable whether he, even under the most favorable circumstances, would have shown himself possessed of the necessary precious acquirements.

This same George Jones, who had never set foot in America, had more to say. When his book appeared dedicated to his grace, the Archbishop of Canterbury, a book which he entitled most modestly *An Original History of Ancient America*, he solemnly declared

> The soul of history is wanting in Mr. Stephens. . . . He has given indeed by his pen and the artist by his pencil, a reflection of the Ruins, but it is from a mirror of polished ebony, simply a fac-simile resemblance – light and shade – only . . . a specimen of Daguerreotype! No one can mistake the rapid manner in which the true copy is impressed upon the mind, and that by the most easy and agreeable means – viz., the fascination of style; but the colouring of life is not there . . . the soul of history is wanting!

And so on and on . . . this Mr Jones* who had wafted Tyrians and Israelites to America's shores with St Thomas.

'We may thank heaven for Stephens' fault,' said one American, 'when we consider the said Promethean spark in the work of the immortal Jones.'

---

*George Jones, *An Original History of Ancient America, Founded Upon the Ruins of Antiquity; the Identity of the Aborigines with the People of Tyrus and Israel*, London, 1843.

PART 3

YUCATÁN REVISITED

CHAPTER XIV

Yucatán Revisited

It was now clear that Stephens and Catherwood would make another expedition to Central America. At first there had been some hesitation for, following the publicity of his first discoveries and first book on the Maya, Stephens' political image began ascending and he was offered a high political post.

He wrote to Prescott: 'I was perplexed by an offer which had been made for me to be Secretary of the U.S. Legation in Mexico, but fortunately I declined . . .'

Catherwood also had a change of mind. At first, mending slowly under his wife's careful administration, he vowed that he would never again face the perils of malaria but he eventually succumbed, for, like Stephens, he felt that there was still 'more out there'. Then too his panoramas were doing well under his manager George Jackson (the account books are still extant), so much so that he felt that he could leave his family in Jackson's care.

Since the last book was a financial success, one must assume that Stephens made another contract with Catherwood for the second planned edition, though no such contract has surfaced in the years of research. It certainly was not only for the money involved that Catherwood returned. It must have been that daemon of creative ambition that helped to propel him.

Whatever the circumstances, Catherwood agreed. And then so did Dr Samuel Cabot.

So they were now to be three. For on his last trip Stephens had felt his lack of knowledge of natural history and had vowed, when being punted through a paradise of bird-life in the Laguna de Términos on the way down from Palenque that the next time. . . .

233

47. Façade of stonework from Kabah.

The next time came in September 1841. Stephens had placed an advertisement in the venerable *Boston Courier* for a naturalist to 'accompany a gentleman to Yucatán.'

The best of the respondents was Dr Samuel Cabot Jr. His qualifications were excellent. He was a Harvard graduate (class of 1836), where he had taken a medical degree. He had been to Paris to study tracheotomy; still, his greatest interest was ornithology for he had corresponded for many years with the great naturalists of Europe.

Samuel Cabot's mother wrote to her other son Elliott, then in Germany studying medicine:

> Sam . . . sailed with Stephens and Catherwood for Central America the middle of this month, it was quite unexpected. Your father went to New York with Sam and saw Stephens and Catherwood; he was much pleased with their reception of Sam, they were in the midst of packing all sorts of things, amongst others, two daguerreotypes. . . . just what they want for copying the ancient monuments found in Central America.

Stephens instantly warmed to the modest young doctor, and Cabot returned the compliment. 'They remained very warm friends,' said Cabot's son, 'and he greatly admired Stephens's resourcefulness, dauntless courage and determination.'

Cabot was a well-built, athletic young man taller than Stephens (he had been a champion bare-knuckle boxer at Harvard for two years). Set in a fine head, high and broad, the blue eyes were kindly and the mouth wide with well-shaped lips. It was a studious sort of face and one which reflected his shyness. Dr Cabot was destined to become one. of America's most distinguished surgeons. As the United States drifted into the inevitable Civil War he was to become also one of the more militant abolitionists helping slaves to escape to Canada.

On 9 October, 1841, the party left on the bark *Tennessee* bound for the port of Sisal in Yucatán.

They went off quietly, almost secretly. Stephens had warned Prescott:

> You would oblige us . . . by not mentioning our purpose. We wish to get off without any newspaper flourishes, and without directing attention to our movements. . . . We wish to complete what we have begun before others can interfere with us.

The capital of Yucatán, titled by the king as 'The Very Loyal and Very Noble city of Mérida,' had been one of the first cities built after Yucatán's conquest by the Montejos. They had, it is true, begun the conquest on the ground floor; Francisco de Montejo, the elder, had landed with Hernán Cortés at Cintla in 1519, fought in its first battle, and had been chosen a year later to take back to Charles V the first loot, to impress the council with the wealth to be found in the Mexican land ruled by Montezuma.

An amiable gentleman, this Montejo, with his blue eyes and a scar across his face which gleamed scarlet when he was angry, and a conquistador with connections at court.

Montejo, after successfully accomplishing his mission, remained in Spain, where he married a widow troubled by the weight of a fortune and a demanding womb.

Then in 1524, just before Cortés was to make his heroically quixotic march across one thousand miles of Mexican geography to find and punish those who had revolted against him in Honduras, he sent for Montejo.

He could refuse nothing to his old companion in arms and agreed to make yet another representation for him before the Court. While he was on his way back to Spain, in skirting the jagged littoral of Yucatán, the sirens of conquest called again to Montejo, and this time he was unwilling, as Ulysses was, to stuff his ears.

He returned to Salamanca, where he enticed his rich wife to sell her estates and pawn her jewels. The madness of conquest possessed him.

In those halcyon days – before the age of reason – the King of Spain, by virtue of the papal bull, was outside of God the greatest real estate holder in the world. He owned all the lands in the 'new founde worlde' (except those of Brazil) west of the arbitrary line drawn by the papal geographers.

The new conquests operated something like realty subdivisions. Montejo, whose qualifications were well established, paid a sum of money to the Crown, agreeing to conquer and then colonize the whole of Yucatán at his own expense. He was named Capitán-General – only one of his sonorous titles – and given a grant of arms with a bequest of one thousand square miles of land, *para siempre jamás*, that was his 'for ever more.'

The Crown, as was the usual practice, was to have its 'royal fifth,' which was to be used to build schools, convents, roads, and a host of other complicated projects which would weld the newly conquered province to the state. And so it came to be, or factually, not to be.

The conquest of Yucatán took fifteen years, fifteen years of close battle, for the Maya had learned to take the measure of the Spaniard.

They had among them a talented practitioner of perfidy, Gonzalo Guerrero, a Spanish captive of the Maya* who had lived through the rituals and tortures to emerge a war chieftain. The Maya turned to him when pressed by the Spaniard, and he devised defenses that blunted the offensive power of horse and gun.

By posing as a captive slave, unwillingly held, he smuggled to the Spaniards scrawled messages always ending: 'I remember God, and you, Sir, and the Spaniards. I am your good friend. . . .'

*Gonzalo Guerrero, the Spaniard, rose from Maya slave. He married, fathered two children and was made *Nacom* war-*capitán*. He refused to be repatriated by Cortés, and conducted the unified defense of Yucatán against the *conquistadores*. For many years it was highly successful. In the siege of Omoa, Honduras, he was killed by a shot from a Spanish *arquebus*.

Still there was no staying the conquest. Tutul Xiu, one of the most powerful chieftains of the Maya, was induced into alliance with the Spaniards, in the promise of their aid against his traditional Maya enemy. That marked the end of Maya independence. In January 1542, Montejo chose the site for his capital, the Maya religious center of T'ho; its huge plaza of stone buildings reminded him of Mérida in the Spanish province of Badajoz (the ancient Augusta Amerita of Lusitania) with its Roman ruins and he called the new capital Mérida. In the rigidly prescribed 'manner of founding a town', the town council was appointed, streets laid out, a gallows erected, and the Indians employed to tear down their temples so that the stone might be used in building the cathedral.

On the south side of the plaza, the Montejos, uncle and nephew, selected the site for their palace.*

Over the doorway was an elaborate carving; the Montejo coat of arms in the center, and on the sides two mailed knights standing on the heads of conquered Indians.

It was not truly symbolic. The conquest of Yucatán was long drawn out and bitterly waged by the Maya, who never really submitted.

They resisted the conquest of their souls as they resisted the conquest of their land. On Sundays they went through the ritual demanded by the white man's God, and on weekdays in the shadows of the jungle they still worshipped as they had always worshipped.

In the deep recesses of the forest they carried images of the Maya gods that had escaped the rapacity of their new masters;

---

*There were three Montejos in the conquest of the Maya. The first, Francisco de Montejo (1479–1548) sailed with Grivalja in 1518. Later he took part in Cortés's conquest of Mexico and was selected to bring back the Aztec treasure to Spain. There he married a rich widow, sought and won a contract with the title 'Adelantado' for the conquest of Yucatán. The first campaign in 1527–1528 ended in disaster; he tried Tabasco to the north first, won and then lost in 1511–1515. He gave over his titles and the conquests to his son, known as Montejo el Mozo (younger) who finally conquered part of the Yucatán by 1546. The third Montejo succeeded him and built the famous Montejo mansion in Mérida, Yucatán.

and here in the blue haze and the aromatic perfume of burning copal incense they sought solace.

There was little progress in their spiritual conquest until Fray Diego de Landa appeared on the peninsula. A rigidly efficient monk lacking humor and proper humility, Landa with one hand lighted the torch that helped destroy Maya culture, and with the other hand preserved it.

He assiduously studied the Maya language, and armed with it, and it alone, walked the riverless land of Yucatán attempting through these pagan shibboleths to bring the Maya around to his ways.

When this method did not succeed, in terrible fury he tore down with his own hands any vestige that remained to remind the Maya of their gods. In this way the beautifully built stone pyramid at Izamal was destroyed under his direction and used to build the Franciscan monastery. Landa spared no one, not even the Spanish authorities, when he found them violating the principle of the Laws of the Indies. For failure to appear at Mass, they were lashed. For continuation of their pagan ways, they were given soul-breaking tasks to perform.

When Diego de Landa learned that the people at the village of Maní, the font of the Tutul Xiu dynasty, were still offering obeisance to their ancient deities, he descended upon the village, and found to his horror idols of clay and wood and books, folded books, on which were written glyphs (such as Stephens found carved in stone), histories, calendars, tables astronomical and astrological, illustrated to assist their mnemonic processes.

These were the cornerstone of Maya learning, books which had so far escaped the zeal of the missionaries' hands.

Landa gathered them together under his own *auto-da-fè*. 'We found among them a great number of books . . .' he said, 'and because they contained nothing but superstitions and falsehoods about the devil we burned them all.'

'We burned them.'*

The accretion of two thousand years of knowledge perished in those flames at Maní. Landa had dealt the blow at Maya culture. For while socially important secrets are never in the hands of a single man, as Aldous Huxley aptly pointed out:

> In many communities elements of higher culture are in the hands of a few. The [first] world war has given more than one example of how delicate is the balance of civilization, how easily it can be uprooted. The very existence of an industrialized and urbanized society depends on the knowledge and skill of, at most, 1 per cent of its members. . . . a selective massacre of three to four hundred technicians would bring the whole economic and social life of England to a standstill.

Yet paradoxically, the same person who helped so generously to stamp out Maya culture also did the most to preserve its history.

Diego de Landa carefully compiled – with a host of Maya amanuenses – all the details of their lives, as well as – and this is the most important – an analysis of their written language.

When the Spanish authorities learned of his self-administered burning of Maya antiquities, he was recalled to Spain and made to answer before higher ecclesiastical authorities. Confined at the convent of San Francisco in Guadalajara he wrote a manuscript, in reality his *apologia*, which he called *History of Yucatán*.† This proved to be of value in the deciphering of the Maya glyphs.

Stephens, who begged for a Champollion to unravel the linguistic mysteries, little knew as he looked upon the monk's

---

The Aztec and Maya Papermakers by Victor Wolfgang von Hagen (edition limited to 220 copies), J. J. Augustin, New York, 1943.

†See the excellent edition of Landa's *Relacion de las Cosas de Yucatán* – translated with elaborate notes by Dr Alfred M. Tozzer, Peabody Museum publications Cambridge, 1941.

tomb in the cathedral at Mérida that his 'Jean François Champollion' lay there under the name of Diego de Landa.

In Mérida, Doña Micaela was delighted to have back in her pension Señor 'Esteebens' and his two friends. She met them at the door on the cobblestoned 'Flamingo corner' in a red-embroidered, freshly-pressed huilpil, together with the latest style of high-heeled shoes from Paris.

In high spirits Stephens gave Doña Micaela an *abrazo*.

Music, celebrating the last hours of the fête of San Crístobal floated down from the plaza as the three expeditionists raised their hammocks in the cool, sparsely furnished room which was for a short period to be their home, and having arranged their mosquito netting they went out into the streets of Mérida.

White-clad, broad headed Mayas with eagle-hooked noses and dark epicanthic eyes filled the streets.

The women, short and sturdy inspiringly neat in their gay huipils, hurried by with graceful, lissome carriage.

Young Dr Cabot, his face more boyish than ever under his large panama followed these strange people with wondering eyes; from the very first he was delighted that he had come with the expedition, for the sight of the egrets, pelicans, and ducks (not to count his first wild ocellated turkey) on the Yucatán coast at Sisal, where they had arrived on 25 October, 'was alone worth the voyage,' he told Stephens.

The air of the fête was about them. The narrow, cobblestoned streets were garlanded with pine sprays, the pastel-shaded houses exhibited portraits of their particular saints, lanterns hung from balconied houses, and pretty, dark-skinned girls peeked out from their grillwork.

On the Alameda, the place of promenade, where the broad stone avenue was shaded by *ramón* trees, the expeditionists sat down and watched the ladies, with their flower-bedecked hair, ride by in red-wheeled carriages.

In the rush of progress Stephens had almost forgotten

the charm of this 'primitive Knickerbocker State,' but he had hardly forgotten how much, on his previous short visit, he had been charmed by the women. Let Stephens catch sight of a woman or a ruin and his pulse began to beat wildly. With the eye of a connoisseur, he wrote:

> Near . . . us was a bevy of young girls beautifully dressed, with dark eyes and their hair adorned with flowers, sustaining, though I was now a year older and colder, my previous impressions of the beauty of the ladies of Mérida. . . . All these mestizas exhibited . . . a mildness, softness, and amiability of expression that created a feeling of promiscuous tenderness.

There was so much charm about the mestiza dress – no stays, flounces, furbelows petticoats, or garters . . . it was so clean, simple and loose, leaving 'every beauty free to sink or swell as Nature pleases,' quoth Mr Stephens. 'I was particularly alive to these influences.'

Catherwood was experimenting with the daguerreotype, at the edge of the plaza trying to expose a picture of the palace of the Montejos.

The daguerreotype caused a sensation in Mérida. Many had heard of the new invention, for Mérida had good communications with New York, Cuba, and the outside world, yet with the exception of the Baron von Friederichsthal, who had arrived with one in the previous year, none had ever seen one.

At first the expeditionists had experimented on themselves until they grew tired of seeing their own faces. 'It was a new line for us,' explained Stephens, 'but no worse than for an editor of a newspaper to turn captain of a steamboat; besides not like banking – we could not injure anyone by a failure.'

Catherwood raised no objection to Stephens's suggestion that they photograph, in their rooms – purely for experience, of course – the ladies of Mérida.

They took down their hammocks, pushed back their baggage, and opened the shutters. Into the room poured the warm 'creative sun' of Yucatán, further 'lighted up,' said the irrepressible Stephens, '. . . by the entry of three young ladies with their respective mamas and papas.'

The women were dressed in the Creole, Yucatán-style; the huilpil cut square at the neck and low, low enough to show the shadow of the division of their olive-tinged breasts. Their hair was pushed back and tied in a bun exposing ears bejeweled with elaborate earrings.

There could be, in the Stephensian logic, no better method to experiment with daguerreotype for its proposed use, the photography of the Maya ruins, than the taking of portraits of attractive señoritas.

The first effort was an unqualified success, so Frederick Catherwood put the whole unwieldy black apparatus into a high wheeled *volán* and drove to the home of the next experiment. For Stephens proposed for science that they picture the whole household, from mother down to the Indian servants.*

It was at this moment that the people of Mérida discovered that the amiable young man, Dr Cabot – who spoke French but no Spanish and who seemed more interested in bird-skins than ladies – was a surgeon. He had studied in Paris, under Docteur Guerin, they soon learned, and knew how to cure the 'squint-eye.'

Mérida, as most of Yucatán, had an unusually high quota of persons who were cross-eyed, an atavism doubtlessly of their Indian ancestry; for, in the Mayan world it was deemed attractive to be cross-eyed.

---

*The perfected daguerreotype, made public in 1839, was introduced to America by John Draper and S. F. B. Morse. In 1841 Baron Emmanuel von Friederichsthal appeared in Yucatán and there for the first time he exposed daguerreotypes of Maya ruins. These were exhibited in New York, London and in Paris, where Friederichsthal succumbed to a tropical disease. So the first photographs of Maya ruins evanesced; Catherwood was the first to extensively use the daguerreotype for archaeology.

Maya mothers attached small balls of red-feathered wax between the eyebrows of their newly-born to cause the eyes to cross. So beloved was the 'squint' among Maya that Itzamna, the god of writing (among his other protean aspects), was always represented as fiercely cross-eyed.

A fourteen-year-old boy, the son of a Mérida family that had befriended Stephens, was the first strabismus patient.

A handsome, liquid-eyed boy, his features were singularly spoiled by the squint. After honing off the rust that had gathered on his finely tempered Parisian instruments, Dr Cabot explained to the parents, through Stephens the *modus operandi* of the strabismus technique.*

The eye was secured in its orbit by six muscles, which regulated its movements up, down, inward, and out. Any overcontraction or underdevelopment of one of these eye muscles produced an obliquity in the eye called in their language *bisco*.

He, Dr Cabot, was now to cut one of those eye muscles, without, unfortunately, any anesthesia, after which, God willing, the eye would 'fall' back into its normal position.

As these muscles lie under the surface of the eye it would be necessary to pass through its membrane. It was obvious that for so delicate an operation one could not use either a broadaxe or a machete.

'In fact,' Stephens concluded, 'it requires a knowledge of the anatomy of the eye, manual deterity, fine instruments; and Mr Catherwood and myself for assistants.'

A cut of Cabot's knife, a piteous scream; and the boy, his eyes bleeding, got off the improvised table without the squint. Cabot's miracle swept Mérida.

The next morning betimes, their room was surrounded by a regiment of people and many squint-eyed boys. With two

---

*Strabismus (from the Greek 'to squint') is a defect in the eyes in which the optic axes cannot be directed toward the same object due to an undue relaxation of the muscles of the eyes. French surgeon Guerin perfected a simple method of undoing the squint, and Samuel Cabot learned the surgical technique in Paris after graduating from Harvard Medical School.

local medicos, Dr Sado and Dr Muñoz, in attendance, patients selected at random yielded their inheritance of Itzamna to Dr Cabot's knife. One, a Gargantuan fellow, almost lost his eye when he jerked away from the incision; the voice of one small boy, clad in the traditional white Yucatán shirt and drawers, could be heard above all the others: '*Yo quiero, yo quiero*' – I wish it, I wish it.

The boy climbed on the table and lay heroically immobile while he was cured of strabismus. Then came an old general, the oldest in the Mexican Army. He was followed by a pretty young girl with her dueña.

After that Dr Cabot declared he had had enough. So did Stephens whose head 'was actually swimming with visions of bleeding and mutilated eyes.'

But it was not as easy to stop as it had been to begin. . . . Their doors were crowded throughout the day with numbers sufficient to blot out the warm Yucatán sunlight, with clamoring people, all with squint-eyes, demanding to be treated.

'They became . . . as clamorous as a mob in a western city about to administer Lynch law.' Everywhere they went in Mérida after the strabismus operations, they were followed by small boys who shouted: 'There go the men who cure the *biscos*'.

The reception of Messrs. Stephens, Catherwood and Cabot by the people of Mérida was in the warm extravagant Spanish manner. The local papers, *El Boletín Commercio* and the *El Siglo Diez y Nueve*, had reprinted most of the news stories emanating from New York of Stephens' discoveries in Central America, and contrary to Madame Calderón de la Barca's observation that 'his *Travels* are criticized as being incorrect by those who know the country,' the people of Mérida were pleased with the accuracy of his descriptions, '*Ilena de la verdad*' – 'full of truth,' as one editor expressed himself.

The publicity attending them, the daguerreotype, the strabismus operations, not to forget the personal charm of

Señor Stephens – all were to be of inestimable importance to their archaeological discoveries. They were assisted by almost everyone.

Just before they left for the ruins of Uxmal, Don Simón Peón, who was to provide them with generous and indispensable aid, suggested that he present Stephens, officially, to the governor of Yucatán. Don Simón himself possessed great power, for he was an *hacendado* of great holdings, enough in Yucatán to be classed as fabulous wealthy.

He actually owned the site on which were the ruins of Uxmal. Don Simón had been a gentleman of the Order of Calatrava, but when independence arrived, he was one of the members of the junta which proclaimed the Yucatán peninsula free from Spain.

Even though Yucatán was nominally a republic, attached to Mexico or not, as political caprice suggested, Don Simón still retained all the prerogatives of the aristocracy.

His dress was simple and elegant, his suede roundabout jacket had buttons of chased gold. Although he had not the slightest interest in Mayan antiquities, evidences of which were scattered everywhere on his great estates, he none the less recognized their importance in the history of the land and the people.

His excellency the Governor, Don Santiago Méndez, had read of Stephens's travels in the papers and was honored to welcome him again to Yucatán.

Although he did not now come in any diplomatic capacity, the Governor informed him that his search for the horizons of the Yucatán's ancient history assured him of every consideration within his country.

Learned, facile, and gracious, Don Santiago was about forty years old, although his tall, thin body, and somewhat cadaverous appearance, suggested a more advanced age.

Later in life, influenced by the renaissance of Maya interest created by Stephens' writings, he was to write a book on the customs of the Maya Indians.

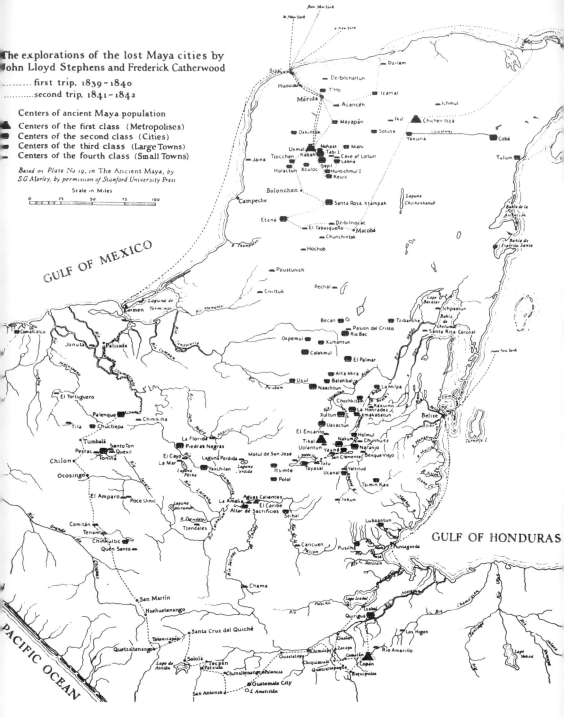

48. *Maya explorations of Stephens and Catherwood.*

At present his head rested uneasily on his political shoulders, for he had proclaimed Yucatán a separate republic in 1840, and Yucatán was now seeking political union with Texas. For his audacity Méndez expected an attack on Yucatán by Mexican troops under the command of Antonio López de Santa Ana.

In fact Méndez was to survive Santa Ana's attacks as well as the War of the Castes that was to break out in 1846 (when Indians, stung by three centuries of ill treatment, rose in successful revolt) and die in the place of his birth.

Stephens was not in the least deterred by the political situation. They were going into an unknown land, a region almost entirely devoid of white population; into an ancient land, where the natives were making their first mutterings of revolt. They loaded their brace of pistols, tied their baggage to pack animals loaned by Don Simón, received from Doña Micaela an *abrazo* and a large manuscript map of Yucatán, and prepared to set off in a blazing sun into the scrub jungle of the interior. To complete the idyll, their landlady refused to accept money from them.

'The pleasure of your society,' she said, 'was compensation enough.' Between friends house rent was not to be thought of.

'We shall never see her like again,' said Stephens.

Since they had been stopped at Uxmal on the last expedition by Catherwood's illness, they were to begin the new one from there.

The view of Uxmal, from the top of the House of the Magician, inspired a moment of great exhiliration

. . . richly ornamented without a bush to obstruct the view and in picturesque effect almost equal to the ruins of Thebes . . . on the Nile.

They had climbed the two hundred feet and there opened before them a vast panorama of flattened jungle. As far as the limits of the senses allowed, until the horizon was opaqued

49. *Panorama of Uxmal by W. H. Holmes in 1895.*

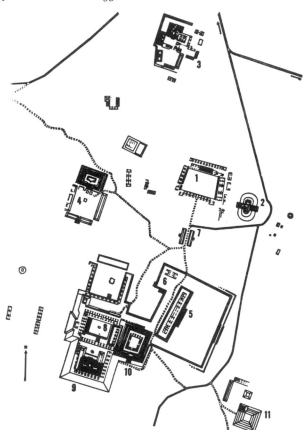

Modern Map of the Central Section of Uxmal

1 Nunnery Quadrangle	7 Ball Court
2 House of the Magician, or Dwarf	8 House of the Pigeons
3 North Group	(Casa de las Palomas)
4 Cemetery Group	9 South Group
5 Place of the Governors	10 Great Pyramid
(Casa del Gobernador)	11 House of the Old Woman
6 House of the Turtles	

50. *Modern map of Uxmal.*

by a purple haze, they could see the limestone land of Yucatán stretching out, tortilla-flat, mile upon flat mile. Not a river, not a stream, not even a rivulet broke the flatness of the land. Only below and immediately about them, was the eye relieved. Scattered over a two-mile-square area were stone buildings mounted on terraces completely faced with precisely cut stone, and still revealing something of their once elaborate façades; mounds, now amorphous and indistinct, that were once the meeting-places of the Maya people. This was Uxmal, built by a history-less people who once dominated the land.

All about them, under the sinking sun, the world seemed preternaturally quiet, as if nature wished to impress upon its visitors the dread monotony of space and time.

The House of the Magician, dominated by a magnificent doorway before which the travelers rested, was a truncated pyramid on which a rectangular building had been built. Stone stairways mounted its sides, leading into rooms, thick walled and windowless. The ornamental doorway, an allegorical mask, had for its mouth an open door, while about its sides, in an elaborate contrapuntal pattern, were other masks, symbols of the long-nosed god, Itzamna. It was wonderfully conceived. The broken surface of the decoration still bearing the violent polychromy of barbaric colors stood out dramatically from the unornamented limestone wall. In the moment of Maya greatness, it was without question, the most beautiful in the whole cultural realm.

From these heights one looked down upon a quadrangle about which lay the House of the Nuns, the Nunnery in short, so called by the padres because of the cell-like chambers of the architectural complex. The buildings, resting on an asymmetrical artificial terrace, turned their ornately carved façade inward to the enclosed court entered through a grand archway.

Each side differed in decoration. One, as decorative motif, had small models of Maya houses; on another side an entwined feathered serpent wound in and out of a frieze of ordered design; and in yet another, the masks of the rain god, the nose fantastically elongated, dominated the corners of its severely plain sides. No one knew the purpose of the building.

South of the Nunnery were the remains of the ball court, and beyond it, all but swallowed up in the scrub brush and raised on an earth podium, a rectangular building called the House of the Turtle from a decoration of turtles carved, unusually realistically, in the upper cornice. And far beyond this, enveloped in the blue haze of evening, were the hulks of two pyramids, truncated in the typical Maya style, topped by pinnacled buildings ruined beyond all form. Destroyed, too, was the building at their western base, the serrated nine-gabled roof comb, the House of the Doves, named in analogy by the perforations in the roof comb that recalled a dovecot.

It was the Palace of the Governor, the greatest building of Uxmal and perhaps the most impressive in the entire Maya area, that commanded most attention. It was a huge trapezoidal building, three hundred and twenty feet long by forty feet in width, covered in its entire length by a façade of exquisitely cut stone, so intricate in design that it was in fact a mosaic of some twenty thousand sculptured stones. The recessions and projections of the white stones were set, much like 'flecking' of the impressionists' canvases, so that the façade would be enlivened by the subtle play of light and shadow along its entire length. Seven hundred and twenty feet of gigantic counterpoint in sculptured stones! It is one of the greatest monuments the Indian has left in his walk across the American earth. The Palace of the Governor was doubtless meant for occupancy, since the length was pierced by nine doorways which led into rooms and two gateways that permitted egress into the alternate courtyards.

In its original state, the lintels of the doorway had been fashioned out of a single piece of *chicozapote* wood, hard and richly brown, carved with glyphs, until time, termites,

51. Doorway of the Temple of the Dwarf, Uxmal, as drawn by Catherwood.

fungus, and dry rot destroyed them. Their collapse left ragged arches above the doorways to mar an otherwise resplendent unbroken façade of carved stone.

None of these architectural features escaped the trained eyes of Catherwood. There were certain aspects of the buildings, technics of a civilization which he recognized as stemming from the same source as that which had reared other stone cities such as Palenque.

Uxmal had nothing of the massiveness of Copán. With its sculpture carved in full round, nor did it possess the lovely sculptured stuccoes they had found at Palenque. There were no monolithic stelae bearing glyphs. Still there were unmistakable features in the structures that proclaimed that the civilization that had reared all the others had also erected Uxmal.

They were to spend six weeks here, from 15 November until 1 January, six weeks of painstaking surveying, mapping, and drawing.

Stephens expanded in Uxmal. With the huge folio of

251

Cogolludo's *Historia de Yucatán* (loaned to him by William Prescott) under one arm and in the other hand a machete, he was raveling out the enigma of yet another mysterious ruin.

Uxmal, unlike the ruins of Copán and Palenque, was endowed with history. Fray Antonio de Ciudad Real, a priest of facile intelligence, had visited Uxmal in 1585 at the conquest's end, following vague rumors of a great city buried in the jungle. He thought Uxmal looked in the distance 'like a painting of Flanders.' He had written *Of the Very Renowned Edifices of Uxmal* in which in terms of unassuming modernity he had described the Temple of the Magician and its 'one hundred and fifty stone steps, which are very steep,' and all the other 'muls [sic] carved with wonderful delicacy.'

He saw and marked well the high lintels 'made of the wood of the *chicozapote* tree which is very strong and slow to decay', and noted too, that the glyphs had 'certain characters and letters which the Maya Indians used in olden times, carved with so great a dexterity as surely to excite admiration'.

But this information was not available to Stephens, for it was not yet rooted out of the Spanish archives where it was to lie for three hundred years, until 1875. Only when Stephens had set the character of the Maya Renaissance was it published.

The discoverer of Uxmal was born in 1551 in the city of his name in the province of La Mancha. He had been one of the youthful God-inspired frailes that had been sent to Yucatán at the discretion of Bishop Diego de Landa. After the Bishop's death in 1582, Ciudad Real was elevated to commissioner general and secretary of the Franciscan order, in which exalted capacity he traveled much over the land of the Maya. As soon as he had familiarized himself with the Maya language, he began a compilation which he called *Calepino*, six volumes of linguistics, history and ethnology with variations on a theme of Jehovah.

Before his death, in 1617, he had written a *Brief Relation,* in which, among theological excursions, Uxmal was examined in some detail. He found, in the ancient rooms of fetid smell, murals of naked Indians dressed in ancient Yucatán huilpils, 'by which,' the padre wrote, 'it is shown that these buildings were built by the Indians.' 'The Indians,' said Ciudad Real, 'know that it was more than nine hundred years since the buildings were built.'

He consulted the Popul histories of the Chilam Balm Maya. So he knew! For the original Uxmal had been built sometime in the seventh century, which (since Ciudad Real was writing in the sixteenth century) made the Indian's time estimate of Uxmal's foundation a most remarkable coincidence, for Uxmal, which means 'thrice built,' had begun to lay its foundation at the very century that disaster was overtaking the Maya 'Old Empire.'

Stephens' excursus into history had the object of finding 'who were the people who built these ruins.' Uxmal for the first time provided him with proof, real proof, that the buildings were erected by the people inhabiting Yucatán at the time of the conquest.

Although he knew nothing of Padre Ciudad Real, he looked about in the archives of the villages and discovered a Spanish transcript of the Books of Chilam Balam, verbal Maya histories recited to a Maya-Spanish amanuensis in the sixteenth century. There he learned that 'on the Tenth ahau

52. *Catherwood's general view of the House of Nuns and the Temple of the Dwarf, Uxmal.*

Ah Zuitok Tutwl Xiu founded Uxmal.' He found at Maní 'a large volume which had an ancient and venerable appearance being bound in parchment, tattered and worm-eaten, having a flap to close like that of a pocket-book,' written in Maya, dated 1556. He had it translated to him by a Maya-speaking padre, and again had confirmation that Uxmal was part of modern Indian tradition. Later Stephens discovered an Indian map at Maní. Drawn in 1557, Uxmal appears therein, not as a drawing of a church, but in the unmistakable symbol as one of the Maya ruins.* Stephens also dug into the title deeds of Don Simón Peón – 'a formidable pile compared with which the papers in a protracted chancery or ejectment would seem a *billet doux.*'

Sometime after A.D. 900 it is presumed that all Maya activity was centered in the northern tip of Yucatán. Chichén Itzá had first been built in the fifth century. It was reoccupied in approximately A.D. 987, since the Maya found two huge-mouthed, sixty-foot-deep *cenotes:* an inexhaustible water supply. Southward other cities were rising in splendor: Kabah, Labná, Sayil, Izamal, Uxmal – wherever, in fact, a *cenote* was found, a religious center arose in the scrub jungle.

For two centuries, the Lords of Chichén Itzá ruled this new cultural empire. Trade, an essential part of the cultural growth, was under their dominance; large canoes, carrying the manufactures of their realms, set out southward beyond Honduras on trading expeditions. Indian slaves, smothered under mounds of produce, proceeded into interior Mexico.

Chichén Itzá levied tribute. It set calendaric festive days. As the religious center it rose to Old Empire splendor.

Then on the horizon of the Maya came competition.

*Uxmal, A.D. 900, lies in the Puuc of Yucatán, a range of low hills, rolling limestone ridges, with alternate pockets of soil. It is not only the most uniform of Maya cities; it is also the most beautiful. Moreover, it is quite probable that 'Uxmal' is what it was called .by the Maya themselves. It has a history, written, recitative, traditional. Uxmal was part of the League of Mayapán. It even has a date in the literature: 'In Katun 2 Ahau (A.D. 987) the Maya Lord Ah Suytok Tutul Xiu was established in Uxmal.'

The highland people of Mexico did not stand still, culturally or materially, while the Maya moved forward. Most of Mexico, broken up into tribes or confederations of loosely strung temporary alliances was building, expanding, and learning to dominate nature.

Most of interior and coastal Mexico was spotted with religious centers, built with the same precision although not with the artistic mastery of the Maya.

Gradually, through trade and contact, all facets of Middle American culture were becoming common currency. Although indirect, contact had been made with the people of South America, and metal, in the form of weapons of bronze and artifacts of gold, was dribbling in along the long narrow neck of the Isthmus.

In Padre Cogolludo's *Historia de Yucatan*,* that thick folio of foxed pages, Stephens read that he had visited Uxmal while it was still

> Smirched with offerings of cacao, and marks of copal, which is their incense, burned but a short time before, an evidence of some superstition or idolatry recently committed although we could not find out anything about it among all of us who were there.

So Stephens asked himself rhetorically: 'What was Uxmal?' It was 'clearly beyond all question' an ancient city built by the Indians who were in Yucatán at the time of the arrival of the Spaniards, who frequented it, long after the conquest, to pay homage to their ancient gods. Neither Roman, Greek, Jew, Carthaginian, or Egyptian built these cities: they were built by the American Indian.

---

*Diego López de Cogolludo, a missionary, worked in Yucatán during the latter part of the seventeenth century. His *Historia de Yucathan* (Madrid 1688) gave much attention to the Maya culture, especially to religion. A critical edition of Cogolludo did not appear until 1867, the manuscript of Diego de Landa's *Things of Yucatán* was not discovered until 1864 so that the 'Cogulludo' published in 1688 seems to have been Stephens' only source of contemporary history.

Stephens did not yet fully grasp the connection between Uxmal, in Yucatán, Copán in Honduras, and Palenque in Mexico, except that the structures were built of stone. But there was then one obvious link – the glyphs. The mysterious ideographs that filled the stones at Copán, that he had seen in the awesome grandeur of Palenque, he also found at Uxmal. Even though he could not read them, there was no doubt that they were the same pebble-shaped glyphs ('the general character is the same'). In the extreme northeast chamber of the Governor's Palace they discovered a wooden lintel, carved with glyphs, which 'so far as we could understand them were similar to those of Copán and Palenque.' In the whole ruins of Uxmal here was the 'one definite point of resemblance.' They found the lintel in the darkened corner of the room where Count Waldeck had hidden it in 1836 and Stephens resolved to preserve this beam and take it back to New York.

Even then, before they determined by architectural analogy the homogeneity of the cultures they had discovered, to Stephens and Catherwood, Uxmal was related to the other ruins they had found.

Residing in the sumptuous Governor's Palace, they were miserable, hungry men. until the arrival of Chaipa Chi. She had been promised to them by her patrón, the owner of Uxmal, as one of the ways out of their impasse, since food meant mainly the maize corn-bread tortilla which only a woman could prepare. The boy who had been assigned to them could speak no Spanish, they no Maya; moreover he could not cook.

Their conquest of the Maya could not begin until Chaipa Chi arrived.

They saw her coming through the brush, 'with a small boy as her dueño.' Dark-skinned, ample-rumped and bosomed, she had the profile of a thousand stone Maya portraits, hook-nosed, slanting forehead, dark almond-shaped eyes. She came up the steps, carrying her clothes on her head, nodded a greeting to them – for she spoke little Spanish – and retired to a makeshift kitchen. From then on they were in her hands.

As they lived in it and it was close at hand, the Governor's Palace was the first to feel the measuring rod of scientific accuracy.* They had spent some days making a map of the ruins (a work impaired by the thick scrub jungles and the distractions caused by Dr Cabot, who, at the precise moment of reading, would drop the surveyor's tape to take off after a bird).

Once the survey was finished, they could turn to the Palace. Catherwood seemed the most content of the explorers for he was at least in his element. At night, by the flickering lights of candles, he worked upon the Uxmal map, while during the day, as Stephens and Cabot cleared the other buildings, he limned the Palace.

He began by making a panoramic drawing, done to scale, of the front of the building. (When it appeared in Stephens' books, it was engraved so as to extend beyond the book format.) In this, his past experience with panoramas had come to his aid. He made detailed drawings of the whole building, supplemented by daguerreotype views, and soon he had in his possession 'the architectural materials for erecting a building exactly like it.' He sketched the stone tracery of the façades, made a floor plan of the building and measured the walls, performing incredible feats of architectural labor.

As an architect he recognized that the massiveness of the construction was necessitated by the lack of knowledge of thrusts, strains, and stresses. He marveled that while their priests could calculate the advent of equinoxes, solstices, and eclipses, and invent a complicated hieroglyphic language,

*The Governor's Palace at Uxmal is considered to be 'the most magnificent single building ever erected on the Americas in pre-Columbian times'. It was in all probability the official residence of the ruler (of Toltec antecedents) who built the city. The Maya chronicles have it that in Katun 2 Ahua (A.D. 987) Uxmal was one of the three that formed the League of Mayapán.

53. *Catherwood's drawing of the Governor's Palace, Uxmal.*

the Maya had been unable by some architectural blind spot to conceive the wheel or the principle of the arch. It was not their inability to use a keystone that would co-equally divide the stress that made the Maya fall back on massive walls. These were tapered into an inverted V of stone, making it almost impossible to construct rooms of any great size.

Eventually the pressure of the walls and the overhead roof combs, weighted down by the great mass of rubble, pushed in the roofs, yet left intact the wonderfully conceived friezes of cut stone: 'a sculptured mosaic,' Stephens called it, 'ornaments, I have no doubt, with a symbolical meaning – each stone a part of history, allegory and fable.'

After the Palace they went to work on the House of the Turtles, a rectangular box-like building lying to the right of the Palace on an earth-stone podium. Then after the Turtle House, the Nunnery. By the time this building was reached, Stephens, with the aid of Cabot and a fifteen-year-old squint-eyed Maya boy called Bernaldo had cleared much of the ruins for Catherwood's inspired brush.

While Catherwood worked, Stephens rode off to the fair at Jalacho and discovered more ruins, including the site of Maxcanú.

Don Simón Peón, the liege of Uxmal, then paid them a visit, attired in tight-fitting buckskin breeches ornamented with silver lace.

He had a practical view of the ruins of Uxmal and dilated on them at some length, bidding them picture the immense fortune one might have if these ruins were situated on the banks of the Mississippi by selling the sculptured stone blocks for paving the streets of New Orleans!

Don Simón did not long remain at Uxmal. The Maya ruins had an unhealthy reputation, especially in the rainy season when all the dry *aguadas* were filled with noisome water and the air hummed with mosquitoes.

Dr Cabot, to preserve their health, had suggested the burning of fires in the Palacio, hoping to kill the 'malaria'

54. *The Governor's Palace, Uxmal, modern view.*

within the ancient stone walls, for the fever was thought then to be just that, *malaria* – bad air – fetid humors that seeped up from the earth. They took the precaution of sleeping under fine-netted *pabellones* to save themselves sleepless nights.

But these precautions fell short. During their third week at Uxmal, Stephens was visited by the old enemy. It did not come at him in the open, with lowered lance, to do battle on honorable grounds, but moved with stealth, carried in the long probosces of the night-loving mosquitoes; it insinuated into his blood stream 'millions of malarial parasites.' There was no warning of its presence until his teeth shook and he grew pale and cadaverous.

That night Stephens' body was on fire and his blood boiled. In the morning the fever subsided and he quaffed quantities of water. Then came the great cold – the second phase of malaria. Stephens shivered violently even though Chaipa Chi took off her shawl and added it to the heap of clothes piled upon him. At that moment, like the presage of death, a tall thin priest, in the habit of a Franciscano, walked slowly into the Governor's Palace.

The *cura* of Ticul, a village midway between Uxmal and Mayapán, was paying his promised visit. He was mortified to find his host, the temporary liege of Uxmal, suffering from *calentura*, and immediately administered a simple concoction of sour orange juice flavoured with cinnamon and lemon juice to allay Stephens' great thirst.

Fray Estanislao Carrillo was worthy of his cloth, a man of rare integrity of soul, beloved equally by slave and master. He still wore the frayed blue habit of the Franciscano with its huge cross for he had refused to abandon it even though in the time of social revolution it was not considered physically safe to wear it. For many years he had interested himself in the Maya, and was eventually to write several important historical papers on the ruins of Nohpat.

As curate of the village of Ticul, he had transformed it

into a small oasis of prosperity in a desert of indifference. But now at forty-three years of age, this ascetic life had taken its toll; his brilliant eyes lay sunken in his head and his habit hung loosely on his thin frame.

Padre Carrillo was all kindness. He insisted that Stephens must leave the *Palacio* and return with him to his convent at Ticul where he could nurse him back to health, and when Stephens weakly objected, he raised a long, bony hand and worked his index finger back and forth like the ticking of the pendulum of fate. Stephens was hypnotized by that moving finger and made no further remonstrance as the padre issued an order in Maya to his Indian retainers, and they quickly ran down the tumbled steps of the *Palacio*, eager to comply with his wishes.

As they waited for a palanqyin to be built to convey Stephens to Ticul, the padre told his story. He had been born in 1798 in the village of Teabo in Yucatán. There he received elemental instruction. At ten years of age he decided to join the priesthood and attempt to alleviate the sufferings of the Indians. In 1823 he entered the Franciscan Order. After the destruction of the convent of Mérida and the scattering of the Order, friends tried in vain to have him secularize. He refused. Now he resided in Ticul on the $40.00 a month allowed him by the Order to live on and extend hospitality to strangers.

Unusually active in mind and body, without affectation, he had, fortunately for science – and for Mr Stephens' reputation – interested himself in the antiquities of the country. Stephens owed him much, as he fully acknowledged in his book.

Three days in the cool gardens of Ticul with warm infusions of the cinnamon-orange-lemon concoction had worked wonders. Quinine was not then used in Central America, nor was it known as a malaria specific; when fevered, one merely rested, waiting for the fever to abate, as it did in time, when the malarial germs took temporary refuge in the spleen, ready, at the moment of bodily exhaustion, to swarm out again into the main blood stream. On the third day, Stephens was taking his first stroll in the garden, when an Indian ran into the monastery and, between violent pantings, told them that another *inglés* had taken the fever.

They found Dr Cabot on the convent floor. His eyes, staring out of their sockets, were wild with fever; his face was flushed brick red, and even his sturdy body seemed to have dehydrated.

He did not recognize Stephens. Too weak to stand, he was crawling about like a wounded animal, and when Stephens weakly leaned over to pick him up, they fell together in a twisted pile of fevering legs and arms.

On the third day, out of hearing of Cabot, the padre told Stephens, in a hoarse whisper, that the expression of the young doctor's face was *fatal*. In Spanish, this meant 'unfortunate' but to Stephens the word 'fatal' conjured up a terrible picture.

The next day Albino, their newly acquired retainer, appeared – also with the *paludismo*. He had become so pallid that his swarthy-bronze skin seemed depigmentized.

Catherwood was now the only survivor of the expedition and held the ruins alone with only the ceaseless *tortilla*-slapping of the wordless Chaipa Chi to break the silence.

A very heroic figure in the annals of American archaeology this Frederick Catherwood. For two years he had endured revolution, sickness, and the bites of thousands of insects; malarial fevers, bad food, sleepless nights – during all the time, without cease, copying with amazing fidelity and with charming composition the ruins of the Maya culture. Now, once again alone, he kept at his drawing, spending days tracing out the intricate stone sculptured frieze of the House of the Nuns.

But as the sun entered Capricorn, the malignant influences of Uxmal were working on Catherwood. On New Year's

Day, 1842, after six weeks of demoniac activity, he finished his work and was carried, in delirium, from the ruins.

It was at Kabah that Albino, their Maya-speaking guide, first exhibited his worth. Ever since he had entered their service at the suggestion of Doña Jacquina Peón, Albino had done little expediting, since he, like the more vulnerable white men, was constantly under siege of 'that devil malaria.' An amiable cut-throat, Albino was a blacksmith by trade, and soldier by avocation. He had been at the siege of Campeche, where he had received a saber-cut on his brown rump, 'which,' said the observant Stephens, 'rather intimated that he was moving in an opposite direction when the saber overtook him.'

Albino's army career ended abruptly. Having received neither salary nor pension for his services, he renounced the army and entered the employ of Señor Stephens.

A thick-set, dark-skinned man with lustrous, amorous eyes, he was an important adjunct to the expedition. His broad-bladed machete had cut down the scrub jungle around the ruins of Nohpat, where they found a frieze of skulls and crossbones; he had chopped down the trees that hid the ruins of Xcoch, revealing a huge pyramid, and so he went from new ruin to new ruin until he was finally affected by the same enthusiasms as the archaeological explorers.

He soon found it an exciting game.

Kabah, which lay only a few miles from Uxmal, just outside of the modern village of Nohcacab, had been discovered by Stephens' reconnaissance even while Catherwood was finishing his work on the previous ruin.

Its discovery also revealed the latent talents of Albino, for he knew how to handle the natives, being, as Stephens noted, removed from the Indians only by a tiny rivulet of 'white' chromosomes (externally shown in his fierce *mustachios*).

Stephens had desperate need of Albino's diplomacy, for

55. *The masked façade from Kabah.*

56. *Stephens at the ruins of Kabah.*

their arrival at Nohcacab, where the pure Indian populace had never before seen strangers, was as sensational as would have been the return of Kulkulkan.

The Indians poured out like ants from their wattel-and-daub houses, followed the mule train to the convent, where, crowded into the patio, they chattered in excited Maya sibilants, pointing to the tripods, sextants, camera lucidas, and the mysterious black-boxed daguerreotype.

Rumor, skimming over Yucatán, had already told the people of Nohcacab that there were loose in the land men who 'cured the squint-eye,' who captured the visible souls of people in a black box, and, who, in a final madness, searched for stone cities in the jungle.

Albino applied himself at once to dissipating these diabolical illusions, for not only were their very lives in danger so long as these ideas persisted but, as the Indians were the only source of labor, the proposed excavation of Kabah was in the balance.

'Great-place-of-good-land' had lived up to its name, the *milpas* annually yielded several corn crops, and, swollen by food and giving themselves over to the pleasant madness of rutting, the Indians were not at all tempted to work.

Albino therefore applied himself. He managed to acquire Indians with mattock and crowbar who filed out to the ruins every morning, there to do the bidding of these white-skinned madmen who cured the squint-eye.

Kabah was now the new word. Gone from the travelers' vocabulary were Palenque, Copán, and Uxmal, for at Kabah they discovered a site whose very existence, even in Yucatán, had been unknown.

Stephens took as much delight in his new ruin as if it were the first that they had discovered.

An important religious center in the tenth century (to judge by the number of its monuments) Kabah was part of the tri-citied League of Mayapán. It had been connected, at the height of the League's power, by a road to Uxmal over which runners once carried messages – and over which commerce and people alike flowed.

It extended over a vast area. Where cattle cropped the sparse herbage, great buildings had once stood; remains were still to be seen of immense terraces, a triumphal arch, stately palaces, and pyramids, badly ruined and mutilated by man and time alike, yet still preserving enough of their grandeur to quicken the pulse of the discoverers.

Combined operations of axe and machete soon cleared most of the tan structures of vegetation and this allowed full sight of the buildings.

The first, which Stephens described as *Palacio 1*, was a one-hundred-and-fifty-foot-long structure; unusual, even in Yucatán, for the ornamentation of its façade – entirely constructed of 'horridly smirking stone masks' – an ornamentation so elaborate that the architecture entirely disappeared under it.

There were six tiers of open-mouthed stone masks revealing a rounded object which was the conventionalized tongue. It was a bold and daring conception.

Equally ingenious was the stone molding, conceived so that the chiaroscuro of the Maya day could enliven the whole fantastic stone mosaic. Stephens was deeply impressed by this pattern:

> . . . The cornice running over the doorways . . . tried by the severest rules of art recognized among us, would embellish the architecture of any known era, and, amongst a mass of barbarism, of rude and uncouth conceptions, it stands as an offering by American builders worthy of the acceptance of polished people.

Kabah, which was joined to Uxmal with a causeway, lies nine miles south-west of Uxmal. As it now stands it seems to consist of three groups of buildings, still only partially restored, but since the whole area had the greatest population density in the Puuc it is fully possible that further exploration will reveal more structures.

Kabah is dated A.D. 879 from the two stone doorjambs which Stephens carried to New York.

The scalloped zigzag design that flows around the Temple of the Masks so impressed Catherwood that he had it stamped on the binding of the *Yucatán*. The same design was repeated by Pal Kelemen in his *Medieval American Art*, New York, 1940, as 'a homage to these pioneer explorers.'

Kabah yielded other archaeological surprises. They discovered a solitary monument, a form of triumphal arch, which Catherwood pictured.

Stephens thought it something like 'the proud memorial of a Roman triumph.'

Latter-day archaeologists politely smirked at this monument because they could not find it. It is now known to be very real. It was rediscovered in 1941, just as Catherwood had drawn it.

They found more carved lintels in sapote wood such as they had found in Uxmal, and superbly worked wood panels, a great rarity in Yucatán.

At Kabah, too, they had further proof of the Maya architectural unity (whether found in Honduras, Guatemala, Mexico, Yucatán). There was for example a striking resemblance in details between the figures and ornaments of Palenque and those at Kabah. They found again the mysterious enigmatical glyphs carved now on wooden lintels. They found, in three sections, a beautifully conceived figure carved on sapote wood, ornamented by a headdress of quetzal plumes.

So unusual was the subject that Catherwood – fortunately for archaeology – drew the carving. Fortunate since it was one of the objects burned in the calamitous fire that destroyed his Panorama.

Another singular architectural feature at Kabah was the

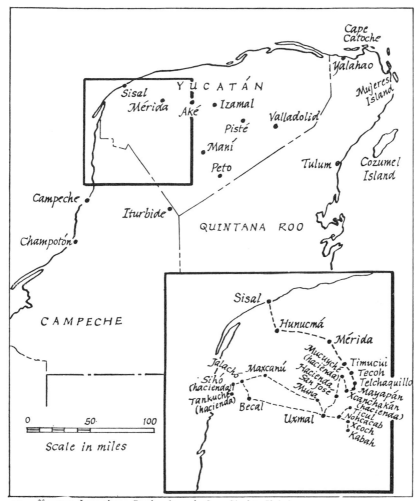

Map labels:
Cape Catoche
Yalahao
Mujeres Island
Sisal
Mérida
Aké
YUCATÁN
Izamal
Valladolid
Pisté
Maní
Peto
Tulum
Cozumel Island
Campeche
Iturbide
QUINTANA ROO
Champotón
CAMPECHE
Sisal
Hunucmá
Mérida
Mucuyché (hacienda)
Timucui
Tecoh
Telchaquillo
Mayapán
Xcanchakán (hacienda)
Jalacho
Maxcanú
Hacienda San José
Sihó (hacienda)
Muna
Tankuché (hacienda)
Becal
Uxmal
Nohcacab
Xcoch
Kabah
0   50   100
Scale in miles

57.   *Yucatan. Inset shows Stephens' travels from Sisal to Kabah.*

carved stone door jambs which Stephens found in the structures on the grand terrace at the south end of the site.

The slabs, six feet high by two feet in width, were delicately
carved in low relief out of a pinkish-grey limestone representing
a curious allegory: a kneeling figure holding a mask, dominated by a warrior priest enveloped in headgear out of which
carved quetzal feathers seemed to flow in rhythm.

Stephens decided then and there that these slabs should
form the base of his projected Museum of American Antiquities. Accordingly the five-hundred pound monolith slabs

were lowered from their niche in the palace, wrapped in grass and straw, and under the supervision of Albino removed for shipment.

By running a long tree trunk along the stone and tying it to the limb by means of strong lianas, Indians in relays laboriously carried it to the coast.

Catherwood remembered the incident when years later he published his famous lithographic *Views*; Stephens in full beard and short blue jacket is seen directing the removal.*

After Kabah, the explorers traveled light.

Catherwood was mounted on a horse of so placid a disposition that he could sketch without dismounting, Dr Cabot rode an ugly-headed sorrel of so lethargic a spirit that he could discharge his shotgun without its registering more than a flick of its ears.

Stephens drew a trotter. Even Albino traveled like a

---

*These Maya sculptures had a singular odyssey. Arriving in New York they were to have been exhibited at Catherwood's Panorama. They came too late. The rotunda had burned down and with it all the other specimens of Maya art collected so laboriously in Yucatán.

So Stephens gave the stones to his friend, John Church Cruger, who carried them by steamboat to his estate, Cruger's Island, on the Hudson near Tarrytown. There he had built, under the influence of the 'romantic agony,' a moldering cuspidated wall, constructed to simulate a ruin, surrounded with a glade of trees, so as to weave a texture of mystery and romance. Here in the wall he embedded the 'Stephens stones,' and there they were seen by the Swedish traveler, Frederick Bremer, in 1884:

> On a point projecting into the river a ruin has been built in which are placed various figures and fragments of walls and columns discovered in Central America. . . . This ruin and its ornaments in the midst of a wild romantic rocky and wooden promontory was designed in the best taste.

Perhaps, but hardly the place envisioned by Stephens for his Museum of American Antiquities.

In 1918 Stephens's wish came true – posthumously: Dr S. G. Morley, the great Maya scholar, pondering the disappearance of the 'Stephens stones,' read the travels of Frederick Bremer, visited Cruger's Island and found, still embedded in the 'romantic wall', the slabs of Kabah along with other Maya sculptures.

The octogenarian daughter of John Cruger, 'who remembered Stephens patting her head when she was a little girl', agreed to their removal. For $10,000 the American Museum of Natural History purchased the 'Stephens stones,' and they formed – as they were originally intended to form – the nucleus of a Maya exhibit now to be seen in the Middle American Hall at that Museum.

caballero, as the word suggests, mounted; he put his cicatrized rump in a wooden saddle.

Little Bernaldo walked for after all someone had to retrieve Cabot's birds. The only pack animal carried the daguerreotype and the mosquito nets and hammocks. This strange procession traveling south-east, 'moving toward Campeche,' was to perform an archaeological reconnaissance never matched in daring. For revolution troubled the land. Indians were stirring from serfdom and the authorities were bringing reprisal.

The creative sun as they rode across the land, was a great molten ball burning its way through the first days of February.

This was the transitional time between wet and dry periods. The sky, sometimes blackened by rain-bearing clouds, heralded the preludes of the other season. The flatness of the Yucatán plain was now broken by limestone reefs and depressions over the undulating ground.

They were passing through the section called a *dzekel*, 'a place abounding with loose rock,' a well-drained calcareous land with pockets of deep, heavy, waxy clay.

They rode through the groves of *ramón*, a mulberry with small yellow berries shaped like miniature oranges, that were fed to mules in absence of other forage.

These trees alternated with the spiked pads of the agave, for in the Yucatán, the immortal maguey of the Aztecs yielded its tough grey fibres for a hundred uses.

In the straggling village they met with *ceibas*, the Maya's 'god trees', thick trunked and hugely buttressed trees whose shadows offered the traveler cooling succor from an oven-hot day.

In appearance and purpose, the native houses, oval-shaped, constructed of reddish clay over a wattle of branches, and roofed with palm leaves, were as unchanging as the landscape, for in the time of Diego de Landa, of immortal memory.

271

58. *Oval modern Maya house.*

59. *Maya house sculpted in a frieze at Uxmal.*

They built their houses . . . covered with palm leaves and they have steep slopes so that the rain may not penetrate. Then they build a wall in the middle dividing the house lengthwise . . . half of which they call the back of the house, where they have their beds.

It was the same form of 'thatched house' structure that the sculptor-architect had used as a decorative motif in the frieze ornamentation at the Nunnery at Uxmal.

Around each house were planted bananas. There were also papayas, with acanthus-shaped leaves shading the melon-sized green fruit; sour-oranges and spined fruits of the chayote-vine.

These were their gardens. Basic food came from the *milpas* fashioned out of the scrub jungle which they burned in April and planted in May when the rains came, insinuating the corn grains into the reddish soil as their ancestors had done for centuries, with a fire-hardened, pointed stick. Beans used the growing corn as support, and between the rows of corn, later in the season, sweet potatoes and cassava, were cultured to add to a diet wholly vegetable. The land here in the Puuc was not a hard task-master. Modern agronomists have adequately demonstrated that 'even in the bleak-looking and thin-soiled north-east enough maize could be grown to support the average Maya family of five with only forty-eight annual man-days of labor.'

In every house there was the incessant patting of the *tortilla* maker. It was a sound above all else heard over the land, as the Indian women molded the lime-swollen corn grains, into greyish dough which became rounded corn cakes of the size and symmetry of a stove lid. These were put to bake on the hot *cumal*.

Stephens liked the sound. It brought visions of food, and the travelers were almost always hungry. It evoked visions of women bent over the stone *metate*, furiously kneading the corn mass, while within their loose-fitting huilpils their breasts kept time in fearful agitation.

They passed from village to village, from ruin to ruin, until they came upon Sayil (Stephens wrote it as 'Zayi'), another site once bound to the League of Mayapán.

Here they found a palace of three beautifully proportioned and ornamented stories, graced by a broad thirty-two-foot grand staircase, leading up from terrace to terrace.

Then not far distant they found another ruin at Zabacché, smothered by flowering plants which grew out of tumbled stone walls.

Later still, when they passed beyond the checkered *milpas* of a village they discovered another ruined city, which too, had once been in the order of Mayapán. This was Labná.*

Labná, famous for its arched gateway, was a city contemporary with Kabah and Sayil and like them to be

*Labná (A.D. 869) which was one of the constellation of cities about Uxmal, is only six miles from Kabah. Its architecture is characteristic of the Puuc. But Labná lacks architectural continuity and one feels that the project was larger than the labor supply and that the buildings grew by accretion; many structures were left unfinished. There are only two known dates from Labná. One of these, A.D. 869, is carved on the elongated proboscis of the god Chac.

60. *The Temple of Zabacché from an engraving by Catherwood.*

61. *The ruins of Xlah-pak between Sayil and Labná.*

62. *Façade of the principal temple at Sayil.*

converted into a necropolis even before the white man appeared to spread his tale of doom. It had a spreading, complex of buildings.

At 'the Palace' neatly cut columns set off the doorways, along with serpent motifs, incised rosettes, and frets in relief with human heads emerging from the opened jaws of alligators.

The building, set off by the russet-colored hills behind it, rested on a stone podium, and rose to several stories. It spread its length over four hundred feet of the scored land.

The façade still held fragments of its stucco figures and exhibited some of the vivid colors with which it had been painted.

Stephens wrote:

> If a solitary traveler from the Old World could by some strange accident have visited this aboriginal city when it was yet perfect his account would have seemed more fanciful than any in Eastern story, and been considered a subject from the Arabian Night's Entertainments.

As they rode southward toward the Campeche border, they discovered, in a single month, a dozen more ruined cities: Kivik which reflected the influence of Mayapán, and Chunhuhu with its single-storied building, and Champón where, in the overcast of an approaching storm riven by flashing lightning, Catherwood drew, with the dramatic overtones of a Piranesi, a ruined temple, even while before his eyes, a deer with blood-frothed tongue was set upon by ravenous dogs.

Reaching the village of Iturbide they found 'the grandest structure that now rears its ruined head in the forests of Yucatán,' the elaborate three-storied edifice of Santa Rosa Xtampak which Stephens called simply 'Lab-pahk.'

In many rooms of the ruined building, where roots had broken through the interstices, the walls still held the polychromy of its murals, which reminded Stephens of those he had seen on Egyptian tombs. About the ruins, the natives had leveled the forest to grow tobacco, and the rooms of Xtampak were reduced to housing drying tobacco. Xtampak would have been easier to draw than all the previous sites, since it was open and free of the entangling web of the jungle, but it was not to be.

For Catherwood fell ill again. He had collapsed the week before, and Stephens had found him lying in the road, Albino by his side, 'with the ague upon him,' cold and pallid, wrapped in all the clothing he could find, including the stinking saddlecloths of the horses.

Carried to a convent, Catherwood took the simples offered him by Dr Cabot, yet resolutely refused to allow his fever to abate before he was up again. But he no longer

63. *Catherwood's drawing of the Gateway at Labná.*

could bear the sun's glare and while he worked, the patient Bernaldo held a sunshade over him.

Worse, Catherwood's personality had undergone a change. Always of a retiring nature, never given to impassioned colloquy except when enraptured by a superb piece of architecture, Catherwood had grown moody and querulous.

So came the serious quarrel with Dr Cabot, himself unwell.* It had developed over a knife, for news had come that an Indian had crushed his entire hand in the toothed jaws of a cane-crusher, and Cabot, always giving generously of his skill to whosoever asked it, thought an amputation necessary.

He then discovered that he had left his own amputating instruments behind, and the only knife available was Catherwood's spring knife, Paris-made, of admirable temper, which Cabot proposed to hone down to lance thinness.

Catherwood, who had acquired the knife twenty years before when he was in Rome, would not hear of it being converted into a surgical instrument.

The argument developed fiercely and for a while was serious enough almost to break up the expedition.

Even when the moment passed, with Catherwood refusing to sacrifice his knife to save the Indian's hand, the tenseness between them did not relax.

Then at the ruins of Santa Rosa Xtampak, Catherwood became ill again. Stephens suggested that they break up the expedition, but Catherwood, in a surprisingly firm tone, would have nothing of it. They must go on.

While Cabot and Catherwood were beset by malaria and sought to regain their strength, Stephens 'determined at once to change the scene,' and set off for the festival at Ticul 'with only a sheet, hammock, and Albino.'

Music was already filling the air about the small plaza,

*A similar incident arose between Catherwood and Joseph Bonomi, the English artist, who was with him in Palestine in 1835. In his unpublished diary Bonomi wrote: 'I had a row with Cath . . . his conduct always appeared ungenerous and in some cases unjust . . . we propose to separate at Beirut.'

which, tastefully planted with hibiscus and palms, was ablaze with spluttering pine-wood light.

The dance of the mestizas had already begun in the plaza. The good-natured padre Carrillo was there, fully recovered from his attack of malaria, and the English-speaking member of the Peón family, Don Felipe.

They came up to Stephens, took his hand, and led him to a chair where he could see the dancers.

> After a month in Indian ranchos, toiling among ruins, driven to distraction by *garrapatas* clambering over a frightful sierra . . . I settled down to a fancy ball amid music, light, and pretty women in the full enjoyment of an armchair and cigar. For the moment a shade of regret came over me as I thought of my invalid friends, but I soon forgot them.

All that next morning, as he rode to the Wells of Bolonchen, Stephens thoughts were on the festival of the mestizas at Ticul, for an extraordinary thing had happened. Between the other nonarchaeological episodes of the fiesta, he had met a very unusual man. His name was Juan Pío Pérez, and he had journeyed all the way from Peto to see Stephens.

Before Stephens left, Pío Pérez pressed into his hands a manuscript copy, expressly prepared for him, of *Cronologia Antiqua Yucateca – The Ancient Chronology of Yucatán*. While he was a local administrative official at Peto, Pío Pérez had copied this from the ancient Maya chronicles, the Book of Chilam Balam.

The numeration of the Maya which he had worked out (extraordinarily carefully when one considers that he was on unknown ground), was the system of Maya chronology.

The Maya had a lunar, solar calendar based on twenty months of eighteen days each, with an extra five-day month called Uayeb (the 'five empty days of the Aztecs'), which made the 365-day year.

The leap year was calculated but not interpolated. The Maya starting point of creation was placed at 3300 B.C. (just as the mythical date of the Biblical creation was once set at 4004 B.C.). The Maya calculated their time sequences in an elaborate pattern of the face-glyphs which Stephens had found on stelae at Copán, on the sculptured stucco reliefs at Palenque, and on the carved wooden lintels of Kabah.

The outstanding feature of Maya science was the perfection of their calendar, combining day names, month names, and numbers figured from their mythical genesis, by which they were able to designate a particular day which could not be mistaken for any other day throughout thousands of years. This elaborate time-counting system, which went beyond the sterile accomplishment of day counting of tables of solar and lunar eclipses, was lost – or more accurately destroyed – by the Spanish conquerers.

The Maya 'Rosetta stone,' which was to assist in the deciphering of the Maya glyphs, still lay in the archives in Madrid; for the manuscript of Fray Diego de Landa was not to come to light until 1865.

John Lloyd Stephens took the studies of Pío Pérez out of unmerited obscurity, had them translated, and put them in his second publication on the Mayas. He did not know it then, but Stephens was himself supplying a piece of the Maya Rosetta stone.

Juan Pío Pérez, born in Mérida, of a Maya-speaking family, and of pure Spanish origin, was made official interpreter to the government.

After the revolution he was sent to Peto, in Central Yucatán, as administrator. There, and at the ancient Maya town of Maní (the last capital of the Maya after they fled Uxmal and where Diego de Landa burned many of the Maya documents and books), Juan Pío Pérez found in the town archives, an ancient painting on cloth along with other records written in Maya-Spanish script. These, dating from 1557, showed the titles which the Spaniards gave to the

Maya chiefs to replace their lost prerogatives. It proved unequivocally that it was the Mayas who had built the ruined buildings. When Pío Pérez fell into disfavor with the government at Mérida and was deprived of his sinecure at Peto, he remained at Maní, making the copies of these manuscripts, which eventually were placed in the hands of Stephens. They were to become the historical woof of the great tapestry of archaeological discovery. This small gentleman, Don Juan Pío Pérez, who spoke of his scholarship with a deprecating air, turned over all of his material to Stephens (it still exists in manuscript in the archives of the New York Historical Society), and Stephens honored him by having him elected to three important American scientific societies.

Although racked by a dry cough which seemed to tear him apart, Don Pío outlived both Stephens and Catherwood. Self-effacing to the last, he allowed most of his work – his Maya grammar, his *Cronología Antigua Yucateca* – to be used by others.

He finally coughed up his lungs in Mérida in 1858.*

Stephens' brain was still whirling with ancient astronomical systems when he rode into Bolonchen. He found to his great delight that both Dr Cabot and Catherwood were now 'free of the ague' and eager to continue their explorations.

They had heard of the mysterious underground wells of Bolonchen, and these were marked as next on their exploratory itinerary.

The mouths of the Wells of Bolonchen opened up in the small plaza of the village, a village of oval-shaped houses with

---

*Juan Pío Pérez (1798–1858) was the first to see the value of local genealogies as a clue to Maya history. Pérez believed, and time has proved him correct, that the so-called *Books of Chilam Balam* were survivals of Maya glyph-histories although written in European script. Stephens gauged their importance and Pérez wrote for him a *Cronología Antigua Yucateca* which was translated and used in *Incidents of Travel in Yucatán*. After Pérez's death in 1858 books written by him, e.g., *Diccionario de la Lengua Maya* (Merida, 1866–1877), continued to appear.

grass-thatched roofs. There were nine wells, hence, the name of the village: Bolon (nine), chen (wells).

Every afternoon Maya women of lithesome carriage, draped with black *revozos*, would come to the wells to draw water.

Here the newly gathered gossip was exchanged, so that water-drawing had, to these quiet, simple people, an important social as well as a life-giving function. All over Yucatán water was taken, as in Bolonchen, from cisterns.

Wrote Diego de Landa:

God provided Yucatán with many very nice sources of water. . . . Nature worked so differently in this country in the matter of rivers and springs which in all the rest of the world run on top of the land, that here in this country all run and flow through secret passages under it.*

And so it is. The fifty thousand square miles which is the Yucatán peninsula is one gigantic limestone shelf. This limestone is unable to retain water on its surface, and rain percolates through it to gather some fifty feet below the surface of the land.

During the dry season, while the land above is as dry as a desert, below, underground rivers rush to the sea.

What made human culture possible in Yucatán was the presence of these huge-mouthed, natural wells which here and there opened in yawning chasms, as Landa says:

On land God provided openings in the rock which the

Cenotes (Maya *dzonot*) was the only source of water in Yucatán. There are no rivers, no surface streams, and rain percolates through the porous limestone; water reaches the ocean by means of underground rivers. *Cenotes* are natural openings in the limestone (the one at Chichén Itzá is one hundred and fifty feet in diameter. Water, usually salubrious, is found sometimes on the surface at other times sixty feet below the land surface. Cole, Leon, L., *The Caverns and People of Northern Yucatán*, American Geographical Society, Bull. 42, New York, 1910.

Indians call cenotes which reach down to the water, through the cut in the living rock.

Around these natural *cenotes* or wells, Maya society first took root. Cities and religious centers were in fact hypothocated about such a well. And, as might be expected with water as the alpha and omega of Maya economy, it took on, naturally or supernaturally, a mystical flavor. Sacrifices were made periodically to the water gods; victims, jeweled and bedecked as befitting one's visitation to the gods, were hurled into the *cenotes*. They were expected to commune with the water god and return to the surface with a prophecy; for a community's rise or fall depended on the water supply.

Bolonchen was one of these ancient villages founded about a *cenote*. Once in the past it had had its great city, now it was ruined and covered with corn-milpas. The wells in the center of the village were active only eight months out of the year, the reasons for which were a complete mystery to the Indians. To supply themselves with water the other four months of the year, the Indians fell back on the most ancient of the wells which lay a half league from the village. It was these huge wells that Stephens and his friends – guided by fantastic rumors – had come to explore.

They came, with a large retinue of Indians, to the mouth of Bolonchen in the flush of a quiet dawn. On the edge of a rise of ground was a huge, gaping, jagged hole large enough to have swallowed the Astor House Hotel of Stephens time. The three, surrounded by a horde of torch-bearing natives, slipped off most of their clothing and followed the Indians down the steep ladder. Bats startled by the light fluttered by. It was close and hot. The sounds of their footsteps echoed deep down in the unseen bowels of the cavern. Paced by the Indians, they came to a second ladder, so steep they had to descend backwards; it was a hundred feet down. The lights below looked utterly unreal, like the flickering lights of lantern-bugs. The ladder, wide enough for twenty men to climb abreast, was without nails; every wooden traverse was bound with withes. Up these, Indians were climbing with water jugs strapped to their heads. At the bottom, the cavern was flooded with a lightshaft, which came from a hole directly overhead at a distance, revealed by the inquiring tape-measure of Catherwood, as two hundred and ten feet. The rock exuded tepid water from all its ramifications, and this formed rills at the bottom from which the villagers gathered their water during the dry season. It was a dramatic setting, 'the wildest that can be conceived,' said Stephens, 'men struggling up the huge ladder with earthen jars of water strapped to back and head, their sweating bodies glistening under the light of the pine-torches.' Catherwood could not resist drawing it. Using the back of Bernaldo as a drawing board he began to sketch, which became one of the finest illustrations of his portfolio. (See p. 288.)*

While Catherwood sketched the posterior of the wells of Bolonchen, Stephens, attended by Dr Cabot, followed another ramification. They were stripped to the skin. Albino, who carried the torch, could only be seen dimly by the white scar on his buttock. They followed a tortuous Sisyphus path, sliding down slippery ladders, going over downward. Cabot took the measurements of descent. They had reached a depth of four hundred and fifty feet and had come, according to Stephens' calculations, one thousand and four hundred feet from the mouth of the cavern. They passed the catch basin called Chac-ha 'red-water' – where they bathed – at another called Putz-ha, meaning that it ebbs and flows like the sea, for the Indians said in whispers 'it goes with the south wind, comes with the north.' Mystically-minded Indians moved silently here when seeking water, for if they made a noise, they whispered, the water disappeared – a legend Stephens promptly punctured by stripping and

*Bolonchen (*bolon*, 'nine', *chen*, 'wells') was the subject of one of Catherwood's watercolors which, when exhibitied in the National Academy of Design, was said to have the 'overtones of a Piranesi.' The original was discovered by the author. It is now in the collections of Yale University.

jumping into it. At each level was another catch basin, each with a specific name. These were the wells and the watery supplement of hell which supplied water to a community of seven thousand in the dry season.

It is strange that the Maya never solved the problem of water. The level of their engineering technics were far enough advanced to build stone-lined reservoirs. This the Maya had accomplished at the ruins of Tikal where at least ten reservoirs for potable water have been found. Doubtlessly they were the result of stone quarrying which were then cemented – for the stone is all porous limestone and water percolates down to the underground rivers.

In the Puuc area they also built reservoirs although time has obliterated the effort. They constructed small subterranean water reservoirs, which Stephens first discovered in the province of Maní. Here at Maní, where the topography of the land changes and where there are ranges of low hills, relatively heavily forested, were what the Mayas called the Puuc lands. Water gathers in the hollows during the rainy season and they are formed into aguadas, filled with blue water hyacinths and animated by the ghostly presence of white herons. Under these the Maya built narrow-throated water reservoirs, lined with mortared stone, twenty-five feet in depth, forming a sort of huge subterranean demijohn. Water was retained here when it evaporated elsewhere. Catherwood, who had extensive knowledge of the whole of Mediterranean archaeology, was astounded by this example of engineering knowledge. They searched for other subterranean passage in the immediate vicinity, finding over forty, which Catherwood stylized into five types and which he made into diagrammatic drawings. After that they quitted the wells of Bolonchen.

It was here that Stephens discovered the stone roads of Yucatán. He had, at first, discounted the rumor of stone roads built by Maya that connected their ancient cities, for one grows skeptical in the face of Spanish hyperbole, but

after discovery of the underground water-cisterns he was
ready to follow these, no matter how fantastic their suggestions. At the ruins of 'Sacbey' he discovered his first road,
'one of the most interesting monuments of ancient antiquity
in Yucatán,' he wrote, 'it is a broken platform of roadway of
stone eight feet wide . . . called by the Indians Sacbé'
(plurally, 'Sacbeob'). The Indians say it traversed the country
'from Kabah to Uxmal.' Then at Chemax, in central
Yucatán, the resident padre again observed the remains of
road 'running to the south-east to a limit that has not been
discovered, but some aver that it goes in the direction of
Chichén Itzá.'

It was not until a hundred years later that archaeologists
following Stephens turned their attention to these roads.
A Mexican archaeologist undertook a traverse of a stone
causeway, the Yuxuna-Cobá road,* and confirmed that
which was known to the early priest chroniclers, that the
cities of the Maya in Yucatán were bound together by well-
kept roads mysteriously winding their way through jungles
and swamps. Diego de Landa had seen them: 'there are
signs today of there having been a very beautiful road from
one (set of buildings in Izamal) to the other'; and Fray José
Degado had traveled over them in 1605: 'I followed roads
through the swamps which had been built in ancient times
and which were still well preserved'; but it was Stephens who
brought their existence to the attention of the modern world.
He believed that most of the cities had been linked by roads.
Investigation showed that causeways, wide enough for
several people to walk abreast, were built of stone filled with
rubble and cemented with white earth cement, called
'sacab' from which the name *sacbeob* ('white roads') was

*The Maya saché causeways (plural, *sacbeob*), which Stephens first explored,
still exist. Although only one of them (The Cobá Yuxuna causeway sixty-seven
miles in length) has been subject to formal study the evidence is mounting that
the Maya had causeways that connected all their important cities. Victor W.
Von Hagen, *The World of the Maya*, New York, 1960, pp. 179–190, and *The
Sunkingdoms of the Americas*, Paladin Books, London, 1973.

derived. As the Maya had no beasts of burden, the roads were built for pedestrians. Priests borne in palanquins passed from one province to another. Rest houses were erected at regular intervals along the road, and small reservoirs of water were built in the shadowed side of the highways. Stone markers guided the travelers. There were no roads in all Europe to compare in the same period with them. With the aid of the *sacbeobs* the Maya wove all their independent realms into a cultural and trade synthesis.

One of these great roads, in actuality, a *via sacra*, wormed its way across the jungle to the environs of the great city of Chichén Itzá. So following it, in part, where its stones still cumbered by the jungle, journeyed Messrs. Stephens, Cabot, and Catherwood on the Ides of March, 1842, and so ended their archaeological survey of the Puuc.

CHAPTER XV

The Wells of Itza

Stephens had heard about Tulum, a ruined city that could be seen by sea from Juan Pío Pérez, of Maní, the same who had given him the ancient Maya documents. A friend had found the ruins some years previous to Stephens' visit, but as he was neither antiquarian nor writer, the site remained for all practical purposes unknown.

Located on the same latitude as the ruins of Uxmal and seventy-five miles from Chichén Itzá; a *stela*, first discovered by Stephens, read 8 Ahua, 13 Pax. It was deciphered as having been set up on 29 January, A.D. 564.

They went to Tulum by sea in a small coastal craft in which they had in turn to paddle and bail with all the press of dynamic death. They skirted the coral-studded shore, windswept and rain driven, and passed the Isle of Women (Mujeres*) where Bernal Díaz del Castillo, the companion of Cortés, landing in 1519, 'went on shore and found in the town hard by, four temples, the idols of which represented human figures of large size, for which reason we named the place, "The Point of Women".'

Stephens found one of these temples of Díaz del Castillo, and Catherwood drew it before they sailed southward to the next island, Cozumel.†

*The Island of Mujeres (Women) lies off the immediate shore of Cape Catoch, Yucatán. It was first described by Bernal Díaz del Castillo and called 'Women' because of stone figures that looked like such. It had several structures similar to the type of buildings found on the east coast of Yucatán. William H. Holmes, *Archaeological Studies Among Ancient Cities of Mexico*, Field Museum Anth. Ser. 1, Chicago, 1895–1879.

†Cozumel (Ah Cuzamil Peten) 'the Isle of Swallows' lies fifteen miles out of the mainland into the Caribbean Sea. One of the Maya sanctuaries, it was at one time filled with temples and shrines; the town of Polé opposite on the mainland was the terminus of a Maya road over which pilgrims came to take boats for Cozumel.

64. Catherwood's drawing of the Well at Bolonchen.

In the Maya period a large number of temple-cities and city-states had been formed on the flat Yucatán limestone land, close to the sea, and the Maya spread along the storm-lashed north-east coast of Yucatán. They took possession of the island of Cozumel, and, during the colonization period, established the walled city of Tulum. There, among screaming petrels and driving blue-footed boobies, they saw what remained of the time-battered Maya ruins, which the conquistadors had seen in 1518. On this island, where Cortés had bivouacked in 1519 on his way to the conquest of Mexico, Catherwood made a single sketch.

Tulum, in the Quintana Roo Province of Yucatán, they found as described hanging, it seemed, on the very edge of a limestone cliff facing the Caribbean Sea. Huge mounds of water broke against the cliff in an agitated froth. In its rear the jungle lapped about the ruins, hiding all but a section of the wall. It was in June 1542, that Juan Díaz and

65. Catherwood's drawing of the Castle at Tulum.

his retinue of bearded *condottiers* bound for conquest and glory saw 'three towns separated from each other by 2 miles . . . many houses of stone, very tall towers and buildings thatched with straw.'

In the few days allotted Stephens *y Compañía*, they made a plan of Tulum, discovering the great wall enclosing the central part of the ruined city and running to the edge of the cliff. Despite the privations – 'the sun beat upon us, moschetoes, flies and other insects pestered us' – Catherwood was able, with the assistance of Cabot and Stephens, to figure at least seven of the principal buildings.

The Temple of the Diving God was dominated by a strange deity made of stucco, which hung over the entrance; it had the tail of a bird and feather wings on the arms, and was flying earthward.

The interior of the temple was covered with geometric figures painted on a barbaric blue and scarlet background. The *Castillo*, also frescoed, was approached by a great stairway, now hugged in the tight embrace of snakelike roots of the strangler-fig tree. 'Watch-towers,' near the end of the wall, commanded the view of the sea.

It was only when they were leaving, unable to endure further the onslaught of the mosquitoes, that they discovered another ruin.

Dr Cabot, in search of the ocellated turkey – made famous by Audubon – had gone off with his shotgun into the jungle where he discovered the Temple of the Frescoes. Catherwood had only time to make the exterior drawings, the frescoes of geometric design, set in a raw blue color.

The real survey was left for a later century.

Eighty years after Stephens and Catherwood had made their first survey, Samuel K. Lothrop subjected this same Tulum to a very thorough archaeological excavation and study which resulted in one more of his superb monographs.*

*Tulum, *An Archaeological Study of the East Coast of Yucatán*, Carnegie Institution, Washington, 1924.

66.   *The Gigantic head of the Pyramid at Izamal as drawn by Catherwood.*

Although they discovered further ruins in the mainland such as Aké,* and Silan, and Izamal (where Catherwood drew a colossal full-lipped head since destroyed), and thus extended the Maya cultural area by hundreds of miles, it was at Chichén, at the wells of Itzá, where the last stages of their discoveries came to a dramatic conclusion.

Chichén Itzá was now the ruling passion.

'Ever since we left home,' Stephens wrote, 'we had our eyes upon this place.' And well they might. For Chichén Itzá was the greatest ruined city in the entire Maya realm; and moreover easy of access. It lay on a flat plain, sixty miles from the sea, close to, in fact connected with, Vallodolid (the second largest town in Yucatán) by road.

As the greatest city of the Maya New Empire and a religious center to which all the Maya, at least once in their lifetime, made pilgrimage, Chichén Itzá rivalled all other cities in the splendor of its monuments. So great was its fame that its tradition remained in chronological order even though the confused memory of events erased all else from Maya minds.

Chichén Itzá was thrice founded, its first beginnings going back to A.D. 432.

Chichén Itzá's buildings lay under the orb, as bright as snow in the glare of the sun; the truncated pyramid of Chichén Itzá rising one hundred feet above the flat, jungle-covered plain, the Nunnery, the most massive structure of them all, a huge solid block of masonry two hundred feet high, covered with ornate sculptures; a Great Ball Court, as large as a football field, where once, man was pitted against man in a Maya Olympiad.

*Aké is thirty miles east of Mérida on the Izamal road. It belonged in 1870 to Don Simon Péon who was Stephens' benefactor at Uxmal. As most important Maya city-states it was built about a *cenote*, a natural well whose water lay thirty feet below the surface. The ruins of Aké are extensive; it has fifteen or more pyramids, one of which is surrounded by thirty-six pillars each four feet square and sixteen feet high, reminiscent of the Temple of the Warriors at Chichén Itzá. Aké was connected with Izamal, by a Maya road. Little has been written of Aké (see Charmay, Desiré *The Ancient Cities of the New World*, New York, 1887).

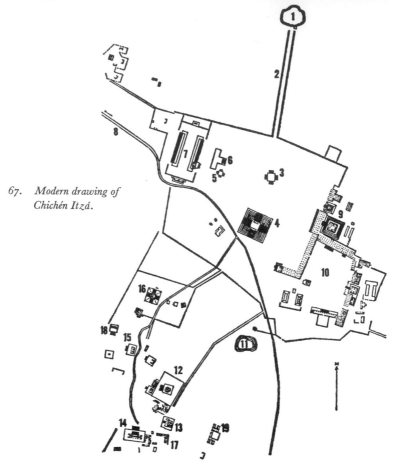

67. *Modern drawing of Chichén Itzá.*

Modern Drawing of Central Area of Chichén Itzá

1 Well of Sacrifice	11 Fresh-water *Cenote*
2 Sacred Way	12 Caracol, or Observatory
3 Dance Platform	13 Temple of the Wall Panels
4 Castillo, or Temple of Kukulkán	14 Monjas, or Nunnery
5 Platform of the Eagles	15 Red House
6 Tzompantli, or Skulls	16 High Priest's Grave
7 Ball Court (Stephens' Gymnasium)	17 Iglesia
8 Modern Road to Mérida	18 House of the Deer
9 Temple of the Warriors	19 Akab-Dzib
10 Market	

For three square miles, they saw from where they sat the most extensive city-state in Mayadom; the Temples of the Warriors, guarded by the strange, reclining figure of the Chacmool, and the circular Caracol, a Maya observatory by deduction if not by tradition.

Although Stephens and Catherwood had seen forty-four

ruined Maya sites, none stirred them as did Chichén Itzá, for here, as at no other, there was a feeling something akin to a European city. The architecture had a lightness, a restraint in decoration with which they almost felt an affinity. They were to remain eighteen days at Chichén Itzá, and to lay down a scientific approach that would endure as long as man was stirred by the antique.

Their fame had already spread across the land. At the hacienda of Don Juan Sosa,* whose great fief included the site of Chichén Itzá, they were welcomed with touching hospitality; Indians squatting by the hacienda gate exhibiting their infirmities had been waiting for days for Dr Cabot to appear; young ladies dressed in their Maya best, with hibiscus-trimmed coiffures, ogled Catherwood so that they might be pictured by his daguerreotype.

Catherwood's fever had abated as had Dr Cabot's and everything – the people, the surroundings – was as halcyon as the turquoise blue sky.

Within a few days they had made the first map of Chichén Itzá.

Here there were no lingering doubts concerning the identity of the people who erected Chichén Itzá. At the first structure they investigated the low, flat, rather undistinguished building, the Temple of Akabtzib, in one of the eighteen rooms, where the sculpture was polychromed in violent reds, blues and yellows, they found an inscribed stone lintel.

Its motif was a seated Indian with quetzal-feathered headdress and outstreched left hand as if in the act of explaining something.

Around this figure flowed those same glyphs they had found at Copán, Palenque, Uxmal, and Kabah, and it was immediately obvious that Chichén Itzá was bound in

*Now owned by the Barbachano family, it was long used as headquarters by various archaeological expeditions. It has now been converted into a hotel from which tourists can make excursions into the surrounding ruins with a leisure denied all early Maya scholars.

68. *The Nunnery of Chichén Itzá.*

cultural relationship with Copán, hundreds of miles to the south; and with Palenque, hundreds of miles to the north.

Architecturally, too, there were specific resemblances. The cornices of the annexes of the massive ruin of the Nunnery had the motif of Itzamna, the long-nosed god. It was at this building, called ludicrously the 'Church,' with its lavishly decorated façade, that Frederick Catherwood's architectural art reached its height; his drawing of the *Iglesia* has never been equaled, in detail or dramatic intensity, by any photograph.

The pyramid, which one reached by following the remains of a stone road from the sacred *cenote*, bore a general resemblance to other structures they had seen, except that this one was higher and more massive. The temple building atop its truncated pinnacle was well preserved. Four great stairways with a continuous balustrades of the plumed-serpent motif led to the top, to its four entrances, which were oriented to the earth's four directions.

69. *The Temple of the Warriors at Chichén Itzá.*

70. *Doorway in the Temple of the Warriors at Chichén Itzá.*

The interior, which Catherwood sketched by the light of Albino's spluttering pine torch, was decorated with sculptured doorjambs; its sapote-wood beams were carved with a delicate tracery of figures.

Stephens and Catherwood spent an entire day within the Temple of Kulkulkan, wandering out at various times during the day to survey the vast panorama of Chichén Itzá.

A few hundred feet to the east of the pyramided temple of Kulkulkan, they discovered, in Stephens' words, 'the most remarkable, unintelligible remains we had yet met with.'

Fighting their way through the incessant web of low scrub, they found groups of small square columns 'in rows of three, four, and five abreast, many rows continuing in the same direction, when they changed and pursued another.'

When Stephens had counted to three hundred and eighty of the six-foot-high sculptured columns, he was completely bewildered; neither he nor Catherwood (who made a single diagrammatic sketch of them) could comprehend their significance.

They had discovered the Court of the Thousand Columns now known as the Temple of the Warriors.

Stephens merely surmised that the columns at one time 'upheld a raised walk of cement, but there were no remains visible,' but a century later the Carnegie Institution of Washington reconstructed the whole of his discovery and found it once had been 'encompassed by a covered colonnade, roofed, like the inner sanctuary of the Castillo . . . supported by the [square pillars] . . . carved and brightly painted with life-size figures of armed warriors.'

It is one of the most magnificent monuments of the Maya, long since restored and the subject of its own complete monograph: *The Temple of the Warriors*.

When Catherwood had drawn the Caracol,* a round

*The Caracol is believed to have been an observatory. Within the central core, which Stephens noted, is a spiral stairway which suggests the convolutions of a snail shell (hence caracol); there are openings in the round forty-one-foot-high tower so placed that observers could fix the vernal and autumnal equinoxes.

structure, rare in Maya architecture, he, and Stephens followed a cow path which led between verdure-covered mounds to a huge structure with twenty-eight-foot-high parallel walls enclosing a field two hundred and seventy feet long by one hundred and ninety feet wide.

At one end of the east wall, forming a narrow esplanade in front of it, was a ruined structure to be known in archaeological parlance as the Temple of the Jaguars.

While Catherwood put up his camera lucida to obtain a panoramic view of the whole structure, Stephens wandered along the great walls.

Overhead black clouds obscured the sun. The mass of vegetation, palms and agave, growing on top of the structure bowed in obeisance to the winds and even as Stephens stood there in the awesome grandeur of Chichén Itzá, the sky was rent, riven by a bolt of lightning.

As Stephens was walking the length of the walls, he pondered their use in the Maya economy, then at a height of twenty feet above the ground, he discovered attached horizontally to the wall a massive circular stone, four feet in diameter, pierced by a large hole. Around its border two

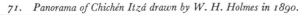

71. Panorama of Chichén Itzá drawn by W. H. Holmes in 1890.

72. *Catherwood drawing of the Ball Court at Chichén Itzá.*

73. *The stone-carved ring in the Ball Court.*

snakes, fiercely entwined like those of the caduceus of medicine, were carved in low relief.*

It was when Stephens found that two identical rings faced each other across the one-hundred-and-ninety-foot-wide court that he remembered he had seen similar rings at Uxmal.

He had discovered the Great Ball Court of Chichén.

'I shall call it, as occasion requires, the Gymnasium or Tennis Court.' He later found, in reading the closely printed pages of Herrera y Tordesillas (the incident-loving Spanish chronicler) that the Aztecs played a ball game called *tlachtli* with hardened rubber balls: 'On the side wall they fix'd certain Stones like those of a Mill stone with a Hole quite through the Middle.'

Herrera had noted, too, that 'every Tennis Court had a temple.' Stephens believed that this was a ball court, and only said 'tennis,'† because basketball, to which the Indian game bears a resemblance, had not yet been invented. It exhibits an excellent analogical sense; to be surrounded by a structure of which man knew nothing, and yet to judge it so clearly.

Time has confirmed Stephens' findings; he accurately described the ball game the Mayas called *pok-a-tok*.

Catherwood could not resist copying down the superb carvings, in low relief, that circled the walls of the ball court; warriors, carrying bundles of obsidian-tipped arrows, accoutred in flowing quetzal-feathered headdresses. The Maya sculptor showed great virtuosity in composing these

---

*Catherwood was deeply impressed by the circular carving. When he designed their second book, he used the circular device on the cover of the *Incidents of Travel in Yucatán*.

†The game *pok-a-tok* has been likened to basketball. In Stephens' time the term did not exist as the game was not invented until 1891. *Pok-a-tok* had opposing players whose hips, elbows and legs were protected by cotton cloth; the object was to put with hips or elbows a six-inch diameter solid rubber ball through the horizontally set stone 'basket.' The game had religious overtones. Courts for this game are found from Nicaragua through Mexico (where it was known as *tlachtli*) up into Arizona.

space-filling figures; and Catherwood, who had seen most of the archaic sculptures of Egypt and the Mediterranean had no hesitation in saying: 'These are as finely conceived as those of the Egyptians'.

The Maya artist seemed capable of much stylistic variation depending upon the geographical milieu in which he worked. Yet no matter how much the variation, Mayan art remained, even at Chichén Itzá (where it was influenced by the Toltec), basically Maya. The reliefs were as barbarically beautiful to Catherwood as Mexican art had been to Albrecht Dürer when he first saw it in 1520.

So it is aesthetic twaddle for the French art-historian Elie Faure to write off this American art as 'something beautiful, almost always monstrous, contorted, blown-up, crushed-in, warped. . . .'

Faure, presuming that the art forms of the Maya were of Eurasian derivation, believed that the American Indian had lost his 'world-memory' and that the Indian sculptors never saw anything but 'mutilated trunks, dislocated members, scalped heads, skinned faces, empty eye sockets and grinning teeth. . . .'

> In Central America, where the earth is soaked with water of hot rains, where the vegetation is heavier, the miasmas deadlier, and the poisonous thorn bushes impossible to traverse, the dream is still more horrible. . . . In sculptured rocks one distinguished nothing but heaps of crushed and palpitating flesh, quivering masses of entrails . . . a confused pile of viscera.

Stephens did not know it then but he sensed that the 'Maya art forms in Chichén Itzá had taken on a different aspect.'

Something had happened. Frederick Catherwood felt it too as he drew the new figures through his camera lucida.

Catherwood then did not possess any of the weapons of – to give an example of the new technical archaeological jargon –

The New Archaeology's morphological paradigm, through which statistics aid interpretation of functional relationships of archaeological finds; an anthropological paradigm through which patterning of archaeological data may suggest possible social organization . . . and ecological paradigm [read prototype] through which ancient sites may be related to their paleo-environments and a geographical paradigm through which inter-relations of sites which natural environments may be postulated.*

Nor had he any inspiration from systematic intuition. What he did possess was twenty years of field experience in the old world and the new where he had drawn and studied every known style of architecture.

From this experience, he sensed that 'something had happened at Itzá.'

That 'something' was the Toltec invasion of Central Mexico into the Maya country. The time: A.D. 987.

The Nahuatl-speaking Toltecs, had their capital at Tula, north of Mexico City, built as their new center in or about A.D. 900. A leader, who called himself after the Plumed Serpent God Quetzalcoatl, became involved in a power struggle and was forced into exile in 987. Under him a fairly large army of warriors drifted down to Xicalango, a famous trading center 'where the language changes.'

That is where the Maya began. Maya sources are explicit about this historical incident:

'In Katun Ahua [that is 987], Kulkulcan [the Maya word for Quetzalcoatl] wrested Yucatán from its rightful owners and established their capital at Chichén Itzá.'

Chichén Itzá, which had first been founded in A.D. 432, had after some centuries been abandoned. It was refounded in 987. Thereafter the record becomes confused. The late Dr Wyllys Andrews wrote with his usual clarity:

*From a Review in the *Times Literary Supplement* of *Models in Archaeology*, David L. Clarke (editor) 1,055 pp. Methuen, 1972 (£16).

The nature of the origins of the Toltec power and the manner of its maintenance in Yucatán remains unknown. . . . it may have been military or religious or secular. On sculpture of the time, the warrior seems to have taken over [this is precisely what Catherwood was sensing as he drew the warriors armed with bow and obsidian-tipped long arrows . . .] The Toltecs brought with them much that was new to Yucatán, including the first copper and gold . . . In architecture, radically new building forms appeared. Forms of sculptural adornment were changed by innovations such as the carved serpent column and the reclining chaoc mool figures, relaxed bearers of distinctive umbilical ashtrays (into which fresh-torn palpitating hearts of sacrificial victims were placed as food for the gods).*

This occupation seemed to have lasted until 1168. Then there occurred a civil war between Chichén Itzá and the new-formed capital of Mayapan. Mexican-Toltecs mercenary troops, stationed about Xicalango, the trading center at Tabasco, were brought into the fight and Chichén Itzá collapsed. Mayapan became the leading administrative center in Yucatán for the next two-and-a-half centuries.†

There were two distinct invasions of Mexican Toltecs into Chichén Itzá: the first were Maya-speaking although of Mexican highland origin. They had lived about Tabasco for several generations, close to Xicalango. There were profound population shifts during the years before A.D. 900; in Mexico, Teotihuacán, the capital of the Toltecs, which had controlled so much of the central highlands, collapsed – some say it was attacked and burned and whole masses of its people were in movement. This was about the same time that the Maya inland cities – Tikal, Palenque, Piedras Negras, and hundreds

*E. Wyllys Andrews, *Archaeology and Pre-history in the Northern Maya Lowlands, an Introduction.*

†S. G. Morley, *The Ancient Maya*, Palo Alto, 1954.

74. *The Temple of Kulkulkan, the plumed serpent God, as seen by Catherwood.*

75. *A modern view of the Temple of Kulkulkan.*

of others – ceased to erect time-markers, and it is believed this was the time of the population dispersal of the 'Great Descent' recorded in Maya traditions.

Chíchén Itzá was then unoccupied. These Itzás took it over and built a new pyramid over the first. 'New' Chichén. This was discovered in 1937 when archaeologists of the Carnegie Institution, while restoring the Pyramid Temple of Kukalcan, found a smaller one underneath it that served as core to the larger.

It was Maya in style, but with Toltec motifs, that is, marching jaguars such as are found at Tula. A secret stairway led to the Red Jaguar Throne Room. Here a life-sized effigy of an open-mouthed jaguar, painted a mandarin red, stood guard. Its spots are seventy-three round discs of polished jade.

The Mayas were tied up with the destinies of the highland Mexicans, when in the twelfth century it was again the center of Toltec culture.

The great Temple of Tula in Mexico has as motif the plumed-serpent, immense snakes rampant, formed into fifteen-foot-high caryatids.

Inside the temple were massive warrior figures as colon-nades, and about the lower portions of the temple were motifs of marching jaguars and rampant eagles.

Over all there appeared the terrible figure of the Chac Mool, a prone stone figure with a vacant expressionless face. Its hands held the stone dish, and into which the freshly torn human hearts were flung during sacrifices.

Quetzalcoatl was the culture-hero of Tula. Before he became divine, he was man, priest, ruler, and demiurge. He had lorded it over Tula for twenty-two years, lost a civil war, and was forced into exile with a sizeable body of warriors.

The date given to this historical fact is A.D. 1115.

He moved south to Cholula, the land of Mixtec, and there acquired fame as a builder and 'bringer of laws.'

The next time Quetzalcoatl appears, he is in Yucatán. Was this the same Quetzalcoatl or was it another who bore the same name? If we are confused, so were the Maya.

'They do not agree upon the point as to whether he (Quetzalcoatl) arrived before or after the Itzás.'

This much is certain: at some time in the eleventh century, Chichén Itzá was re-occupied for the third time and the people were of Toltec-Mexican origin. Archaeology, history, and tradition, are for once in full agreement.

'It is believed' wrote Landa 'that with the Itzá who [re]-occupied Chichén Itzá, there reigned a great lord named *Kuk* [quetzal] *ul* [feather] *can* [serpent] and that the principal building is called the Temple of Kukulcan.'

This temple was erected over the first, at the top of the truncated pyramid, the Toltec builders introducing carved wooden beams to provide more space, since Maya rooms were severely restricted by the use of corbeled arching.

The walls were muraled and enough still survive to show many aspects of Maya-Toltec life. An open-mouthed plumed serpent is on the balustrade of each of the four stairways ascending the pyramid.

On top, at the Temple, the serpents appear again, this time as sculptured columns – very much like those at Tula, in distant Mexico.

To make doubly certain that people knew it was the Temple of Kukulcan, the top of the building is decorated with the symbol of the sky god, Quetzalcoatl.

The square where the Temple rests is a huge, roughly trapezoidal walled area, 1,600 feet by 1,400 feet. Within this is a gigantic ball court, its tribunes carrying architectural motifs derived from Tula. There are low platforms, and a 'theater,' reached by stone stairways (Landa refers to 'two small stages of hewn stone where they gave farces . . . and comedies for the pleasure of the public.' Nearby is a 30-foot-wide ceremonial causeway, leading 900 feet to the sacrificial *cenote*.

As the last line in his huge, two-volume, work Stephens wrote 'I will now bid farewell to Ruins.'

Far from being a leave-taking, it was an invitation to generations of archaeologists yet unborn to follow in his footsteps and enlarge upon his discoveries.

One hundred and thirty years later, the literature on the Maya and their neighbors is so immense that even to acquire the book-materials is a life-long task.

Yucatán as a book is a time-tested classic. When one considers that Stephens was trampling unknown ground, his deductions on the possible date of the Maya ruins he visited are strikingly near those now accepted by the professionals.

He was the first in modern times to note that the native written Maya histories could be used to document Maya archaeology.

Stephens and his party visited forty-four sites, all of which were new. Catherwood made a general map of the whole of the area and provided drawings of almost all.

The newly discovered Yucatán is still the best archaeological Baedecker to the Puuc area.*

At Mérida the travelers finally bid farewell to ruins and boarded a vessel for Cuba. After ten months travel in Yucatán, Havana was an oasis of delight.

In the four days given them before the *Ann Louisa* sailed for New York, they were able – despite the yellow fever that placed Havana in a sort of state of siege – to 'do the rounds.'

Cuba, one of the last Spanish strongholds in America, was overflowing with an entourage of *Condes* and *Marqueses*.

There were masked balls, Italian opera with Fanny Elssler as its danseuse. There were drives along the Malecón, particularly in the evening, in open *voltantes*, where Stephens could ogle the pretty girls, 'black-eyed and with beautiful figures.'

*Incidents of Travel in Yucatán by John Lloyd Stephens, with engravings by Frederick Catherwood, edited with an introduction by Victor Wolfgang von Hagen, 2 vols, University of Oklahoma Press (Norman, 1962).

But difficulties soon developed at the customs office over the collected material to be transferred from the *Alexandre*, which had brought them from Yucatán to Havana, and this posed seemingly insurmountable problems.

First there were Dr Cabot's bird skins, hundreds of them, the first ornithological collection ever made in Central America by an expert; and Catherwood's huge portfolioes of drawings of forty-four ruined cities, his archaeological note-books crammed with drawings, observations, maps and diagrams; and Stephens' collections from Kabah, Uxmal, and Chichén Itzá, together with his burgeoning notebooks.

Finally the Spanish customs officials, warming to Señor Stephens' *simpático* nature, bridged the difficulties and allowed all their collections to be taken from the *Alexandre* and transferred without going through customs to the *Ann Louisa*.

On the night of 4 June, they were bound for New York City.

CHAPTER XVI

Incidents of Travel in Yucatán

Life in New York City in 1841 had noticeably quickened since their second Maya tour. They both felt it at the moment of return from the quiet, lost worlds of Yucatán. New York's streets were longer, noisier, and dirtier. Business was brisk, money flowed freely. There was, too, cultural gold.

Ralph Waldo Emerson, who had published his first book, *Nature*, in 1836, was beginning to feel his writer's strength; Nathaniel Hawthorne, after publishing two books, gave up his sinecure at the Customs House in Boston to go to Brook Farm and devote himself to writing; Walt Whitman was a reporter on the *Brooklyn Eagle*; Herman Melville was living with the cannibals in Tahiti; and the historical Titans – Bancroft, Tickner, Prescott, and Sumner – were beating the sonorous brasses of America's literary world.

Now John Lloyd Stephens was pointing out yet to another direction, 'the visible past of a Pan-America,' as Van Wyck Brook has written, 'scarcely aware of its own existence.'

As a book, *Incidents of Travel in Yucatán*, was more demanding than the other, for it required wider reading.

Stephens researched the Spanish chroniclers – Cogolludo, Herrera and Bernal Díaz del Castillo. He called out the old Spanish historiographers from their limbo to make them witnesses to his theme: that the civilization of Yucatán was American, built by native Americans, the same people who built them and occupied them during the Spanish conquest; that these civilizations took nothing direct from China, nor Egypt, nor Greece. That their art was indigenous.

The book on Yucatán was going to be filled with many archaeological 'firsts': the first accurate map of Yucatán, the first illustrations of Maya sites, the first descriptions of forty-four ruined sites, the first publication of Juan Pío Pérez's *A True Exposition of the Method Used by the Indians for Computing Time*.

At Catherwood's Panorama, in the meanwhile, there was placed an exhibition to an excited public the carved wooden beams from Uxmal, Kabah, Labná, along with other pieces of Maya sculpture that they had collected in Yucatán.

These were put beside his Panorama of Thebes, so that New Yorkers might themselves see both cultural similarities and differences between the two civilizations.

People poured into the circular Rotunda to Catherwood's Panorama to see with their own eyes the wonders that had been discovered.

Then, on the night of 31 July, 1842 after closing time, the building caught fire. Philip Hone, the famed New York diarist, was an eyewitness of the events:

Catherwood's Panorama of Thebes and Jerusalem were burnt last evening about ten o'clock and these two valuable paintings were destroyed together with the other contents of the building, among which were a large collection of curiosities and relicks and other precious things collected by Messrs. Stephens and Catherwood in their recent travels in Central America. This will be a severe loss not only for these enterprising travelers, but to science and the arts in general. The edifice being perfectly circular and without windows and the contents of peculiarly inflammable nature, the appearance of the conflagration was like that of a huge cauldron.

Up, consumed by flames, went all of the Yucatán collections; utterly consumed were the priceless and irreplaceable Mayan wooden lintels with their carved hieroglyphics; up in smoke, too, went a huge section of Catherwood's life. The personal loss was calamitous.

New York papers, the next day, 1 August, 1842, announced the Panorama's destruction:

Destruction of the Rotunda by Fire. A few moments after closing of this building in Prince Street last evening at half past nine o'clock, it was discovered to be on fire, and in less than half an hour, owing to the combustible state of the paintings and other materials in it, the interior was entirely consumed INCLUDING the panoramas of Jerusalem and Thebes. In addition to this loss by Messrs. Catherwood and Jackson, the owners, the former met with an almost invaluable loss in the total destruction of a large portion of his ancient relics and original paintings, obtained and produced while on his visits to Mexico and the surrounding country. . . .

The story continued on the following days:

The Fire at Catherwood's. This fire is likely to prove much more disastrous than we at first anticipated. For we find that Messrs. Catherwood and Stephens returned to this city from their last trip to Central America and deposited their valuable collections of curiosities, pieces of ruins, specimens, drawings, plans and everything that they had collected in their painful and perilous tour. These things are a great loss; no money can replace them. Mr. Catherwood thinks that if the water had been directed as he had desired at the fire these things might have been saved. He was insured for only $3,000, his own private loss will be at least $10,000 more.

The fates had been unkind to Catherwood. His great work on the Dome of the Rock at the Mosque of Omar was left unpublished; his pioneer work among the Egyptian tombs swallowed up in the anonymity of the unpublished folios of Robert May, still lying in the British Museum collections, and now his great work on the Maya was destroyed.

Yet Catherwood did not allow his contretemps to entirely possess him. Fortunately for him, many of his drawings had been given to the publisher Harper and Brothers and these, with his archaeological notebook and other sketches in his home at 89 Prince Street, had survived. So to assuage his loss he gave himself fully into the work of illustrating Stephens' book. Harper and Brothers turned over to Catherwood the complete control of this phase as well as the design of the book. It is stated in a special preface that: '. . . the illustrations were made from Daguerreotype views and drawings taken on the spot by Mr Catherwood and the engravings executed under his personal superintendence.'

However, it took Stephens several weeks to pick up the thread of his narrative. Then, *Yucatán*, at last, was done. The illustrations, as might be expected from the dispatch of the work, were too hastily executed to be excellent, of too many hands to be uniform; yet, *Incidents of Travel in Yucatán*, with its one hundred and twenty engravings, was produced in six months. It was off the press and in the book stores by March 1843; a copy was sent to William Prescott on 23 March, 1843:

I sent you yesterday, by Express, a copy of my Yucatán, before passing judgement upon it I beg to remind you that you committed yourself before I set out on my expedition by saying that if I should make half as good a book as the last, my voyage would not be in vain.

Prescott replied:

I am truly obliged to you for your welcome present. It opens rich and promising, and I am sure from the sample will be worthy of the elder brother *Incidents of Travel in Central America*. 1841.

A month later Prescott wrote again:

I have accomplished one volume of your work and a part of second. I read slowly, or rather it is read to me, which is a slow process . . . It is all interesting to me as the old ruins have ever more attractions than the lively narrative of adventure. Most readers find the adventures told with even more spirit than in your preceding work. You have made a good advertising sheet for our friend the doctor. *I hope he may live to profit by it.* . . . I know not what to think of the ruins, they leave my mind in a kind of mist, which I shall not attempt to dispel. . . .

The reviews stimulated purchase and, like its 'elder brother,' the two-volume work on Yucatán galloped its way through edition upon edition, until Catherwood's engravings became worn from use. This made the last editions in 1865, only ghosts of the originals.

The plates having been destroyed in Harpers' disastrous fire in 1854, the type was reset and reprinted by the publishers every two years until the Civil War.

Yucatán was then forgotten and buried under a hail of grape-shot.

In England, John Murray printed an edition, and translations appeared in France, Germany, Sweden, and in **the very theater of Stephens' operations** – Mexico. The work has had a good life: over one hundred years after its publication translations still come from Mexico's presses.*

After the success of *Incidents of Travel in Yucatán*, a new publishing venture was launched by Stephens and Catherwood. It was to be on so monumental a scale that only John James Audubon's folios of *The Birds of America* could stand up to it in bibliographical measure.

*In Germany it was translated as *Begebenheiten auf einer Reise in Yucatán·* Deutsch von Dr N. N. Meissner, Leipzig, 1853, 438 pp., plates, maps, plans.

A new edition of *Incidents of Travel in Yucatán*, in two volumes was issued by the University of Oklahoma Press, Norman, Oklahoma, 1962. Engravings by Frederick Catherwood; edited with an introduction by Victor Wolfgang von Hagen.

The projected work was to be an all-embracing study of Central American Archaeology. A letter dated 25 March, 1843 from Stephens to Prescott outlines the scheme:

. . . A few words upon a new subject. I am thinking of sending out a prospectus for publishing by subscription a great work on American Antiquities to contain 100 or 120 engravings fol. to be issued in four numbers quarterly. *PRICE $100!* Nine hundred subscribers will save me from loss, which is all I care for. I have no room for details and can only say that Mr Catherwood has made several large drawings, which in the grandeur and interest of the subjects and in picturesque effect are far superior to any that have ever appeared. It is intended that the execution shall be creditable to this country as a work of art. From the specimens of engravings which we have seen on Audubon's new works [he had issued a smaller edition of his *Birds of America* in seven octavo volumes] we think that ours can be done in this country; if not, Mr. Catherwood will go over to Paris and have them executed there. Albert Gallatin [Jefferson's Secretary of the Treasury and in his later years an excellent ethnologist] will furnish an article, and he will endeavor to procure one from Humboldt with whom he formed an intimate acquaintance while Minister to France. I have written to Mr. [John] Murray . . . requesting him to apply to Sir John Wilkinson the best authority on all points of resemblance between American signs and symbols and those of Egypt. . . . The fourth and only other person to whom I have thought of applying is yourself. I do so purely as a matter of business and in my estimate of expenses have allowed $250. and a copy of the work for an article from you. It need not contain more than 20 or 30 of your octavo pages and will not be wanted in less than a year.

How grandiose was the project can be felt even at this

distance of time. The mere prospect of bringing together in one work Humboldt, Prescott, Gallatin, Wilkinson, and Stephens with 120 of Catherwood's drawings can still stir a bibliophile. For its time the cost of $100 a copy was staggering.

Prescott, to suggest the high esteem in which he held both Stephens and Catherwood, replied:

> The AMERICAN ANTIQUITIES . . . is a noble enterprise, and I hope it may find patronage . . . I will supply an article of the length you propose.

The project began under excellent auspices. A meeting of the executive committee of the New York Historical Society was called on 2 May, 1843 to consider giving the project sponsorship.

Catherwood's drawings were exhibited in the library, and Stephens, in rare good form, explained the project. Thereafter, the venerable Albert Gallatin took over.

Still speaking with the slightest trace of French accent, his eighty years did not curb his enthusiasm he said:

> Stephens having accomplished his principal task, of giving to the world a full, graphic and faithful description of these ruined cities and temples, now proposes to complete his valuable contributions to the cause of Historical and Scientific research by publishing an edition of the drawings on the scale here represented. . . .

Exhibiting to the executive committee the fifteen large watercolors that Catherwood had made of the ruins, a fraction of the intended number that were to grace the work, Gallatin went on:

> This would certainly be a work in which every American must feel a just pride, and it ought, in fact, to be considered a national production.

He then asked that the New York Historical Society sponsor the 'great project.'

Resolutions were formulated in which it was stressed

> That the recent discoveries of ruined cities and the remains of a people and history entirely unknown have given a new aspect to the American continent.

Professor Edward Robinson, a member of the committee and the founder of Palestinian archaeology, who was intimately familiar with Catherwood's work in the East, enthusiastically seconded the resolutions. Another member felt that the great project was calculated to call forth the highest enthusiasm and that the works of Stephens and Catherwood would create a new era in the science of ethnology. Catherwood's drawings afforded

> Means of solving doubts and testing theories with regard to the origin of these races which inhabited the continent at the time of its discovery by Europeans.

Finally it was

> Predicted that Stephens and Catherwood, the first investigators in this field, would be followed by hundreds of others and that though the fame gained for their distinguished countryman for his former volumes, was scarcely second to that of any name in our literary annals, he was destined, as a discoverer of these hidden treasurers, to a still more exalted position.

In a glowing tribute to Catherwood, Albert Gallatin closed the session, thanking the members for their endorsement of a work that would take its place beside Audubon's immortal *Birds of America*.

Thus nobly launched, the 'great project' sailed immediately into the disturbed commercial waters of the United States. The political scene was turbulent and this uncertainty was reflected in financial circles.

Manifest Destiny, the shibboleth under which the United States was to launch a war of aggression upon Mexico, gaining thereby ten million acres of real estate (and the enmity of the entire Latin-American world), had already been formulated.

At first Harper and Brothers, thought of publishing this new project, but, as they stated in the Press they were 'not willing to undertake so great a work without some prospect of remuneration'.

As the necessary three hundred subscribers were not forthcoming Harper and Brothers dropped the project.

It was taken up at once by Bartlett and Welford, booksellers, and in an attempt to awaken public interest, Catherwood's dramatic drawings were exhibited in bookstores and elsewhere throughout the Eastern seaboard.

Catherwood now had good cause to curse his outrageous misfortune. The requisite number of subscribers could still not be found, and even John Lloyd Stephens, obsessed by some soul-disturbing problems in his immediate family (and pressure from that ogre, politics), seemed to have lost interest.

Nonetheless, this time Frederick Catherwood resolved that he *would publish*. He would not again allow his work to be usurped by others.

In July 1843 after consultation with Prescott, Catherwood sailed to England.

American antiquities had drawn Prescott and Catherwood into close intimacy, for Prescott, in the throes of writing *The Conquest of Mexico*, had been helped immeasurably by Stephens and had been confirmed in his deductions as to American origins by Catherwood.

Working as he must, half-blind among the manuscripts he had gathered from the dark corners of the world's libraries,

Prescott, too, came to the conclusion that the American civilization was indigenous to the continent and that the structures that had been discovered in Central America were built by the people of these civilizations. He now completely rejected the idea of the American Indian having his origin out of misty voyages of Phoenicians, the Lost Tribes of Israel, or wandering Carthaginians.

He was delighted that his views on the ruins had been reaffirmed by Catherwood, and was therefore more than willing to assist him in his new project.

In a letter to Edward Everett, the American Minister to the Court of St James, dated 15 June, 1843, Prescott wrote:

> . . . A literary project of some magnitude is set on foot here by Messrs. Stephens and Catherwood. It is the publication of the magnificent drawings made by Mr. Catherwood of the ruins of Central America. The intention is to have them engraved on a scale corresponding to that of the original designs. Mr. Catherwood will embark for Europe in July to confer with the English publishers who have intimated a willingness to be interested in the undertaking. I have taken the liberty to give him a note to you, at his desire. . . . Mr. Catherwood, who is a truly modest and well-instructed man, desires only to have your approbation of this important undertaking and the interest you take in every liberal enterprise of your countrymen will, I have no doubt, interest you in the success of this. . . .

In London Frederick Catherwood took up residence with his family at his old home at 21 Charles Square, Hoxton, from where his brother, Alfred, carried on his medical practice.

From there the artist of the Mayas, portfolio in hand, went out to see the booksellers and publishers.

He met with little encouragement – a strange reception

for so original a work, since this was the age of the illustrated book and of handsome folios of handcolored lithographs.

Not many years before, D. T. Egerton had published with much success his *Views in Mexico*, and John Bateman, his magnificent book on tropical orchids.

At that very moment George Catlin was in London making final arrangements for the publication of his lithographic portfolio on the American Indians of the Plains.

Yet Catherwood was rebuffed.

He wrote to Prescott:

As regards the large work of Stephens and myself, nothing has finally been agreed on. The booksellers say trade is bad etc., the old story and I fear a very true one. . . . I delivered your letter to Mr. Everett who received me very cordially but I have not yet attained my object, an audience of the Queen and Prince Albert. It would seem nowadays that nothing is successful here with the rich and aristocratic without the patronage and sanction of royalty which ill accords with my *loco foco** notions.

Frederick Catherwood's disappointment became very real when Stephens decided for reasons not clear (since the Stephens-Catherwood correspondence is lost) to withdraw entirely from the 'great project.'

Catherwood now wrote to Prescott:

My own work (for Stephens has declined having anything to do with it) is getting on, several of the plates are finished in the best style of lithography and others are in hand. I have no publisher and do not intend to have one on this side at least . . . *I shall be my own publisher.*

*Loco focos, a derisive term for a splinter group of the Democratic Party. They were against bankers and their practises, opposed monopolies, stood for pure democracy and were united with the Working Man's Party against privilege. Their name came from the fact that the gas was turned off during their meetings and they had to be continued by the light of candles and long stemmed matches.

He gathered together six of England's outstanding artists – Andrew Picken, Warren, Parrott, Bourne, Thomas Shotter Boys, and George Moore – to lithograph his drawings. Andrew Picken was given the largest number of plates to lithograph, ten in all, since he was a superb artist.

Strangely enough we know precisely what this work cost.

'My book,' Catherwood wrote to Prescott, 'consists of 25 plates and a Title Page' [the great project of 120 plates with text by Humboldt, Prescott, Gallatin, Wilkinson, and Stephens, had been narrowed down to this] and 'the estimate was £10 per plate making the total estimate £260.'

The actual cost of the plates 'eventuated into £307.10.0,' and this was a large outlay for Catherwood, who only in the previous year had lost his life's fortune in the burning of his Panorama.

The printing of the work, to be called *Views of Ancient Monuments in Central America, Chiapas and Yucatán* was executed by Owen Jones ('an intimate friend' of Catherwood) at his studio at 9 Argyll Place, London.

Owen Jones, now famous for his study on the *Grammar of Ornament*, was the son of the celebrated Welsh antiquarian and had been a pupil of Vuilliamy. He had published his first work on the 'Alhambra' the previous year, a work he had had to sell his patrimony to complete. Forced into all forms of remunerative work, he consented to print Catherwood's *Views*.

The imprint bears his name.

The publication had proceeded far enough along by December 1843 for Catherwood to send Prescott 'a few proofs of the work' through Stephens. This was in return for Prescott's gift of a copy of his *Conquest of Mexico*, of which Catherwood 'could almost wish that subject had been of less absorbing interest, that I might have had a prolonged pleasure of its perusal.'

In this letter came the first indication that Stephens,

who had promised to write the text for the *Views*, would not be able to do so.

'Mr Stephens has kindly offered to write an introduction and the descriptions, but I fear they will scarcely be in time, as I am endeavouring to get [it] out by the beginning of March.'

On 25 April, 1844, *The Views of Ancient Monuments of Central America, Chiapas and Yucatán* with its twenty-five lithographs, map, introduction, and description, 'dedicated to John Lloyd Stephens, esq.,' was published in London. Catherwood, who had been explorer, archaeologist, artist, author, then publisher, was now finally reduced to be his own bookseller.

So, at the age of forty-five, Catherwood published his first and only book. It was limited to three hundred sets. The ordinary edition sold for five guineas, and a small number of hand-colored sets, delicately done by an expert hand, decidedly his own were issued at twelve guineas. Bartlett and Welford of the Astor House Book Shop in New York City became the American distributors of the work and took a number of copies.

Catherwood wrote in an unusually enthusiastic letter to Prescott:

> I have been doing very well so far with my book in London, but look with anxiety to the accounts from your side. If they are favorable I shall be highly successful. Of my £12.12.0 Copies I have sold considerably more than I expected.

Unexpected, too, was the quality of the text from Catherwood's pen, for writing was not his métier, and there exists only one other contribution to archaeology written by him.

Scarcely a literary stylist, since his brush was his eloquence, Catherwood's text is still noteworthy. In a century in which antiquarians believed, through the published works of Lord

Kingsborough and Count Waldeck, that the buildings discovered in the Central American jungles were the work of either Egyptians, Greeks, Carthaginians, or Semitic tribes, the conclusion of Frederick Catherwood in regard to their origin is astute; moreover, his conclusions have stood the test of over a century of the evidence yielded up by the spade and trowel of archaeology.

Although he was possessed of none of the documentation we have today nor the evidence of extensive excavations, the general outlines of Catherwood's conclusions remain quite unchallenged. In sum they represent, with slight modifications, the position of American archaeology today.

Catherwood wrote in his introduction:

With regard to the various theories that have been formed to trace the nations that peopled the American continent, through their migrations to their original habitations in the Old World, we find them all resting for support upon a few vague similarities of rites and customs, more or less common amongst every branch of the human family. Besides the idea that civilization and its attendant arts, is in every case derivative and always owning to a transmission from a cultivated to an unpolished people, is eminently unphilosophical, as it only removes further back without explaining the original difficulty of Invention, which must somewhere have taken place. . . . Mr. Stephens and myself, after a full and precise comparative survey of the ancient remains [concluded] . . . that [the ruins] are not of immemorial antiquity, the work of unknown races; but that, as we now see them, they were occupied and possibly erected by the Indian tribes in possession of the country at the time of the Spanish conquest – that they are the production of an indigenous school of art, adapted to the natural circumstances of the country, and to the civil and religious policy then prevailing – and that they present but very slight and accidental analogies with the works of any people or country in the Old World.

In the whole range of literature on the Maya there has never appeared a more magnificent work than *Views of Ancient Monuments.**

At a London meeting of the Royal Institute of British Architects after publication, Frederick Catherwood, with his drawings as a background, read to a distinguished gathering his paper on the 'Antiquities of Central America.'

He stressed that, before his explorations, it would have been considered a flight of fancy to suggest that the Mayas as builders were in no wise inferior to the Egyptians, and that their painting could be regarded as superior to that of the Egyptians, and 'more nearly like the paintings found at Pompeii and Herculaneum.'

This was a strong statement. Yet those present knew that Catherwood, who had spent ten years in the East, was qualified, as none other, to speak of comparative archaeology.

Catherwood perorated on the manner in which the Maya cut the stones, their knowledge of mortars, stuccoes, and cements; he entered into the architectural techniques and then explained the Mayan 'arch.'

He called it this, as he said, because it answered the purpose of an arch, and he felt that the Mayas had been on the very threshold of discovering the principles of the true arch.

'With regard to the age of these monuments,' the Secretary reported, 'Mr Catherwood differed from Del Río, Du Paix,

---

*Because of the renewed interest in Catherwood after the publication of the author's first biography, *F. Catherwood Architect*, Oxford University Press, Introduction by Aldous Huxley, New York, 1950, *The Views* completely disappeared from the antiquarian bookstores. To meet the interest *Views of Ancient Monuments in Central America, Chiapas and Yucatán* was reissued with the color plates in offset by Barre Publishers, Barre, Massachusetts, 1965, priced at $275.00.

Lord Kingsborough and Waldeck, who would give them great age – antediluvian antiquity.' The amount of debris covering the ruins 'suggested nothing.'

Catherwood did not think he would be safe in ascribing to any of those monuments which still retained their form a greater age than 800 to 1,000 years, and those perfect enough to be drawn more than 400 to 600 years.

The accuracy of such deductions does much to gauge Catherwood's knowledge, for Copán is slightly over 1,400 years old, Palenque, 1,300, Uxmal, not much beyond 900, and the last archaeological additions to Chichén Itzá doubtlessly within the 600-year figure placed on it by Catherwood.

It was just this calm judgment that led James Fergusson, the architectural historian of that period, to rely on Catherwood's work when he attempted, in his *History in All Countries*, to make something out of the chaos of ancient American culture.

> Hitherto the great difficulty had been that the drawings of American monuments – especially those published by Humboldt and Lord Kingsborough – could not be depended upon. The one bright exception to this censure are those of F. Catherwood, both those which he published separately, and those which he illustrated for the works of Mr. Stephens. . . . There seems no good reason for doubting the conclusion at which he and Mr. Stephens arrived: that the cities they rediscovered were those that were inhabited and in full tide of their prosperity at the time of the Spanish conquest.

Such was Frederick Catherwood's position in the world of art, archaeology, and architecture. He had at long last come into his own. His *Views* were apparently a success and there was talk of doing a future work on Central America. Peru was mentioned.

Now, Peru was suggested as a new area for Catherwood's talents.

Prescott wrote:

> Stephens tells me that you have talked to him of a trip to Peru. This is *my ground* [Prescott was beginning to write *The Conquest of Peru*] but I suppose it will not be the worse for your mousing into architectural antiquities, and I wish I could see the fruits of such a voyage in your beautiful illustrations.

It is always to be regretted that Catherwood did not act on this first impulse; certainly American archaeology would have been enriched. So well-known in London was the figure of Frederick Catherwood, lecturing before his drawings of Central American ruins, that Wilkie Collins had him in mind in his novel, *The Woman in White* (1806), when Walter Hartright goes to Central America in the 1850s to make architectural pictures for an archaeological expedition.

So famous had Catherwood's *Views* become that when Alexander von Humboldt sent a copy of his *Kosmos* to Prince Albert, Catherwood's work was chosen as a reciprocal gift.

The Prince Consort wrote to Humboldt on 17 February, 1847:

> I have been constantly impressed while gradually reading the first volume of your *Kosmos* with my desire to thank you for the high intellectual enjoyment its study has afforded me . . . to give some substantial character to the expression of my thanks, I present you the accompanying work, Catherwood's *Views in Central America*. It may serve as an appendix to your own great work on Spanish America and thus become worthy of your attention . . .
>
> ALBERT

PART 4

YOU CAN'T GO BACK

76. *John Lloyd Stephens in 1859.*

CHAPTER XVII

Manifest Destiny

There were many who were caught up in it. It was called 'human progress.'

'We are a nation of human progress,' wrote the Editor of the *Democratic Review*, 'and who will say and what can set limits on our onward march?'

In a single ten-year span – 1840–1850 – Americans received in bewildering succession the telegraph, the Daguerreotype, steam as mechanical power, railways, the trek of the mormons across the plains to the empty lands of Idaho, the absorption of Texas into the Union, the Mexican war – with the states of New Mexico, Arizona, California and Oregon as the prize – and at the end of the expansion rainbow, as an unbelievable climax – the discovery of gold in California.

These were the voices of *Manifest Destiny* and the siren call of expansion. It was not peculiar to Americans; it reached far over to Europe, and no less a person than Henry Schliemann (before he became infected with the virus of archaeology) went to California to seek out his brother's holdings in the gold fields.

Frederick Catherwood also listened to the siren voices of *Manifest Destiny* but in another milieu. The published *Views* (1844) had been a success and had gained him some profit but it was not enough to maintain his family. Railroads were the new avenues to riches; financiers thought them sound investment, the public rushed to purchase the proffered bonds and in this there came into being a new profession: the railroad engineer.

So the protean Mr Catherwood – draftsman, architect, classicist, explorer, panoramist, archaeologist – had kept pace with the shifting moods of the times, and since his training with T-square and compass and surveying instruments was basically sound it allowed this shift in emphasis. After 1845 his title of architect (he always wrote it Archt.) was discarded; his calling card now read 'Frederick Catherwood, Civil Engineer.'

In that capacity he had worked briefly in the construction of the Sheffield-Manchester Railway. Then, in the autumn of 1845 he was asked to appear in London before the Committee of the Demerara Railway Company, organized to build and operate a rail-line between Georgetown and the interior of British Guiana along the Demerara River so that the planters could more easily market their rum, molasses, sugar and cotton.

The money for it being quickly over-subscribed, the board of directors, which included the sons of Gladstone as well as Sir Robert Schomburg, the eminent German-born explorer of British Guiana, suggested the name of Catherwood.

The Committee's report states that they 'consider that they have been particularly fortunate to obtain Mr Catherwood who resided for years in North America where he was employed upon railroads and extensive public works.'

The contract was for one year and he departed at once for British Guiana.

In his own cryptic statement: 'I was obliged to absent myself for several years on a professional engagement.'

For six months Catherwood surveyed the route of the proposed rail-line and his twenty-page report was excellent and most professional in tone. He studied similar projects in Jamaica and the United States, as he wrote in that report, so that he might 'escape their errors.'

The Committee met again in Old Jewry Chambers on 15 April, 1847, after reading the report which went far beyond the mere survey: plans for drainage, suggestions for the establishing of a central factory for all the sugar plantations, so that the Chairman informed the stockholders that upon reading this able report they had 'resumed the engagement of Mr. Catherwood by which his exclusive services have been secured to the company.'

He returned to British Guiana in March 1848 where Henry Light, Resident Governor of the Crown Colony told everyone that 'a scientific gentleman who proposes to remain in the colony for some time is Mr Catherwood, who has gained some eminence as a scientific traveler and who has come out to superintend the progress of the Demerara Railway. . . .'

So began the first railway to be built in the entire continent of South America or more correctly, so it did not begin.

There were labor troubles. The dollar-a-day wages were not sufficient incentive for the Blacks to leave the sugar plantations even though the London Committee 'thought that the novelty of the work alone would attract.'

It did not. Now the pitch-pine rail sleepers which Catherwood had ordered from America were instantly devoured by termites. Then Catherwood's old nemesis – the 'malaria' – returned.

Frustrated by climate and the disease which alternately chilled him and fevered him, his querulousness was aggravated.

This unruly demiurge which had poisoned his relations with his colleagues in the Mid-east, and almost broke up the second expedition to Yucatán, now caused Catherwood to be singularly unpleasant when crossed.

Said an official report 'There was considerable disagreement with Mr Catherwood' when the site for the rail terminus in Georgetown was discussed and there was 'considerable perturbation over his other decisions.'

Although the planters thought he was most thorough and his ideas sound, Catherwood's verbal affronts to the colony came on with alarming frequency.

The official ceremonies were another instance. The Resident Governor ordered a silver plated spade to turn the soil for the first railway built on the South American continent, but as it did not arrive on time he decided to make the ceremony a private one, reserved only for the Executive Committee.

'But,' said the report 'this arrangement was spoiled by Chief Engineer, Mr Catherwood, who issued invitations himself, much to the annoyance of the Chairman . . . and the local shareholders who expressed their dissatisfaction in no uncertain terms.'

Still Catherwood had laid down three miles of rail-line in time for the arrival of the first three locomotives, all insectivoral by name, Mosquito, Sandfly and Firefly, and along with them hordes of Black laborers recruited from Jamaica.

Then the local Black gentry complained fiercely to Catherwood over the free and easies taken by the new comers with the women of the colony.

So Catherwood's proposal that the Committee set up state-organized bordelles of course brought down more upon his head.

So unhappily bogged down with flies, floods and floosies, he wrote in nostalgic weltschmerz to his friend John R. Bartlett, of the famous Bartlett & Welford Booksellers in the Astor House:

September 27th, 1847 . . . I shall be *very* glad of any news (not political or relating to the Mexican-American War) that you will be pleased to send me. I have heard nothing of Stephens . . . Tell me how business is going, whether you are publishing any more books and if the American Ethnological Society is still in existence. How is Mr Gallatin? How is Mrs Bartlett? Have you been able to sell any more copies of my Views of Central America? . . .

You must not be surprised to see me back some day in New York and trying to start anew in business. . . .

Then the money began to run out. The budget had been exceeded by over a hundred percent and to worsen matters one of the members of the Committee, Mr Wisart by name, one of the most popular members in the colony, was run over by the locomotive called the Sandfly, and although poor Mr Wisart obtained in death the dubious honor of being the first man killed in South America by a railroad machine, it did not raise the esteem of Mr Catherwood, who was now blamed for everything that occurred on the railroad. The May 1849 report said: 'Mr Catherwood's agreement was terminated for reasons of economy.'*

Meanwhile John Lloyd Stephens had also succumbed to Manifest Destiny. The war with Mexico was already in its second year when as Vice President and Director of the line, he sailed on the newly built S.S. *Washington* to Europe. Although not one of the original incorporators of the Ocean Steam Navigating Company, Stephens had followed its development closely and invested some of his book profits in it and so was its representative on its maiden voyage. The S.S. *Washington* sailed for Bremen as advertised on 1 June, 1847, with one hundred and twenty passengers, and its three special passengers, including Major Hobbie of the Post Office Department, who was to attempt to make postal agreements with the Hansa Free States.

Unfortunately for the *Washington*'s reputation, it was beaten by the British steamer *Brittania*, which had left Boston after she sailed. *The Times* in London, even though $390,000 was spent upon her, called the *Washington*, 'about as ugly a specimen of steamship building as ever went through this anchorage.'

But the reception at Bremerhaven was very different. The whole harbor was in a gala mood; banners flew from the ships, American and German flags flying side by side.

*These details of Catherwood's construction of a railroad in South America were taken from reports discovered by the author in Georgetown, British Guiana, and were typed for him from the originals:
  1. 'Report of the London Committee,' April 15, 1847, by Frederick Catherwood, Esq., C.E.'
  2. 'Report of Mr. F. Catherwood C.E., on the Construction of a Railway from Georgetown to Mahaica.'
  3. 'Sidney H. Bayley, "Railways in British Guiana".'

An official dinner was given at the Hunter's Club, where Burgomaster Schmidt introduced 'Herr Stephens' as the 'great American Traveler, who opened New Worlds and Old.' And as almost everyone present had read a summary or heard of the German translation of his first book, and the second which was eventually to be published,* they welcomed Stephens with a standing ovation.

After the reception, Stephens left for Berlin.

'There was but one object in it,' he wrote of his quick trip to the German capital '... to see ... Baron von Humboldt. I might visit Berlin again,' he added, 'the other monuments of the city would remain, but Humboldt might pass away.'

Stephens had called upon the American minister, to see if he might arrange an introduction to Humboldt, but there he learned much to his regret that the great man, in feeble health was with the King at Potsdam and unable to receive visitors.

Visiting Baron von Ronne, formerly Prussian Minister to Washington, he expressed his disappointment at not being able to visit the famous explorer.

> He stopped me abruptly and, with friendly earnestness, said that I must not leave Berlin without seeing Baron Humboldt, at the same time looking at his watch, calling up my servant, telling him that the cars for Potsdam started at twelve; and hastily writing a line of introduction, without allowing me time for acknowledgements, he hurried me off to my carriage. A brisk ride brought me to the depot, just in time for the cars; three quarters of an hour carried us to Potsdam and, almost before I had recovered from my surprise, I was at Baron Humboldt's residence.

All his life Stephens had heard the name Humboldt.†

*John Lloyd Stephens, *Begebenheiten auf einer Reise in Yucatán*, Deutsch von Dr N. N. W. Meissner, Leipzig, 1853.

†Victor Wolfgang von Hagen, *South America Called Them* (A. A. Knopf, New York, 1945).

The man who had made more contributions to positive sciences was above all a friend of America. Colonel John C. Frémont, not many years before, had sprinkled the name Humboldt on rivers, mountains, and cities until it was famous throughout the American earth.

Time was riding fast now for the celebrated Humboldt, who, born in 1769, was at the time of Stephens' visit seventy-eight years of age. Even then he was to outlive the discoverer of the Maya and to die ten years short of a century of existence. Stephens wrote:

I was entirely mistaken in the idea I had formed of his personal appearance, and was surprised at not finding him bowed down and bent by age. He spoke of Mr Prescott's History of the Conquest [of Mexico] and said that I might, when the opportunity offered, say to that gentleman, as from himself, that there was no historian of the age, in England or Germany, equal to him.

I had occupied, without any interruption, more than one hour of Baron Humboldt's time, when Seifert, his Majordomo entered to summon him to dinner with the King . . . he urged me to remain a few days for the purpose of making certain acquaintances at Berlin, and pressed as he was, insisted upon giving me a line to a distinguished gentleman of Berlin, without seeing whom, he said, I ought not to leave. Circumstances did not permit me to deliver the letter; but I had the satisfaction of bringing home with me, written in German, in a strong firm hand, an autograph of Humboldt.*

At the suggestion of Stephens, then President of the Line, the Ocean Steam Navigating Company later named one of their boats *Humboldt* in his honor; this drew a reply.

* John Lloyd Stephens, 'An Hour with Humboldt,' *Little's Living Age Magazine*, Vol. XC, 1847, 151 ff.

Berlin, 21 September 1847

Monsieur le Président (of Ocean Steam Navigation), Through the mediation of my old friend, Mr. de Gérolt, our Minister to the United States, I have today received, while occupied with preparations for a trip to Paris, your amiable letter, dated August 21, with which you have been so kind as to honor me. It informs me that a favor has just been accorded me, of which I could not believe myself worthy, in comparing my name to that of a great Citizen who, from my earliest youth, has been the object of my liveliest admiration. I dare to beg you, Sir, to be so kind as to present the testimony of my respectful acknowledgement to the Directors of the 'Ocean Steam Navigation' who, on the flattering motion of Mr. Stephens, have decreed that the 4th ship destined for communication between New York and Bremen will bear my name... Devoted, as I am, through my studies to the noble destiny of the New Continent, keenly interested in the most direct and intimate commercial relations between the United States and my Fatherland, I place the highest value on the honor which you have deigned to pay me. . . .

CHAPTER XVIII

Troubles with the Railways

After Stephens' first adventure in the steam age, he was caught up in the web of the new era. John Lloyd Stephens was one of the founders of the Panama Railroad Company. The Document* which he prepared to be read to both Houses of the United States Congress, although couched in the formal language of an official Document, was still the prose of Stephens. It is instructive to listen to a portion of it:

> That the acquisition of California and the settlement of our boundary line in Oregon have opened a new era in the history of this country . . . the mildness of the climate, the richness of the soil, the great promise of mineral wealth and above all, the long coast with the magnificent harbors of the Pacific. . . . At this moment, hundreds of young men full of enterprise, from our Eastern States, are buffeting the storms of Cape Horn, while, with the coming spring, the hardy pioneers of the west will be moving by thousands over the desolate prairies, or climbing the rugged steeps of the Rocky Mountains . . . no means of returning, except by the stormiest passage ever known at sea.
>
> In view of this condition of things, and to hold out some encouragement to emigrants that they might not be virtually expatriated when upon their own soil. . . . there was established a monthly mail steamer from New York

* Memorial
of
Wm. H. Aspinwall, John L. Stephens and Henry Chauncey
in reference
to the Construction of a Railroad across the Isthmus
of Panama
30th Congress, two sessions, Senate misc. Doc. No. 1, Memorial, 11 December, 1848.

to Chagres [Panama], on the Atlantic . . . and on the Pacific side, to California and Oregon.

The Isthmus of Panama is about fifty miles in breadth – less than on any part of the Continent of America; and from the falling off of the great range of Cordilleras, running from the Rocky Mountains to the Andes, it has always been considered as the region in which, if ever, an easy communication would be effected, either by canal or road, between the two seas. . . . The route over it is probably worse now than in the early days of Spanish dominion . . . no wheel carriage has ever attempted to cross it. . . .

There had been, in the past, a plethora of talk of railways and canals; and the public, as was to be expected, was apathetic, not because communication across the Isthmus was not desired, but because they had heard about it without cease. Every year it seemed new companies were formed to break the back of the Isthmus. But investors lost their money, and the ill-conditioned travelers left their corpses in the amoral embrace of the jungle. There was a difference, however, with this, the latest project: Stephens, 'the eminent traveler,' was connected with it.

There had been much international interest in an Isthmian canal, French, English, Spanish, Dutch and the Americans had essayed ventures that had made New Granada, that is the Republic of Colombia, very uneasy over her nominal sovereignty of the Isthmian route.

The French first seized the initiative when Baron Charles de Thierry, the London-born scion of a French *émigré* family, with a Cambridge education, had arrived in the United States in a penurious position. Finding that there one must work for a living, he departed for the West Indies and at Guadeloupe he met Augustin Salomon,* a Jewish merchant

*Gerstle Mack, *The Land Divided: A History of the Panama and other Isthmian Canal Projects*, New York, 1944, wherein is summarized from the literature the historical connections of Augustin Salomon and the Panama Canal, pp. 126–127.

capitalist, to whom he expatiated upon the advantages to be derived from an Isthmian Panama canal as a shorter route to his holdings in New Zealand.

He managed to convince M. Salomon et Compagnie and for the next ten years they held a monopoly on all Isthmian projects.

But after years of comic-opera suggestions, the climax came when their engineer, the great Napoleon Garella, famous for his engineering works in the Alps, suggested they tunnel the Isthmus for ship passage.

The canal – definitely beyond the techniques of the time – gave way to the more practical one: a rail-line. In 1846, the Government of New Granada signed with M. Mateo Klein, an emissary of Salomon et Compagnie, an exclusive contract to build (and to operate for ninety-nine years) 'an iron railroad track across the Isthmus of Panama.'

On paper, at least, the organization, called 'The Panama Company', appeared as potently financial with a British banker, William Henry Dainbridge, and Sir John Campbell, an official of the Oriental Steam Company, named to the directorate.

Had this organization been able to carry through this project, the 'passage' would have been in the hands of a non-American power and would eventually have stifled the American control of passage to California, when the whole American structure of an ocean-to-ocean nation would have been endangered.

Providentially for the United States, France was suddenly precipitated into the Revolution of 1848 and with the closing of the *bourse* M. Augustin Salomon fell with it. He was unable in July 1846, to comply with Article IV of the contract: 'The Company shall give as security for the fulfilment of the obligations six hundred thousand francs.' So the whole contract was forfeited. America was given one more opportunity over control of its manifest destiny.

Stephens and Humboldt had conversed over the 'canal

idea' when they met at Potsdam. Even at that time Stephens apparently believed that the French syndicate could not carry through their project. Humboldt had always desired to see the Americans build their own canal, and had read Stephens a passage from Goethe's *Conversations with Eckermann*.

Wrote the aged Goethe from Weimar in 1827:

> Humboldt with his thorough knowledge of the problem, has indicated several places . . . But I ask myself whether the United States will let this opportunity slip through their fingers. It may be foreseen that this young state, with its decided predilection to the West, will, in thirty or forty years, have occupied. . . . the land . . . beyond the Rocky Mountains. . . . It is absolutely indispensable for the United States to effect a passage from the Mexican Gulf to the Pacific Ocean; and I am certain that they will do it. Would that I might live to see it!

It was to be John Lloyd Stephens who would give substance to Goethe's wish for he was to be the motivating force behind the formation of the Panama Railroad Company.

The contract called for the building of the road in eight years. Stephens wanted it done in three. The reasons were obvious.

The British were out to checkmate Manifest Destiny and had seized the Mosquito Coast, including the mouth of the San Juan River which led to the interior Nicaraguan lakes.

Lord Palmerston, who had returned to power in the Foreign Office, was not going to allow America to have a monopoly on the passage to the Pacific. There had already been clashes between American and British ships at Greytown in Nicaragua, a turbulent international situation that ended in the Clayton-Bulwer Treaty.

In view of Stephens' leadership, he had been made Vice-President of the railway, the building materials were gathered, ships chartered, and the whole complex plan put into movement for the building of the first transcontinental railroad.

There had been considerable correspondence between Stephens and Catherwood over the railway. After Catherwood's experiences in British Guiana, he was not too easily won over to the idea. Writing from his London home on 18 August, 1849, he said:

> All Railway enterprises here are looked upon with great and distinct suspicion . . . I have not yet made up my mind as to what I shall do, but shall wait to hear of your movements. My children are well, and my boy is as tall as myself and a good classical scholar and arithmetician, so I intend to educate him as an engineer. . . .

Later he showed himself interested in Panama:

> I shall be glad to hear from you respecting your Panama railway and whether there is any chance of getting the appointment to survey the lands.

It then became imperative for Stephens to have an alter-ego, a man of trust in Panama, since he himself had to take the long journey to Bogotá, the capital of Colombia, there to re-negotiate certain aspects of the treaty between the Panama Railway Company and the Government. Would Catherwood therefore be willing to come out for a year to 'take charge of the works' during his absence?

For a while Catherwood hesitated. He explained to Stephens, writing from the family residence at 21 Charles Square, Hoxton, that he had only $15,000 capital and the interest from it was not enough to care for his wife and three children.

He first suggested to Harper and Brothers, the American publishers, that he would be willing to invest that sum if they were to open up a London branch under his management;

he had then refused an English publisher to do a book on the Maya 'since I do not know how to write books.'

The offer from Panama was very meager ($1,500 with certain allowances) but since he did not wish to 'dig into capital' Catherwood went out.

This trip in 1850 has, curiously enough, a definite time-table. John Bigelow, Editor-owner of the *New York Evening Post*, author of many books and Minister-to-be in France during the American Civil War, noted while going to Jamaica in 1850 that:

> Among our fellow passengers (on the voyage down) was Mr. Catherwood, the artist, who was on his way to Panama whence after a sojourn of a few months, he proposed to embark for California on a professional visit. His large experience as a traveler in every quarter of the globe rendered him an interesting and useful addition to our mess.

The Panama Isthmus, lying between the seventh and ninth latitudes north, is a jungle-choked nexus of land. Assailed by winds of the *Chubasco* from its Caribbean side, Panama is deluged between April and December by an annual rainfall of one hundred and fifty inches.

Nurtured by these rains, the earth's warm and luscious body throws out an exuberant wealth of vegetation. Trees crowd closely upon one another, with delicately flowered parasites hanging from their branches; great aerophytes hold up spined leaves, cable-thick *lianas*, rooted somewhere in the humid earth, twist from tree to tree until whole sections of forest seem woven into a single element. So humid the atmosphere, so moisture-laden the air, so luxurious the warm embrace of the jungle that earth is not a requisite for growth; a year unattended and man's work is smothered by a bewildering complexity of growing plants. The whole of Panama's four hundred and thirty long miles of twisting earth is covered, from seashore to jagged antillean peaks, with insistent verdure.

The Indians came to terms with this environment and developed relatively high cultures and left in the disarray of their graves beautiful, fantastically cast gold ornaments encrusted with emeralds, or plaques of hammered *repoussé* gold, representations of ancient Coclé gods: this profusion of golden ornaments Columbus saw, and for this reason he called the land 'Golden Castille.'

White man first came to Panama in 1509. Nuñez de Balboa who then crossed the Isthmus to discover the Pacific Ocean was followed by other Spaniards, who built Panama City.

Haughty and brave men as they were, they could not come to terms with the jungle, as had the Indians who had lived with it for centuries.

White man opposed it. It was not the nocturnal jaguar that emptied his ranks, nor the herds of *peccaries* with their knife-sharp hoofs, nor the Indians whose ranks were quickly thinned by the steel-tipped 'partisans.'

White man's enemies were smaller, each in itself insignificant, yet in the myriads in which they abounded in the jungle habitat they, in the end, overwhelmed him.

The enemy were insects; the large, the small, the buzzing, the crawling, the droning, flying, swimming, ubiquitous insects. They governed the green world. There was the black-haired tarantula, four-inch-long praying mantis, large yellow-bellied wasps and huge scorpions that carried their stings overhead. And ants – harvesting ants, weaver ants, solitary ants, umbrella ants – the terrible-mandibled army ants that moved in solid black columns through the jungle. There were cryptobiotic termites, working within all cellulose, night and day, day and night. Panama was an entomological Elysium.

At all the hours of his tropical day and night, there were insects to plague. At mid-day a mosquito – the *Aedes aegypti* –

which introduced into the bloodstream the yellow-fever scourge, the *vomito*, the Spaniards called it, since in one's last life-consuming fever there was painful retching, convulsive vomiting, until one's entrails were wrenched loose.

At dusk, came the thin whine of the *Anopholes* flying in from the stagnant pools where it had pupated from an aquatic form into an insatiable blood-sucking mosquito, the bearer of malaria, and introducing into man's bloodstream microscopic armies of flagellated protozoa.

A dull pain in the back, a fierce headache, then the victim paled, the finger nails turned blue, the body cold, the eyes bloodshot, and the infected one's teeth chattered as if he had just been fished from Arctic waters.

Then, without prelude, heat, fever, an inferno raging, sweat pouring from every pore. After that – death. If not from malaria, or *vomito*, then typhoid, dysentery, typhus, sprue, bubonic plague, filariasis, or encephalitis. All these feverish plagues the American lumped into one generic name – the *Chagres fever*.

Catherwood immediately found himself concerned with more than railroads. The Isthmus swarmed with gold-seekers, California-bound, attired in the accepted style of slouch hat, red shirt, cowhide boots, and Colt revolver.

There was more to do than guide the building of the road and pay the workers: 'charge of the works' meant digging Americans out of difficulties, attending to fainting ladies' handing out quinine to those infected with malaria, and, when that failed, arranging burying parties to inter the mounting number of dead.

The Rio Chagres once flowed in twisting caprice for many miles through the Isthmus: beginning as a tinkling rill near the Pacific and gathering hundreds of streams into its darkly sedimented body, it brawled its way through the heavy parapets of the jungle until, many leagues later, in a surging flood of dark water, it debouched into the Caribbean.

Since the Chagres was the one navigable stream into

Panama's interior, it had been used since the beginning of the Spanish occupation. The Spaniards had built a fort at its Caribbean mouth to guard it, a huge, solid pile, meant to be impregnable.

Now, in the memorable year of 1850, when the Isthmus was to undergo its final siege – the assault of Big Business – the fortress stood gaunt and blackened on its Chagres hill, strangled by the grey roots of ficus trees and smothered by the smooth green leaves of wild heliconias.

This was the Panama which Stephens and Catherwood and their people were to defy; this was the Panama which was to hold the rails of the first transcontinental railway; this was the Panama which was, in effect, to be Stephens' deathbed.

James Marshall's discovery of gold at Sutter's Mill in 1848 did not bring, at least in the East, any immediate migration to the gold fields. The eastern newspapers printed the fantastic news without fanfare, merely as news items:

Said a writer in the *New York Herald*:

Oh this California, this gold fever. It is turning the Californian country upside down, people are leaving their wives and daughters and laugh at an offer of ten dollars per day.

But letters from California were being printed with precipitous editorial fervor:

. . . the immense quantity of gold daily gathered by the people . . . exceed in romance and riches the ancient stories of El Dorado.

So the Gold Rush gained momentum. By autumn 1849 the fever was in full spate.

At first vessels were chartered to carry their passengers around Cape Horn, but this voyage was both dangerous and slow, and soon the Harnden Express Company was making arrangements to get people to the goldfields of California via Panama for two hundred dollars.

Hotels sprang up on the sand bar below the Chagres fortress; express companies, using native dugouts.

When the builders of the Panama Railroad needed labor most, their workmen caught the gold fever, for men take thoughts from one another as they catch disease.

The Rio Chagres was now flooded with people California-bound. Women came, too, with their children; the builders of the railroad merely suffered the gold-seekers, for they impeded the work.

Thousands continued to pour down upon the Panama Isthmus. In vain did the editors of the *New York Herald* tell them:

> Hurry out of the village of Chagres, which is pestilential . . . avoid the sun, do not sleep out of your boat, bear the heat, bear the mosquitoes, do anything rather than expose yourself to the night air. Take from two to four grains of quinine every morning.

And yet they came on.

By autumn of 1851 so many lay dead on the Chagres trail that the coleopterous burying beetles had to work overtime.

By February 1850 Catherwood had fully taken over the 'works' in Panama.

He wrote to Stephens, who lay bed-ridden in Bogotá from a severe fall from his horse:

> My surveying about the City of Panama, in conjunction with the arrival of the iron rails has created a considerable sensation and I am often surrounded by crowds of persons enquiring what it is all about and where the Terminus of the railway will be. . . .

The depot and port facilities to handle the maritime traffic to connect it with the rail-line had begun and after this Catherwood was putting down the plank road which he planned would run along side of the proposed rails so that supplies when conveyed would not bog down in the jungle.

It was all at a high price to Catherwood's health. He had the 'Chagres Fever.'

'I have had my share of sickness,' he reported to Stephens 'and I am still under medical care.'

But in spite of this, Catherwood kept on with and beyond the terms of the contract. The plant road was beginning to edge its way eastward toward Chagres on the Atlantic side. 'And,' he wrote

> Main Street in Panama City was somewhat improved. A few good shops having been opened. In other respects Panama remains the same filthy place it has always been. . . . P.S. I hope this letter reaches you at Chagres [Stephens had returned there from Bogotá] and with a firm determination to carry on the railroad despite all the troubles and difficulties.

This hope was not to be realized. Stephens was ordered by his physician to recuperate in New York City and it was then that Catherwood assured him that:

> I shall remain here until I see you. But with the small salary I am receiving I am not desirous of remaining a day beyond my stipulated time. . . .

When Stephens was unable to make the trip across the narrow isthmus to Panama City, Catherwood expressed his chagrin that they could not spend the Fourth of July together as they had before 'under different circumstances,' since Stephens wished to find a colder climate 'and of course more money.'

In a long, detailed letter about the aims and difficulties of the rail-line, he explained his own dilemma. Since the

347

scheduled contract had run over the stipulated time, he hoped that they would provide him with an extra $1,000 which might be of service to him at San Francisco.

> I pay $650 a year insurance of my life for the benefit of my children . . . and this is a heavy burden with a salary of only $1,500 and 3 children to support at school. In fact, this year I shall have to encroach on my capital, which is small enough. . . .

While Stephens was on the mend in New York City, he was elected President of the Panama Railway Company and with that the gold-fever acted as a stimulus to the financing of the railway.

The company had erected a small hotel in Limón Bay for its own personnel with work shops for the maintenance and construction of the rail-line which by that time had seven miles of usable track.

In November 1851 one thousand California-bound emigrants arrived in two vessels. They could not dock in the port of Chagres and put in at Limón Bay, where they clamorously demanded that the railroad transport them on the cars, even though it was only seven miles away.

At first the rail engineers refused; they had only flat cars and no accommodation for passengers and put an impossibly high price for that transport, $7.00 for 7 miles, hoping that this would discourage. . . . It did not. The passengers eagerly paid the price, rode on open flat cars, crossing over flimsy wooden bridges built of green timber. Some passengers were scraped off by the low-hanging tree-limbs; still they came on.

At once public confidence in the Panama Railroad rose, its stock soared, its credit extended.

The gold rush had saved the rail-line. Henceforth people traveled the railroad. By 1855 the line had earned $12,000,000 – $4,000,000 more than the entire cost of the road. It was to earn twenty-four per cent dividend. Ten years later it was considered the safest investment on Wall Street and by far the most successful American enterprise ever attempted outside of the continental limits of United States territory.

After it had earned millions, the Panama Railroad was sold in 1877, to the French Panama Canal Company for a then formidable $25,000,000.

Stephens made final preparations to return to Panama to push the rail-line to conclusion, but his health continued poor. The germs of tertiary malaria had taken up residence in his liver and kidneys and the intermittent fevers were constant.

Did he know that the infection was making a fatal headway? If he did, it did not change his outward manner, but although he made jests about it, he seemed to sense his end.

At the Benton residence in Washington a few days before his departure, over a third cup of tea, Stephens leaned toward Jessie Benton Fremont and, in a light tone, said: 'You must

77. *Stephens' cottage on the Rio Chagres.*

be very good to me, for some day soon perhaps, I'll be sent to the Isthmus to die.'

Yet he gave no signs of a decline.

Returning to Panama Stephens settled down midway between the two oceans in order to more effectively guide the two rail-lines which were approaching a junction.

At Bujio Soldado (now long since submerged in the canal's waters), thirty miles up the Chagres, he built a cottage. 'It was here,' runs a contemporary account, 'that Mr Stephens, whose fame as a traveler and writer is world-wide, and whose later life was spent in developing this great railway enterprise, loved in his intervals of labor, to rest in his hammock, and enjoy the luxuriant beauties of the surrounding landscape.'*

Yet these intervals of rest were growing increasingly long. Malaria, 'his old enemy,' was shaking him more and more frequently even though he daily consumed quantities of bitter quinine. In a moment of repose, he would suddenly be visited by a fierce headache and then the chills would come over him, shaking him until he was numbed with cold.

Some type of order appeared. Hospitals were put up, quinine was found to be a specific against malaria and in liquid form was placed on all dining tables to be taken as prophylactic, Dr Chauncey Griswold was brought down from New York to organize the sanitation and was put in charge of the main hospital, facing Stephens' cottage at Bujio Soldado.

Dr Griswold found that the 'ague . . . with the judicious use of fifteen grains of quinine, could be entirely removed, leaving patient, after one paroxysm, as well as he was before.'

Diarrhoea and dysentery caused him more difficulties. Pneumonia was not infrequent. But malaria still remained the 'curse' and until it was finally eliminated, along with yellow fever, by the American Canal Commission prior to the full

---

*'The Panama Railroad,' *Harpers New Monthly Magazine*, Vol. XVII, No. IV, January, 1859, pp. 159–161.

construction of the canal, every enterprise disintegrated before it.

To Dr Griswold – as well as to all medical science of that period – 'miasma was the essential cause of the fevers.' One avoided the evening air because of the 'unhealthy exhalation which hover near the earth like smoke and fog.'

Griswold and Stephens saw a great deal of each other:

'Stephens has been, emphatically, the pioneer in this enterprise, and the duties of his office could not have been placed in better hands, not only from his thorough knowledge of the country, and the habitats of the people he had to deal with officially. . . .'

Catherwood, meanwhile, had arrived in San Francisco, and at once wrote a letter dated 28 August, 1850 telling: 'My Dear Stephens, According to my promise, I write you immediately on my arrival. . . .'

The population of the city had risen from a settlement to 50,000. Fire had destroyed the waterfront houses, but Phoenix-like, they were replaced by new ones; false-fronted dwellings, saloons, business houses all mired in the mud-streets.

Indians, Spaniards, Americans, Frenchmen, a German or two, notably Heinrich Schliemann, the one-day discoverer of legendary Troy, gold-grubbers, merchants, gamblers, harlots, with a generous sprinkling of honest men, all scrambling for gold and dollars: **and** all the while trying to build a city.

Into this *olla podrida* of races disembarked Frederick Catherwood.

'I expect next week to set out on a short visit to the Mines or "diggins" . . . for until I shall have been there I shall not feel satisfied to settle down to business. . . .'

This business developed first as a contractor to rebuild parts of San Francisco's houses and warehouses. He then sailed to the new Oregon Territory on one of the newly launched side-wheelers where, spending some weeks at the junction of the Columbia and Willamette rivers, he wrote a report *Relative to the Praticability of forming Settlements on the Columbia River* (but which, like almost all else, has disappeared and only its title preserved). He then became involved in the building of the Railway.

In April 1853, a 'Report of the Engineers of the Survey of the Maryville and Benecia Railroad' was issued. On the last page: 'F. Catherwood, Consulting Engineer.'

Catherwood was now referring to himself as a Californian, for in 1850 California became the 31st State of the Union and whether he willed it or not, he, like all those present in that year, automatically became a citizen of the United States, so that he could be understood when writing to *My Dear Stephens* that '*we Californians* think a good deal of ourselves . . .'

Now Catherwood was pleased with his position, the money and the climate and noted that it was a pity that 'you have not turned your steps towards California and have been a candidate for the United Senate . . . a New man and a man of note would carry all before him. What say you? . . .'

Within a year disillusion was setting in. Land speculations proved the ruin of many – and following his life's pattern, Catherwood had lost $7,000 in the collapse of a merchant – ('I need not tell you of the disastrous state of commercial and monetary affairs here').

The lack of law and order had brought out in 1851 an *ad hoc* committee to suppress lawlessness and people, the guilty and the non-guilty were being hanged all about San Francisco.

As Catherwood observed to Stephens:

Unfortunately California does not improve on acquaintance. I do not mean the country, which is well enough, but the state of the society. To young men who are fond of certain kinds of excitement, it may have its attractions but to a *sober, plodding old fellow like myself*, it is particularly distasteful . . . nothing but direct gain makes it bearable.

However, he re-invested $5,000 more in mining 'either to make a modest fortune or to lose it' and prepared for his temporary departure (on 11 June, 1851). But before he left, he made one more attempt to re-arouse his companion in the discovery of the Mayas interest toward archaeology.

In Lower California he was assured that there were 'some remarkable antiquities of which I have exact information from a most reliable source,' and planned to visit and limn the antiquities 'which are of a massive and impressive character.'

But the whims of fortune wafted his ship past the great isolation of Lower California (which does not possess any antiquities of massive character) and he made the passage through Panama on the rail-line he had helped to build. There he met his friend Stephens for the last time.

In London again, and writing to Stephens in the April of 1852 from his address at 21 Charles Square, Hoxton, he informed him that his adventure in mining in California had taken an upturn.

'We are increasing our capital of Gold Hill to $1,000,000 . . . you do not say whether you will join us or not. . . .'

Yet with all these *sueños doradas*, archaeology still retained its hold on him. He still thought of going to Lower California to 'make drawings of the antiquities found there and put them as an addenda to a new edition of your work [*Incidents of Travel in Central America*]. How does this idea please you?'

The question was rhetorical. By the time the letter had traveled from Chagres to Panama to New York City, John Lloyd Stephens was scarcely in a position to answer.

78. *Stephens' Tree in Panama.*

CHAPTER XIX

Death Meets Mr Stephens

Stephens was paying dearly for the part he was playing in Manifest Destiny. The malaria attacks increased. His body, which had held up so well from the trying days of his youthful travels in Arabia and the more terrifying Central American days, was falling apart.

Yet he seemed to deem it an obligation to keep on assisting travelers across the Isthmus. Many were personal friends. Jessie Benton Fremont, pale and outwardly delicate came through the Isthmus with his personal assistance in order to join her husband in San Francisco.

Then one day Stephens was found unconscious under a huge liana-draped ceiba tree* near Lion Hill beyond Gatun Station. The natives who found him at first thought him dead. No one knew how long he had lain in a coma under the giant ceiba.

As they bore him away, limp and unconscious, to a vessel leaving for New York, rumor had it that he was dead.

And so, for fifty years, this tree was called 'Stephens' Tree,' for legend, more persistent than truth, had it that John Lloyd Stephens, finally succumbing to the tropical hydra, died under the ceiba tree.

In the end, it was Stephens' 'old enemy' that won. The malarial plasmodia that had remained in his bloodstream, unremittingly chilling him and fevering him, had at last taken full possession of his body. But not as malaria. Stephens' liver had become infected. There was a general debilitation. Pains shot through his body. His brain was dull and confused.

---

*'The original lay-out of the road involved destruction of this tree, but the admiration of Mr. Stephens for this Monarch of the woods was so great that he ordered a slight diversion of the line.' Donald Mitchel, *American Lands and Letters*, New York, 1899, pp. 115–116.

He had fallen into a lethargy. The disease after considerable consultation was diagnosed as hepatitis: prognosis was death.

The hot summer days of New York's 1852 gave way to the first breathings of autumn. The sycamores outside 13 Leroy Place, began to lose their russet foliage and the trefoil-shaped leaves glided slowly earthwards and downwards to the streets of Greenwich Village.

Propped up by the window, Stephens' eyes followed these leaves to the ground, watching them with those brilliant 'great eyes' once so admired by Herman Melville.

His eyes now seemed the only element of animation. He was slowly desiccating as if death were emptying all his vital juices.

Yet his ironical humor was maintained to the end, for in playing out the human comedy, he insisted with mock firmness to his doctors that they must have him up by the end of September so that he could be present at the launching of a ship that would bear his name.

The new flag vessel of the Panama Mail Steamship Company, the 'magnificent side-wheeler,' the 275-foot-long vessel destined for the California run, was to be the S.S. *John L. Stephens*.

On 22 September, 1852, the ship was launched from the yards of Smith and Dimon, the ceremonies attended by the Honorable Benjamin Stephens, 'a retired merchant of wealth and probity,' who represented his son.

For many years this ship was John Lloyd Stephens' only immortality. He had fallen into a coma on the day of the launching, and he died on 13 October, 1852, without regaining consciousness.

The *New York Daily Tribune* wrote:

The death of the celebrated traveler, John L. Stephens, which took place on Tuesday evening at the residence of his father in this city, will cause a lively emotion of sorrow, not alone in the large circle of personal friends, to whom he was the object of distinguished pride and affection, but in the far wider sphere of intelligent persons who have been indebted to his admirable writings for rare and valuable information. . . .

Other New York newspapers wrote of:

The American Traveler . . . full of energy, prompt, enterprising, clear-headed, with a constant practical activity which was a necessity of his nature, with the generous 'excelsior' spirit which built our railroads, launched our steamers, extended our domains, wrote our books. . . .

One newspaper, reflecting almost all of them, wrote: 'All this will not soon permit his name to fade from our memories. . . .'

But for some inexplicable reason, it did fade from world memory. He was brought to the Old Marble Cemetery, and, 'temporarily placed,' said a newspaper, 'in the receiving vault.'

And then he was forgotten. He never was legally buried, nor was his grave marked. There he lay, in Old Marble Cemetery, for more than a century until his biographer gathered a group of his admirers to aid in correcting death's oversight.

A plaque, designed by John Howard Benson, was placed where Stephens lay buried, in a small ceremony at Old Marble Cemetery in New York, 9 October, 1947.

This plaque, animated by a Maya glyph which had been taken from one drawn by Frederick Catherwood, reads:

Beneath this vault lie buried the remains of John Lloyd Stephens/1805–1852/Traveler and Author/Pioneer in the Study of the Mayan civilization of Central America. Projector and builder of the Panama railroad.

CHAPTER XX

Mr Catherwood Sinks in the Stream of Time

Frederick Catherwood felt Stephens' loss very heavily, for it had been a long, fruitful and creative friendship.

For fifteen years, stimulated by archaeology and the problems that it presented, there had developed a mutual respect and a rare relationship between author and artist. Up to Stephens' death, their correspondence had been lively and, even during the frenzy of building railways, filled with thoughts of what they could do toward publishing more of Catherwood's brilliant portfolio of Maya drawings.*

Stephens' death in his forty-seventh year ended all this. Yet Catherwood, as a last gesture of friendship edited a one-volume edition of *Incidents of Travel in Central America* (London 1854) to which he contributed a brief affectionate memoir. As it turned out, it was to be Catherwood's tombstone.

He had already written to Stephens in June 1852 that he intended to land at New York on his way to California, for he was needed at Gold Hill 'where something or other was going wrong.' He had put in almost all of his capital, that is $13,000, and 'would not be surprised if he lost the whole of it.'

So, finally, he embarked on the S.S. *Arctic*, sailing out of Liverpool for New York: the date was September, 1854.

The *Arctic* carried 385 passengers, many of considerable renown. The Duc de Grammont was returning to his diplomatic post in Washington; Mrs Collins and her children, the family of Mr E. K. Collins, the owner of the Collins Line,

---

*The author's first biography of Stephens flushed out from their hiding place an immense number of letters and documents. Many are from Catherwood. They had been buried, so to speak, in the archives of the Panama Railway offices in New York City. All these are now part of the collections of the Bancroft Library, University of California, Berkeley, and most of these were copied for the author through the helpful aid of its Director.

held court at the Captain's table; and one could, if one had a mind, pick out on the 226-foot deck, the Drews, Comstocks, Fabbricottis, Howlands, Lockmiranets, Ravenscrofts, and all the other notable New Yorkers that ornamented the passenger list.

On the seventh day, the *Arctic* was to make the landfall of Cape Race, Newfoundland and then follow the coast to New York City.

Her ugly iron hull was wholly obscured by a thick fog-blanket, the only event of a featureless voyage, so that many of the passengers, mostly New Yorkers, were very audible in their complaints that the opaque fog drop-curtain that veiled the sea took from them their first sight of land.

The fog also had broked up a discussion of the war then being waged between Russia and England. Sebastopol had been under siege when the ship had disembarked so that the amateur strategists had used the deck of the *Arctic* as the Crimea battlefield. But the thickening fog had put an end to this harmless military diversion and the men had retired to the main saloon.

'The pilot stood at the wheel,' said the Rev. Henry Ward Beecher many days later, reconstructing for his congregation the events that led up to the tragedy, 'the pilot stood at the wheel, but DEATH stood upon the prow and no eye beheld him. Whoever stood at the wheel in all the voyage, Death was the pilot that steered the craft and none knew it.'

The Captain had just left the wheelhouse at noon when he heard the watch call, 'Hard starboard!'

Then, without warning, the *Vesta*, a French screw-propelled vessel, loomed out of the ocean. The ships rammed head-on.

The *Vesta* pulled away listing badly. The Captain of the *Arctic*, unaware of his own plight, stood by to help the passengers of the damaged ship.

Later, the engineer came on deck in great agitation to report that the hull of the *Arctic* was badly holed and her fires had already been extinguished.

359

Everyone fell to manning the pumps. The *Arctic* slowly settled.

There were not enough lifeboats. The crew, rushing up from below, jumped at once into all the available boats, lowered them, and pulled away from the ship.

Within an hour the passengers were left to their own devices. Those who kept their wits tried to construct a raft out of timber and barrels.

The First Officer, remembering a sinking ship's etiquette, raised the American flag upside down.

Stewart Holland, a young engineer, began to fire the distress-canon. When, after an hour's firing, it was realized that they were a hundred or more miles from shore, Holland solemnly announced that he would fire for the last time.

'The last Gun,' with Stewart Holland pulling the lanyard, is the subject of a famous Currier & Ives print.

At five p.m. the *Arctic* sank with almost its full complement of passengers. Then night mercifully dropped its veil.

As the death lists were posted, New York dropped work to search the newspapers. The Stock Exchange closed, banks stopped their business, flags throughout New York City were held at half-mast.

The Captain of the *Arctic*, one of the survivors, issued his first statement from Quebec, where he was landed. It was addressed to Mr E. K. Collins, President of the line:

'Dear Sir, It becomes my painful duty to inform you of the total loss of the *Arctic*, under my command, with your wife, daughter and son. . . .'

Then followed day after day, name upon name of the missing passengers. For two weeks the dailies swept everything from the first page to bring details of the tragedy that had taken three hundred lives.

The last movements of seemingly all aboard were described.

One by one, the survivors told of the last acts of those who had perished.

Later the newspapers printed obituaries of all victims. All that is, except Frederick Catherwood.

Not a word of one of the pioneer artists of the Robert Hay Egyptian Expedition. No mention of his vast corpus of drawings which still lay entombed in the British Museum.

The architect-draftsman, who repaired and then limned the Mosque of Omar, the panoramist of Leicester Square and later of New York, the co-discoverer of the Maya civilization, about whom New York newspapers had printed much over the period of fifteen years, the engineer of the first railroad of South America, one of the Argonauts of San Francisco, one of the greatest archaeological artists that ever lived, was passed over, one might almost think, in studied silence.

It was not until many days had passed and only when Stephens' family, who knew him well, made pointed enquiries, that the death-notice editor of the *New York Herald Tribune* placed, in an obscure corner, almost, it seemed, as an afterthought:

Mr. Catherwood Also is Missing.

Index

Abdel Hassis (pseudonym) *see* Stephens, John Lloyd
Acre, Manuel Jose 166
Agua volcano 164
Aké 293
Albert, Prince, comments on Catherwood's work 326
Albino 264, 266, 270, 298
Alexandria 54–7, 91
Altar found similar to the Dresden Codex 161
Amatitlan 177–8
Amen-Hotep III 14, 66
Andrews, Dr. E. Wyllys 142
Antiqua 170
Aqaba 76–8
Arabian Deserts 3–35
Arabia Petraea 19, 71–83
Arabia Petraea (Stephens) 94–7
Arctic (S.S.) 358–61
Arundale, Francis 11, 20, 28
Asebedo, Jose Maria 149–52
Atitlán Lake 164, 173
Augustin 147, 163
Authors on Central American subjects 103, 105–8

Baalbek, ruins of 29–30, 99
Bartlett, John Russell 99, 109
Belize 114–17, 120, 122, 125, 127
Berlin, Heinrich 158
Blackstone (lawbook) 37
Bobon (Indian guide) 176
Bolonchen 283
Bonomi, Joseph 4, 6–8, 11, 17, 20, 28, 31
Bradford, Cornelius 67, 76, 89
Bujio Soldado, 350
Burford, Robert 34, 92
Burton, James *see* Haliburton

Cabot, Dr Samuel joins the expeditions, 234
—— gets malaria 263
—— quarrel with Catherwood 278
Caddy and Walker's expedition to Palenque 119–122, 182, 191
Cairo 54, 56–8, 60
Calvéz, Marinas 166
Campeche district 179, 210
—— 12 ruined cities found near 276
Carmen Island 211
Carnegie Institute 153
Carrera, Rafael 124, 163, 167–71
Catazaja lagoon 209
Catherwood, Frederick *passim*
—— at San Francisco 351
—— Chagres fever 347
—— as civil engineer 330
—— contracts with the Demerara Railway Company 330
—— death 358–61
—— malaria 213–14, 216, 331
—— in Uxmal 264
—— personality changes 278
—— publishes on his own account 319–328
—— quarrels with Cabot 278
—— stays on in Copán alone 162
—— to Panama 341
—— United States' citizenship 352
Central America, incidents during visits to 216–30
Chagres trail 344
Chibcha tribe 139
Chichén Itzá 223–4, 254, 289, 293–96, 298–304, 306–7; plan of 294
Cholera in Guatemala (1837) 167
City of St. James, Guatemala, 164
Civilisations of ancient Central America, listed 105
Columbia College 37
Colossi of Memnon 12, 62, 66
Comitán 178
Constantinople 47–8, 58, 60, 87
Contract, formal between Stephens and Catherwood 109–11

Index

Copán 103, 110, 124, 129, 131–4, 145, 147–62, 175, 221, 226: plan of 148
Cortéz, Hernán 105, 164, 182, 208, 217, 235
Court of the Hieroglyphic Stairway 154, 159
Court of the Thousand Columns 298
Cozumel 289
Cyclopean Steps 133

de Alvarado, Pedro 164
de Gayangos, Pascual 217
de Landa, Fray Diego 238–9, 271
Della Magnificenza ed Architettura de Romana (Piranesi) 5
Demerara Railway Company 330
Dendera, Temple of 60, 62
Diaper, Frederick 97–8
Dome of the Rock 21–22, 26, 312
Don Carlos 212
Dresden Codex 161
Du Paix, Capitán 179–80, 202
Dzonotes 142

Egypt, Catherwood's first journey to 3–35
El-Aqsa 21–2, 24
El Dorado 139
Elephantine, Island of 66–7
El Petén 143, 175
'Emblem Glyph' 158
Estrada, 'president' 170
Expedition to Yucatán, account of published 310–28

Friedrichstahl, Baron Emanuel von 222–4
Fuego volcano 164, 170

Genghis Khan, 29
Gold finds in California 348–53
Graffiti 62, 66
Great Ball Court of Chichén 301
Great Plaza, Copán 155
Gregorio, Don 147–8, 151
Guatemala City 126–7, 163–5, 167–8, 171–2

Haliburton, James 11–12
Hall, Mr. (British vice-Consul) 163
Harper Brothers (Publishers) 216, 313, 341

Hatshepsut, Queen 14
Hay, Robert 8, 10–13, 15
Heliopolis 29
Henrickson, Charles 40–42
Homo Americanus 138
House of the Dwarf 214
Hoxton, London 3–4, 319, 341, 353
Huehuetenago 177
Humboldt 105, 334–5

Ice Age 136–8
Idols of Copán, removal negotiated 148–51
Idumaea 84, 92
Illinois 40–2
Incas 138–9
Isabel to Copán, journey from 125–32
Isle of Women 289
Israel, lost tribes of 109, 319
Iturbide, 'Emperor' of Mexico 166
Itzá, The Wells of 289–309
Izmir see Smyrna

Jerusalem 2, 32, 87–9, 98–9: plan of 2
—— in Leicester Square, London 91–100
Juan (Indian guide) 176, 205–6

Kabah 254, 264, 266–270
Karnak 11, 63–6
Katun (7,200 days) 158
Kelemen, Pal 156
Kulkulkan 289–309

Labná, City of 274, 276
Laguna de Terminos (Lake) 180, 211, 233
La Républica, City of 163
Las Cuevas, ruins of 177
Las Playas 208–9
Leicester Square, London 3–35, 91–100
Lembke, Frederich Wilhelm 217
Levant 44–5
Lhullier, Albert Ruz 200
Litchfield, Connecticut 37
London 92
Lord, Daniel 37, 39–40
Los Altos of Guatemala 176, 204
Luxor 11, 62–3

Maler, Capitán Teobert 224
Mary Ann, The, (Ship) 112, 225
Mastodon elephant's remains 177
Maudsley, Alfred P. 153, 203
Maya, calendar 280
—— civilisation ends (900AD) 159
—— country, plan of 246
—— culture 38, 97
—— discoveries, intense interest in 216
—— history 144–5
—— Indians, El Petén, revolt by 166
—— leave the plain of Copán 159
—— the rise of the 133—146
—— Rosetta Stone 156
—— Tribe, start of, in 200 BC 141–2
Meeting between Catherwood and Stephens, the first 92–100
Mehemet, Ali 14, 19, 24–5, 56–8, 72
Memphis 11
Mérida, capital of Yucatán, 212–13, 235, 240–2
Mexican gold rush 348
Mexico revolt (1821) 166
Mico Mountain 123, 125–7
Mixco, City of 170
Morazán, Francisco 124, 167–9, 173
Morley, Dr. S. G. 154, 227
Moscow 49—51
Mosquitos at Uxmal 261
Mt. Sinai 72–3, 75
Mycenae 44

Nakun, City of 144
Naples 5
Napoleon 49, 51, 55
Negro 115–6, 128
New York City 35, 37, 94–5, 97, 150, 217, 310–14
Niguas (a pestilence) 194
Nile 10–12, 15, 19, 47, 52–69
Nohcacab 266
Nuozzo, Paolo (Paul), servant 54, 58, 60, 69, 72, 79

Ocasingo 179
Odessa 48–9
Omar, Mosque of 26

Paesteum, The 5
Palace of Palenque 190—94

Palenque City 103, 110, 119, 121, 147, 158–9, 171–6, 181–214, 221, 226
—— negotiations for the purchase of 206–7, 212
Palestine 84, 88
Palizada village 210
Panama Railroad Company 337
—— sold (1877) 349
Panoramas 31, 92–3, 112, 311
—— destroyed by fire 311–12
Paris 51–2
Pawling, Henry 177–9, 189, 197
Payes, Senor 172
Peabody Museum of Harvard 153
Peón, Don Simón 245–7, 254, 259
Petén Jungle 144–5
Petra, town of 52–3, 60, 71–83
Philae, temple of 15, 67–8
Philip V, King of Spain 117
Piedras Negras 158
Piranesi 5, 276
Pithecanthropos 137
Pittsburg riots 40
Pok-a-tok (Ball game) 155, 301
Pompeii 8
Prescott, William H. 217–8, 220–2, 252, 310–18, 320–28
Proskouriakoff, Tatiana 158
Pyramid at Palenque 205
—— at Uaxactum 143
—— at Uxmal 213
—— in Copán 135
—— of the House of the Dwarf 214
—— The Great Egyptian 11

Quetzalcoatl 306–7
Quetzaltenago 171, 173, 176
Quiché tribe 173, 176
Quiriguá 152, 172, 175, 221
—— negotiations for the purchase of 172, 206
Quitas tribe 139

Rameses II 15
Religion, belief of the Maya 142–4
Río Chico 209–10
—— Copán 133, 151
—— Lagertero 178
—— Motagua 172

Río Usamacinta *see* Usamacinta River
Rock of the Inscriptions 20
Rome 3–35
Royal Institute of British Architects 7
Ruins (Volney) 44–54
Ruins in Palenque district, list of 179, 204
Russell, Charles *see* Don Carlos

Sacred Ball Court 155
San Salvadore 166
Santa Ana, General 178–9
Santa Cruz de Quiché 173–5
San Tomás College, Guatemala 165
Sayil 274
Scoles, J. T. 6–8
Shrewsbury, New Jersey, (birth place of Stephens) 35
Sinai 19
Sisal, port of 234, 240
Smith, Sydney 90
Smyrna (Izmir) 45–6, 48, 60
Soane, Sir John 5
Squints cured 242–4
Stanhope, Lady Hester 90
Stephens, John Lloyd *passim*
—— political post offered 233
—— as minister in Central America 111
—— death of at age 47, 355–8
—— has hepatitis 350
—— ill at Uxmal 260–2
—— in Berlin 334
—— presidency of the Panama Railway 348
—— sails for Bremen 333
—— (with) Prescott, letters of 221–3, 225–6, 233
Stone used in Copán 204
Sun Face Symbol 205
Stucco used in Palenque 204

Tabasco district 208–10
Tapping Reeves Law School 37–8
Temple of Amon 138
—— of Artemis 29
—— of Bacchus 29
—— of the Inscriptions 198–200
—— of Jupiter 29
—— of the Beau Relief 206
—— of the Cross 202–4
—— of the Sun, Palenque 206–7
—— of the Warriors 298
Thebes, ruins of 11–12, 62, 99
Tiahuanacu civilisation 139
Tikal City 144, 159, 175
Titicaca Lake 139
Toltec invasion (987 AD) 303
Tulum, City of 289–91
Tumbalá, heights of 180, 208
Tutal Xiu, Chief 237–8, 254
Tzotzil Indians 189, 195

Uaxactún 143
Udemco, Lands of 21
Ummlugma Mines 20
Usadmacinta River 158, 204, 210
Utatlán, Ruins of 173–5
Uxmal, City of 212–13, 215, 221, 247, 249–64; plan of 248

Vera Paz (Ship) 122–4
Volney, Count 52, 58, 62, 183

Wadi Mokateb 20
Waldeck, Count Jean-Frederik de 186–9, 191, 206, 256
Warsaw 51
Westcar, Henry 17
Western Court, Copán 161
Wilkinson, Sir John G. 7

Xmakabatun City 144
Xtampak 277–8
Xultun, City of 144

Yucatán, first visit to 99, 141, 144, 175, 208, 210–12, 221
—— second visit to 233–288
Yum Kax, Maya Lord of the Harvest 153

Zabacché 274
Zapoluta 178
Zoömorphic Engravings 136